"This is an important book which makes a real contribution to the field of church history and historical theology, with a depth of research enough for scholars but very accessible so that anyone can read it. I found the book very satisfying and enlightening. Well worth the time of anyone interested in the history of doctrine and spirituality, but the book also demonstrates why the study of Gregory is relevant and worthwhile in our time. I especially appreciated the way the author connects christological implications to artistic depictions of Christ, demonstrating that all art teaches something about its subject."

—Jim L. Papandrea
Professor of Church History and Historical Theology
Garrett-Evangelical Theological Seminary

"In *The Doctor of Mercy,* Papazian makes a distinctive contribution by providing the most comprehensive introduction to St. Gregory of Narek, a medieval mystic who experienced and expressed a reality not easily comprehended. The book touches upon everything conceivable about the Saint and his works and does so in an appealingly clear fashion. Papazian acts as a guide who takes the reader on a tour to meet the Saint in his time and place, explaining all along the things encountered on the way and those to be expected upon arrival. Then comes the embrace."

—Abraham Terian
Emeritus Professor of Armenian Theology and Patristics
St. Nersess Armenian Seminary

Michael Papazian

The Doctor of Mercy

The Sacred Treasures of St. Gregory of Narek

LP
A

LITURGICAL PRESS
ACADEMIC

Collegeville, Minnesota
www.litpress.org

1 2 3 4 5 6 7 8 9

Library of Congress Cataloging-in-Publication Data

Names: P'ap'azyan, Mayk'l, author.
Title: The doctor of mercy : the sacred treasures of St. Gregory of Narek / Michael Papazian.
Description: Collegeville : Liturgical Press, 2019. | Summary: "An introduction to St. Gregory of Narek's literary works, theology, and spirituality which also makes the case for the contemporary relevance of his writings to the problems that face the Church and the world today"— Provided by publisher.
Identifiers: LCCN 2019012424 (print) | ISBN 9780814685013 (hardcover)
Subjects: LCSH: Grigor, Narekats'i, Saint, 951–1003.
Classification: LCC BX129.G74 P37 2019 (print) | LCC BX129.G74 (ebook) | DDC 281/.62092—dc23
LC record available at https://lccn.loc.gov/2019012424
LC ebook record available at https://lccn.loc.gov/2019980009

In memory of Robert W. Thomson (1934–2018)
Calouste Gulbenkian Professor of Armenian (1992–2001),
Oxford University

Contents

Acknowledgments

The seed of this book was planted in 2003 at a symposium at Harvard University dedicated to the millennium of the completion of the *Book of Lamentation* of St. Gregory of Narek. I had been asked by Archbishop Oshagan Choloyan, at that time prelate of the Eastern US Prelacy of the Armenian Apostolic Church, to contribute a paper. My topic was Gregory's theology of salvation. Today, having read and learned much more, I would probably question many of the paper's conclusions but the favorable responses from other participants encouraged me to continue my efforts to articulate the theology that informs Gregory's writings. This book is in many ways the fruit of my first very modest attempt to read the saint's works theologically.

But a confluence of events would be needed for that fruit to grow. The most important of these was Pope Francis's declaration in April 2015 of St. Gregory as a Doctor of the Church. That event was for me a powerful impetus that made me recognize the need for a book in English that would introduce Gregory's life, writings, and spirituality to broad readership. The great Armenian *vardapet* was now recognized as a universal doctor whose works belong to the world and not just to Armenian Christians. There are already many very good translations of Gregory's writings in modern languages. But I did not see any book-length work in English or other major languages that addressed the relevance of the monk's theology and spirituality to contemporary world concerns. There is no doubt that Gregory's prayers are powerful medicine, remedies for the spiritual afflictions still present in the twenty-first century as much as in the tenth.

By a happy coincidence, the pope's declaration occurred just before I was eligible to apply for a sabbatical leave by Berry College. I could not have written this book without that generous grant and I am especially grateful for colleagues' assistance beginning with my dean, Thomas Kennedy, and chair, Jeffrey Lidke, who wholeheartedly endorsed my project. I am immensely grateful for the support of all my department colleagues and the faculty of the Evans School of Humanities, Arts, and Social Sciences, who encouraged me and also graciously assumed the duties I was freed from during the sabbatical. A special note of gratitude is due to Peter and Rita Lawler, my best friends at Berry. Peter, who was Dana professor of government, sadly did not live to see this book published. But the influence of his brilliance and devotion to the Catholic intellectual tradition abides in and inspires every page here.

Nor could I have accomplished anything without my family. They nurtured and raised me to love the culture and language of the Armenian people. My maternal grandparents, Krikor and Veronica Pilbosian, my paternal grandmother, Hripsime Papazian, and—though I never met him—my paternal grandfather, Barour Papazian, embodied for me the strength and resilience of this nation that has produced even in times of hardship a rich spiritual and intellectual heritage that includes Gregory's singular achievements. My parents, Pierre and Iris Papazian, made every sacrifice to support my education. My mother taught me with extraordinary devotion to read the Armenian alphabet and modern Armenian and she continues to inspire me. She is the foundation of the learning that led to this book. They along with my aunts and uncle, Margaret Papazian, Elizabeth Pilbosian, Rosely and Wally Stronski, have steadfastly supported my studies. My wife, Andrea Lowry Papazian, was my ever devoted companion and supporter throughout my research and writing. This book is an expression of my profound love for them all.

Many others helped me during my research and writing. I am especially grateful to Hans Christoffersen of Liturgical Press for his enthusiastic interest in my book proposal as well as all of the editors and staff with whom I have collaborated for the care and diligence they have shown in their work. I am also grateful to Abraham Terian, Mike Aquilina, Haig Utidjian, and Stephen Little for their perceptive thoughts and suggestions on my manuscript. All errors herein are, of course, my own.

I dedicate this book to my teacher, Professor Robert W. Thomson. When I went to Oxford in the mid-1990s to study classical Armenian under him, he encouraged me to extend my interests beyond philosophy to theology and biblical exegesis. His initial encouragement led me ultimately to the study of St. Gregory, and his kind yet exacting instruction in classical Armenian made me into the inquisitive if imperfect Armenian scholar I am today.

Michael Papazian
July 6, 2019
Feast of the Discovery of the Relics
of St. Gregory the Illuminator

Abbreviations

BL	*Book of Lamentation* (section numbering based on MH 12, 49–605)
CSCO	*Corpus scriptorum christianorum orientalium* (Paris-Louvain, 1903–)
GCS	Die griechischen christlichen Schriftsteller (Leipzig-Berlin, 1897–)
JSAS	*Journal of the Society for Armenian Studies*
JTS	*Journal of Theological Studies*
MH	*Matenagirk' Hayots' [Armenian Classical Authors]* (Antelias, Lebanon: Armenian Catholicosate of Cilicia)
NBHL	*Nor Baṛgirk' Haygazean Lezui [New Lexicon of the Armenian Language]* (Venice, San Lazzaro Press, 1836)
OCA	Orientalia Christiana Analecta (Rome, Pontifical Oriental Institute, 1945–)
PG	Patrologiae cursus completus, Series graeca (Paris: Migne, 1841–64)
REArm	*Revue des Études Arméniennes*
SC	Sources chrétiennes (Paris: Cerf, 1941–)
TLG	*Thesaurus Linguae Graecae*

Armenian Transliteration

Based on the Library of Congress system

ա	բ	գ	դ	ե	զ	է	ը	թ	ժ
a	b	g	d	e	z	ē	ĕ	t‘	zh
ի	լ	խ	ծ	կ	հ	ձ	ղ	ճ	մ
i	l	kh	ts	k	h	dz	gh	ch	m
յ	ն	շ	ո	չ	պ	ջ	ռ	ս	վ
y	n	sh	o	ch‘	p	j	ṛ	s	v
տ	ր	ց	ւ	փ	ք	օ	ֆ	ու	
t	r	ts‘	w	p‘	k‘	ō	f	u	

Introduction

> Saint Gregory of Narek, an extraordinary interpreter of the human soul, offers words which are prophetic for us: "I willingly blame myself with myriad accounts of all the incurable sins, from our first forefather through the end of his generations in all eternity, I charge myself with all these voluntarily" (*BL* 72). How striking is his sense of universal solidarity! How small we feel before the greatness of his invocations: "Remember, [Lord,] . . . those of the human race who are our enemies as well, and for their benefit accord them pardon and mercy. . . . Do not destroy those who persecute me, but reform them, root out the vile ways of this world, and plant the good in me and them" (*BL* 83).
>
> —Pope Francis[1]

On April 12, 2015, during a mass in St. Peter's Basilica commemorating the centennial of the beginning of the Armenian Genocide, Pope Francis formally pronounced the tenth-century Armenian monk, poet, and theologian St. Gregory of Narek a Doctor (from the Latin word for teacher) of the Universal Church. Gregory thereby became the thirty-sixth of these acknowledged great masters of Catholic faith and spirituality. Among the doctors are renowned theologians like St. Augustine and St. Thomas Aquinas;

[1] Pope Francis, 2015, Message on the 100th Anniversary of the Armenian Genocide and Proclamation of St. Gregory of Narek as a Doctor of the Church, accessed January 1, 2018, https://w2.vatican.va/content/francesco/en/messages/pont-messages/2015/documents/papa-francesco_20150412_messaggio-armeni.html.

mystics and visionaries like St. Teresa of Ávila, St. John of the Cross, and St. Hildegard of Bingen; and Gregory's fellow poet from the East, St. Ephrem the Syrian. Books, both scholarly and popular, about the most prominent doctors easily fill many library shelves. A reader knowing little about any of these august figures would be able to find readily at least one and often many books that would introduce their teachings. Just recently, a new English translation of Augustine's *Confessions* has been published, joining scores of other English translations of this classic.[2] Many books will gently guide anyone desiring to learn more about Aquinas's philosophy. There are several popular translations and presentations of Hildegard, the most recently proclaimed Doctor of the Church prior to Gregory.[3]

Many of Gregory's works have been translated into English in recent years. But, unlike most of his fellow doctors, there has been to date no English language monograph presenting his life and theology to a broader audience. The present book seeks to fill that void. Apart from his now being in very elite company, Gregory also deserves to be better known because of his unusual circumstances. Outside of his native Armenia he is little known and rarely studied. He is perhaps the most obscure of the doctors. Even more remarkably, he lived his entire life outside of visible communion with the Catholic Church. He was a priest and monk of the Armenian Apostolic Church, which had by the sixth century rejected the Council of Chalcedon of 451, the fourth of the great ecumenical councils that defined orthodox doctrine, thus taking his church out of communion with most of the rest of the Christian world. On a number of websites, people responded to Pope Francis's declaration with the question "Is the new Doctor of the Church a Catholic?" The quick answer to this question is negative: Gregory

[2] Augustine, 2017, *Confessions*, trans. Sarah Ruden, New York: Modern Library.

[3] For example, Brian Davies, 1993, *The Thought of Thomas Aquinas*, Oxford: Clarendon, but much earlier also G. K. Chesterton 2014, *St. Thomas Aquinas: The Dumb Ox*, New York: Image (first published in 1933). Interest in Hildegard, declared a Doctor in 2013, has generated numerous translations and original books. For a good introduction to her life and works, see Sabina Flanagan, 1998, *Hildegard of Bingen, 1098–1179: A Visionary Life*. London: Routledge.

was never during his earthly life a member of a church in communion with Rome. Consequently, the declaration of Gregory as the first "non-Catholic" Doctor of the Church is an extraordinary development in ecumenism and a gesture of charity by the Catholic Church toward another Christian church that it once deemed heretical and schismatic.

Gregory's addition to the ranks of the doctors thus has a significance that goes beyond just his writings, as impressive and important as they are. The pope's address at the beginning of the mass made clear that, beyond its ecumenical significance, his declaration was also meant as a message relevant to contemporary world affairs. Gregory bears witness to the presence of a once vibrant and flourishing Christian culture in the Middle East that today is on the verge of extinction. His monastery was abandoned during the 1915 Armenian Genocide and subsequently demolished, as were so many other churches and religious institutions in recent years in nearby countries torn apart by war. Gregory is a witness for us of an earlier period in Middle Eastern history, a time that was certainly not ideal, but when the region was more pluralistic, with members of various Christian communions as well as other religions coexisting and working together. The various ethnic and religious communities were not closed off to each other but interacted both socially and economically, and they inspired each other culturally. Gregory's native land today looks very different. The once prominent Christian presence in eastern Anatolia is almost completely nonexistent today as a result of the genocide that killed over a million Armenians and other Christians, and scattered the survivors into a diaspora that extends throughout the world. The monasteries and churches that filled the landscape of the Lake Van basin are today unused and in ruins. Gregory's life reveals to us today that the destruction and religious intolerance that has engulfed much of the world—and especially the Middle East—in recent history is by no means inevitable.

But besides testifying to a possibility of a different reality in the Middle East and other places where intolerance appears to flourish, Gregory focuses in his writings on a number of themes that are important to Francis's papacy. Among these themes is God's mercy, which Gregory illustrates and celebrates throughout his works. The prevalence in Gregory's thought of mercy, which Francis has remarked on in several of his homilies and addresses, makes him a fitting choice as the first Doctor of a papacy in which God's mercy has been a leading theme. Because mercy is so central to Gregory's works, I have thought it appropriate to refer to him as *Doctor of Mercy*.

In the last few decades, there has been a burst of new scholarship that has brought to light more details on Gregory's background, as well as on his works. This book aims to present some of the results of that scholarship, much of which is currently only available in Armenian. Now that he is a Doctor of the Universal Church, Gregory's wish that his works would reach all the people of the world has begun to be realized. My hope for this book is that it will make a modest contribution toward his goal of composing spiritual poetry to inspire and heal all the nations of the world.

This is a book primarily of theology rather than a biography of its subject. We know very little about the details of Gregory's life, an ignorance that he would encourage due to his monastic humility and his desire to represent, through his penitential prayers, not just himself but all of humanity in its reconciliation with God. Nor is this book a history. Of course, we cannot understand Gregory and his writings apart from the history and culture that shaped him, so there will be considerable attention to the history of the church and monasticism in Armenia. But the purpose of this historical information is to allow us to understand Gregory's teachings and to apply them to our lives and spiritual journey. The only reason he wrote was to offer solace and peace in the light and love of God to an agitated and alienated world. Accordingly, I will try as best I can to honor his wish that his voice may give to all people "tender inspiration, sweet embraces so that the grace of the Lord's light may enter and dwell among us."[4]

I wrote this book not strictly for specialists. Its purpose is to introduce Gregory's poetry and thought to any interested reader having some familiarity with Christian history or theology. To that end, I have attempted to keep details of a more specialized schol-

[4] *BL* 3.3; *MH* 12:67.89–93.

arly nature in the footnotes. Armenian and Greek words will occasionally intrude into the body of the text, but details of a more tangential nature are left in the footnotes. Armenian words are written according to the Library of Congress system of transliteration. However, I use common English equivalents of names whenever they exist. This is in keeping with the custom followed in the cases of names in other linguistic traditions. For example, we are used to encountering in English books not *Iōannēs* but *John* Chrysostom. So, too, it seems appropriate to refer to the subject of this book not as *Grigor Narekats'i*—the transliteration of his Armenian name followed by the name of his monastery's location appended with the Armenian place name suffix *ats'i*—but to the English equivalent, *Gregory of Narek*. In the case of names with no common English equivalents—for example, Gregory's father, *Khosrov Andzewats'i*—I keep to the Library of Congress transliteration.

The footnotes contain references to editions of the primary sources in the original languages. For Armenian authors, most of the texts are taken from the *Matenagirk' Hayots'*. I cite passages by volume, page number, and section number (or in the case of the *Book of Lamentation* and hymns, the line number). So *MH* 12:178.20 refers to volume 12, page 178, line 20. For the *Book of Lamentation*, I also cite the prayer number and section according to the *MH* arrangement. When English translations are available, I give the page reference to the translation, although my translations will often differ, usually not significantly, from the cited version.

Biblical citations and verse numbering (including the numbering of the psalms) are based on the New Revised Standard Version. The only exception is that I translate Gregory's version of biblical passages in those cases in which his text differs significantly from the NRSV.

Reading St. Gregory in Translation

Those readers wanting to read Gregory's writings in English translation now have available to them a number of good translations. His great poem, the *Book of Lamentation*, was translated by Thomas J. Samuelian under its alternate title, *Speaking with God from the Depths of the Heart*.[5] The most recent editions of this translation include revisions made with the Armenian-American poet Diana Der Hovanessian. For those who know French, the translation by Annie and Jean-Pierre Mahé has the advantage of a detailed introduction and extensive annotations.[6] Translating Gregory is a difficult task. Virtually every page of his great poem contains neologisms and obscure expressions. He introduced a large number of words into Armenian, for we find hundreds of entries in the monumental Armenian lexicon *Nor Baṙgirk' Haykazean Lezui (New Lexicon of the Armenian Language)* that cite just a single passage from Gregory's corpus. When I discuss any such words in this book, I designate them as *hapax legomena* or simply a *hapax*, which means that they are words that occur only once in the known body of ancient and medieval Armenian literature.

Beyond just the presence of these singular words in Gregory's poetry, his style is also highly complex and demanding. He makes use of wordplay and equivocation that often defies translation. Although I consulted both of these translations in the course of writing this book, I generally offer my own translations from the Armenian text of the *Book of Lamentation*.[7] When I deviate from other translations, whether of this work or Gregory's other writings, I do not mean to suggest that the other translations are in error. Usually my revisions are done to emphasize a point I wish to make or to bring forward the theological or historical context of Gregory's text. Samuelian and the Mahés have both produced fine translations that allow the reader to get a good sense of Gregory's poem.

For Gregory's commentary on the Song of Songs there is an excellent and elegant English translation by Roberta Ervine.[8] Ervine's

[5] Thomas J. Samuelian and Diana Der Hovanessian, eds., 2016, *Speaking with God from the Depths of the Heart: The Armenian Prayer Book of St. Gregory of Narek*, fifth edition, Yerevan: Vem Press.

[6] Annie and Jean-Pierre Mahé, 2000, *Tragédie: Matean Ołbergut'ean*, CSCO 584, Louvain: Peeters.

[7] Grigor Narekats'i, 2008, *Matenagirk' Hayots'* [*Armenian Classical Authors*] 12, Antelias: Lebanon: Catholicosate of Cilicia.

[8] Roberta R. Ervine, 2007, *The Blessing of Blessings: Gregory of Narek's Commentary on the Song of Songs*, Collegeville, MN: Liturgical Press.

introduction also provides important insights on the historical and theological background of the work. The French translation by Lévon Pétrossian is a valuable resource that includes a detailed set of introductions and notes.[9]

Abraham Terian's skilled and inspiring translations of the festal hymns and encomia make available to English readers even more of Gregory's corpus.[10] The hymns show that Gregory's poetic genius extends beyond the *Book of Lamentation* to his liturgical compositions, while the encomia are important sources of Gregory's theology and his perspective on church history. Thamar Dasnabedian's French translation and more extended treatment of the encomium on the Virgin Mary is also highly recommended especially for those interested in Gregory's Mariology.[11]

It is hoped that more translations and studies, especially of his enormous body of hymns, will soon appear now that Gregory is gaining a wider profile within the universal church.

[9] Lévon Pétrossian, 2010, *Commentaire sur le Cantique des Cantiques*, OCA 285, Rome: Pontifical Oriental Institute.

[10] Abraham Terian, 2016, *The Festal Works of St. Gregory of Narek*, Collegeville, MN: Liturgical Press.

[11] Thamar Dasnabedian, 1995, *Le Panégyrique de la Sainte Mère de Dieu de Grigor Narekac'i*, Antelias, Lebanon: Catholicosate of Cilicia.

Chapter One

The Advent of Christianity in Armenia

The road leading to Khor Virap monastery runs south from the present-day Armenian capital of Yerevan toward the massive peaks of Mount Ararat. At the monastery, they appear to be within one's reach, even though their summits are several miles away on the other side of the closed border dividing Armenia and Turkey. The monastery is named for the deep pit or dungeon in which St. Gregory the Illuminator, the fourth-century patron saint and apostle to the Armenians, was imprisoned for over a decade. The pit is still there beneath a chapel, and pilgrims today can climb down a ladder into the depths of darkness below to Gregory's cell. Just as the new humanity represented by Noah's family is believed to have descended from these mountains to the plain below as the flood waters receded to recreate human life, so too Gregory the Illuminator ascended from the torment of the pit up to the very same plain to bring the light of Christ to the Armenian nation, baptizing the nation in the new and living water. Confined in the pit by order of the Armenian King Tiridates, Gregory was revealed to be the only salvation for the king ravaged by a disease that rendered him into the form of a wild beast.

Or so goes the account in the hagiography of St. Gregory, written by the shadowy figure named Agathangelos.[1] If we relied only on

[1] In Armenian, *Agat'angeghos*, a transliteration of the Greek word meaning "good messenger." For Armenian text and English translation, see Robert W. Thomson, 1976, *Agathangelos, History of the Armenians*, Albany: SUNY Press. The history exists in several recensions and translations, including Greek, Syriac, Ethiopic, Arabic, and Latin translations.

the account found in the Armenian version of Agathangelos's history, we would suppose that there was no Christian presence in Armenia prior to the fourth century. But other narratives speak of a much older form of Armenian Christianity practiced privately and without official sanction, dating back to the missionary activity of two of Christ's apostles, Thaddeus and Bartholomew. Several Armenian chronicles and martyrologies relate Thaddeus's mission. According to these narratives, Thaddeus journeyed to Armenia from the kingdom of Edessa (present-day Şanlıurfa in Turkey) to the southern regions of Armenia after having converted the Edessan king Abgar. There he met with some success even among members of the royal family, when he converted Sandukht, the daughter of the Armenian king Sanatruk. Sandukht refused to apostasize even after her father had imprisoned her in an effort to persuade her to renounce her faith. In the end, she was put to death by order of the king and thus became the first recorded martyr of Armenia. Thaddeus himself is believed to have been killed several days later in Artaz (present-day Manku in northwestern Iran).[2]

The existence of a significant Christian community in Armenia before the conversion of the royal family in the fourth century is supported by the testimony of the Christian historian Eusebius of Caesarea (ca. 260–339), who records the name of a mid-third-century bishop of Armenia, Merouzanēs, most likely a Greek rendering of the Armenian name Meruzhan.[3] The need for a bishop implies a sizable Christian community in Armenia at this time. All indications are that this early presence of Christianity emanated from the south, particularly from Syria. Accordingly, a strong Syriac influence characterizes the most ancient forms of Armenian Christianity not only in terms of language and culture but also theology and the practice of the faith. Among the most significant Syrian imports into Armenia were the ascetic monastics and hermits, whom

[2] For the martyrdom in Armenian, see Mkhit'arean Fathers, 1853, *Vkayabanut'iwn ew giwt nshkharats' srboyn T'adei ar'ak'eloy ew Sandkhtoy kusi* [Martyrology and discovery of the relics of St. Thaddeus the Apostle and the Virgin Sandukht], Venice: Mkhit'arean Press.

[3] Eusebius, 1957, *Histoire ecclésiastique*, trans. Gustave Bardy, SC 41, Paris: Cerf, 6.46.2.8–9.

we will encounter in the discussion of monasticism in chapter two. But the Syriac influence on Armenian Christianity extends to its literature, liturgy, and even church architecture. Syriac literature and theology would continue to inform the development of Armenian Christianity even after the earliest centuries of Christianity. The Armenian translation of the Bible was produced in two stages in the first half of the fifth century.[4] The translators used both Greek and Syriac manuscripts, so the Syriac version of the Old Testament in particular had a profound effect on the Armenian version of the Bible. Beginning in the fifth century, Armenian scholars produced Armenian versions of Greek literature, but they also translated Syriac writings, ensuring that Armenian theology would also have a strong Syrian as well as Greek influence. In chapter nine our attention will focus on Gregory's Mariology and how Syriac writings, especially the Marian poetry of the great theologian St. Ephrem the Syrian (306–73), shaped the Virgin's portrayal in Gregory's own poetic compositions. The examples of Syriac influence include vestiges of a more ancient form of worship that shows continuity with Judaism. Syrian Christianity had a closer relation to Judaism than did Greek Christianity due to a shared Aramaic language and culture.[5] Consequently, some of the Armenian borrowings from Syriac Christianity have conferred on the Armenian rite a closer relation to ancient Judaism. A conspicuous example is the altar curtain reminiscent of the curtain that conceals the holy of holies in the Jerusalem temple. In Byzantine-rite churches the iconostasis has taken the place of the curtain. Armenian churches, by contrast, tend to be marked by a relative paucity of icons.

While Syrian-oriented Christianity in Armenia existed independently of the Armenian political authorities—and was at least sometimes at odds with it—the Greek-oriented Christianity influenced mostly by the church in Cappadocia would gain the support of the Armenian royalty in a dramatic way. The Armenian royal

[4] For a brief history of the Armenian Bible, see Vrej Nersessian, 2001, *The Bible in the Armenian Tradition*, Los Angeles: Getty Museum.

[5] Lucas von Rompay, 2008, "The East (3): Syria and Mesopotamia" in Susan A. Harvey and David G. Hunter, eds., *Oxford Handbook of Early Christian Studies*, Oxford: Oxford University Press, 365–86, especially 367-68.

family enjoyed a close relation with the Persian Empire, whose emperors were members of a branch of the same Arsacid family until the Persian Arsacids were overthrown in 226 CE by the Sassanian dynasty. Because of the suspicion and mistrust that developed between the Armenian Arsacids and the Persian Sassanids, the Armenian royalty began to turn more toward the West and look to the Roman Empire for political and military support. The Armenian shift toward the West, where Christianity was growing rapidly, and away from Iran and its ancient Zoroastrian religion would prove to be consequential. It is within the context of Armenia's westward turn that the most far-reaching event in Armenian history took place. The conversion and baptism of the king and the royal family would touch every aspect of Armenian culture—its art, literature, music, and architecture—and permanently alter Armenia's political relations with its neighbors.

According to Agathangelos, these tensions between the Armenian Arsacids and the Persian Sassanids formed the background to the eventual conversion of the Armenian king. The success of the Arsacid armies in their invasion and plundering of Persian territory enraged the Persian emperor, Artashir, who dispatched a Parthian nobleman named Anak to the Arsacid court on the pretext of aiding the Armenians. His true mission was to assassinate the Armenian king, whom Agathangelos names as Khosrov. Anak succeeded in killing Khosrov, who just before he died ordered his princes to execute Anak's family. Two of Anak's infant sons were saved by their nurses, one being sent to Persia and the other to Greek territory. Meanwhile Artashir had enslaved the Armenian royal family with the exception of the Armenian king's infant son Tiridates,[6] who was furtively dispatched to Rome, where he was raised and received his education.

The son of Anak who had been removed to Greek territory—specifically Cappadocia, already an important early Christian center in central Anatolia—was named Gregory and his caretakers raised him as a Christian. When he had grown up, Gregory learned about his father's crime and decided to offer his services to Tiridates

[6] The Hellenized form of the Armenian name *Trdat*.

without revealing his identity. With Roman backing, Tiridates was restored to the throne of Armenia. Although Gregory served the king, his unwillingness to worship the pagan gods enraged Tiridates, who ordered Gregory to be tortured in an effort to force him to renounce his Christianity. Agathangelos provides detailed accounts of these tortures and Gregory's miraculous ability through prayer to withstand them and refuse to abandon his faith. In his commentary on the Song of Songs, Gregory of Narek refers to his namesake's prayers to God during his torment:

> [T]he saints would have liked, had it been possible, to have died for him not once but ten thousand times; nay, daily, as they said in so many words. Thus, Saint Gregory said to Tiridates, "I have requested Him to make me endure it." Likewise, in his prayers he begged God to make him endure it. Now since the desire of the just is acceptable to Him, He grants them endurance.[7]

After one of the Arsacid princes revealed Gregory's true identity to Tiridates, the king commanded that the saint be confined in a deep dungeon in the city of Artashat, what is now the Khor Virap monastery. The length of Gregory's imprisonment varies depending on which version of Agathangelos's hagiography we read. The Greek version says his imprisonment lasted fourteen years, while the Armenian recensions say thirteen.[8] There are also differing explanations of how Gregory managed to survive. According to one tradition, a pious Christian widow who lived in the castle of the dungeon threw down a loaf of bread for him every day.

Toward the end of Gregory's lengthy imprisonment, a convent of nuns residing in Rome fled the persecutions of Christians under the Roman Emperor Diocletian (r. 284–305). They reached Armenia where they were brought to Tiridates's attention. Tiridates was attracted to one of the nuns, Hripsimē, who resisted his advances and fled from the palace. Eventually she was captured along with

[7] *MH* 12:824.104–6; translation from Ervine 2007, 150–51.

[8] For the Greek version, see Guy Lafontaine, 1973, *La version grecque ancienne du livre arménien d'Agathange*, Louvain-la-Neuve: Université Catholique de Louvain, 54.21–21.

her abbess, Gayanē, and their thirty-three companion nuns, all of whom were executed.

As a result of Tiridates's wickedness, the king was afflicted with a debilitating illness that transformed him into a "wallowing pig."[9] His doctors were unable to cure him, but his sister Khosrovidukht had a vision in which it was revealed to her that only Gregory, now long believed dead in the dungeon, could heal the king. Retrieved from his pit, his skin as black as coal, Gregory was brought to Tiridates, who begged for his forgiveness. Gregory proclaimed that only God could heal Tiridates, and then only if he confessed his sins, ended his persecution of Christians, and was baptized. After Tiridates's penance, Gregory proceeded to deliver homilies to the royal family to instruct them in the teachings of Christianity. Agathangelos includes in his history a text now called "The Teaching of St. Gregory" that purports to be the words of the saint's homilies, but it is most likely a later elaboration and development of Gregory's teachings.[10] Gregory of Narek knows these homilies and cites them several times in his interpretations of the Song of Songs. For example, in his commentary on Song of Songs 8:5—"Under an apple tree I will awaken you"—Gregory inserts a remark on apples drawn from these homilies: "The apple is a wholesome food, and very appealing to the sick, and very appropriate for kings, and through its diverse fragrances makes the palate of those who smell it sweet, as St. Gregory our Illuminator says."[11]

Tiridates remained ill through all this, and it was only when Gregory gave the martyred nuns a proper burial that he was fully healed. In a vision, Gregory saw a man in the form of light descend to the ground and strike the ground with a golden hammer. Interpreting the man of his vision to be Christ, Gregory built on that spot, in the city of Vagharshapat, a church that would be known as Ējmiatsin, or "the Only-Begotten One descended." This was to become the cathedral that is today the see of the catholicos (chief

[9] Thomson 1976, §727.

[10] Robert W. Thomson, 2001, *The Teaching of Saint Gregory*, rev. ed., New Rochelle, NY: St. Nersess Armenian Seminary.

[11] *MH* 12:866.37–39; Ervine 2007, 192–193. As Ervine notes, the passage is from *Teaching of St. Gregory* §347.

bishop) of the Armenian Apostolic Church. Gregory also had built three chapels forming a triangle centered on Ējmiatsin at the locations of the nun's martyrdom, one dedicated to St. Hripsimē, one for the abbess St. Gayanē, and one named Shoghakat' ("drop of light") for an anonymous nun who was discovered and executed apart from her sister nuns.

Now that the king was healed, he declared Christianity the official religion of the realm. He ordered Gregory to be ordained and to begin efforts to convert the people to the new faith. Gregory received his episcopal ordination from the bishop of Caesarea in Cappadocia, the see on which the Armenian Church would depend until it became autocephalous in 374. As an ordained bishop, Gregory was now able to consecrate the church buildings that had already been erected, and he began to destroy pagan temples and build churches in their place. Especially important for understanding Narek's story is that this earlier Gregory also established monastic institutions throughout Armenia. He ended his life as a hermit in the caves near Mount Sepuh near the modern northeastern Turkish city of Erzincan, an area that would later become a major monastic center. He would come to be known as St. Gregory the Illuminator (*Lusaworich'*), for he brought the light of Christ to and baptized the Armenian nation. In order to avoid confusing him with Gregory of Narek, I will henceforth refer to him as the Illuminator.

Armenia's official conversion is usually said to have taken place in 301, although it is impossible to be certain that this is the exact year. We can be confident that it occurred in the first decade of the fourth century and that it preceded the edict of Constantine that gave Christianity a special privilege among the religions of the Roman Empire. For this reason, Armenia is generally acknowledged to be the first Christian nation, a matter of pride and distinction for many Armenians today. Countless churches are dedicated to the Illuminator, and his relics are among the most venerated in the Armenian tradition. Visitors to the Vatican today will see a statue of the Illuminator in one of the external niches in the north façade of St. Peter's Basilica, erected in 2005 and blessed by Pope St. John Paul II.

When the Illuminator withdrew from his office as catholicos, he entrusted the see to his son Aristakēs, establishing a precedent that would continue for several generations as his descendants occupied the patriarchal see. Aristakēs took part in the Council of Nicaea in 325, the first of the ecumenical councils that defined the orthodox faith. Although the royal family was Christian and the church in Armenia enjoyed their support and patronage, pre-Christian beliefs and rituals persisted among the people. The work of converting the people and suppressing those practices that were considered contrary to Christian doctrine continued to occupy the hierarchy of the church, notably during the pontificate of Catholicos Nersēs I (r. 353–73). Nersēs was the great-grandson of the Illuminator and is often called the Second Illuminator for his ambitious philanthropic program of building hospitals, monasteries, and inns throughout the country. Concerned by the plight of the poor, he welcomed to his home and dining table "the poor, the alien, and the stranger."[12] He built houses for the homeless so that they would not need to live and beg in the streets. He exhorted the wealthy to acts of charity and admonished them to be mindful that their "sins must be expiated through compassion and their iniquity through charity and gifts to the poor."[13] In these efforts to serve the people, he was inspired by and followed the lead of his mentor, the Cappadocian Father St. Basil of Caesarea (329–379), also renowned for his philanthropic endeavors.

Nersēs was murdered by the Armenian king Pap in 373. Their enmity was the result of Pap's adherence to the teachings of Arius, an early fourth-century cleric who taught that the Son of God was a created being subordinate to the Father. The Council of Nicaea in 325 proclaimed that Father and Son are one in essence, and thus they are both uncreated eternal persons of the one God. The Nicene bishops declared Arius a heretic. But Arianism still had adherents after Nicaea, and the Armenian king was among them. Like his predecessors and his mentor Basil, Nersēs was a staunch defender of the Nicene doctrine. Nersēs had barred the king from entering any churches until he renounced Arianism. Provoked by Nersēs's rebukes, the king invited the catholicos to a banquet

[12] English translation with introduction and comprehensive commentary: Nina G. Garsoïan, 1989, *The Epic Histories Attributed to P'awstos Buzand*, Cambridge, MA: Harvard University Press, 114–15.

[13] Garsoïan 1989, 115.

under the pretext of requesting penance, but instead had him poisoned.[14]

The Origins of Armenian Writing and Literature

Nersēs's son Isaac (Armenian: *Sahak*) eventually succeeded him in 387, after a hiatus during which catholicoi unrelated to the family of the Illuminator occupied the patriarchal throne. That same year Armenia was partitioned between the Roman and Persian empires. The division of Armenia was a formidable impediment to the unity of the church, with Armenians in the Roman part of the country writing in Greek and those in the Persian sector using Syriac for their written language. Up until then, Armenian was strictly an oral language; there is no evidence of any written Armenian before the fifth century. Since the Bible was only available in Greek and Syriac, priests would have to give impromptu translations of the readings in their homilies. With this problem in mind, Isaac commissioned a monk named Mashtots' to devise an alphabet suitable for the Armenian language.[15]

An earlier attempt to invent an Armenian alphabet proved to be a failure. It was devised by a Syrian monk named Daniel, but the Syriac-based alphabet that Daniel used was not suitable for the unrelated Armenian language. The alphabet designed by Mashtots', which contains thirty-six letters, was unique; while some of the letters vaguely resemble Greek characters, most do not look like the letters of any other writing system.[16] The new alphabet came into use in the early fifth century. Almost immediately after its introduction, Isaac, Mashtots', and their disciples began to translate the

[14] Garsoïan 1989, 203–4.

[15] For Armenian text of the *Life of Mashtots'*, written by his disciple Koriwn, see *MH* 1:229–72. For German translation with commentary, see Gabriele Winkler, 1994, *Koriwns Biographie des Mesrop Maštoc': Übersetzung und Kommentar*, OCA 245, Rome: Pontifical Oriental Institute.

[16] During the late Middle Ages two letters were added to the original thirty-six, but other than that change, the alphabet remains the same today. There is an intriguing similarity between some of the Armenian letters and those of the ancient Ethiopian Ge'ez script but it is not known if the resemblance is the result of some influence or is merely coincidental.

Bible into Armenian. The first version was deemed imperfect, and after some of the disciples brought back other manuscripts, a second, corrected version based on Greek and Syriac translations was produced. Besides translating the Bible, these fifth-century scholars produced liturgical texts. For the first time, the church could speak directly to the Armenian people in their language. For several centuries afterward, scholars belonging to what has more recently been called the "Hellenizing School" translated many Greek texts, both sacred and secular, into Armenian. Some of the works of Aristotle, as well as Neoplatonic commentaries on Aristotle, appeared in Armenian and became the basis of the philosophical curriculum of the monastic academies even as late as the eighteenth century. Armenian scholars translated patristic writings—including those of the Cappadocian Fathers, Basil, Gregory of Nyssa, and Gregory of Nazianzus (known in the Armenian tradition, as in the Byzantine, simply as "the Theologian"), and those from the Syriac tradition. Gregory of Narek draws heavily on the Cappadocian fathers, especially in his commentary on the Song of Songs. In particular, he makes copious use of Gregory of Nyssa's commentary on the Song but also frequently cites Gregory of Nazianzus too.[17] Especially important for the scholars of Narek was the corpus of writings attributed to Dionysius the Areopagite. The Pseudo-Dionysian works, as they are now called, had a significant influence on ecclesiastical organization and practice. Gregory was familiar with these writings and bases various facets of his thought on them.

The new alphabet also advanced the Armenians' sense of belonging to one nation, for although they were divided politically into Greek and Persian jurisdictions, they could communicate by writing in one language and also produce not only translations but original works of theology and literature. The alphabet enabled gifted authors like Gregory to develop a rich literature and forms of expression that both transformed the language and preserved it for later generations.

[17] Because we have a surfeit of Gregories, I will adopt the practice of referring to the Cappadocians by their place names—Nyssen and Nazianzen—while reserving the given name Gregory for the monk of Narek.

Armenia's Isolation

During the remainder of the fifth century, two events isolated the Armenian church from much of the rest of the Christian world while also allowing it to develop its distinctive identity. One was a devastating war with Persia beginning in 451 that grew out of the aggressive policy of the Sassanian monarch to impose Zoroastrianism in Armenia. Earlier in the century, the Armenian satraps—the governors of the various provinces in Armenia, who were always resentful of the Armenian kings' dominance—had persuaded the Persians to abolish the Armenian monarchy. The last Arsacid king of Armenia, Artaxias (or Artashēs) IV, was deposed in 428. Without a strong central government, the Armenians were now more vulnerable to Persian aggression.[18] The Armenians' faith posed a greater threat to the Persians now that the Roman Empire was also officially Christian too, and thus the Armenians living within the Persian Empire would have cause to align themselves with Rome and resist Persian rule. The Persians, with their enormous armed force and the aid of Armenian defectors, had the upper hand militarily, but the vehemence of the Armenian opposition caused the Persians to relent and allow the Armenians to practice the Christian faith without interference. The Persians also needed the support of the Armenians to defend the empire's eastern borders from the incursions of the Huns. In 485, envoys of the Persian king Vagharsh met with the Armenian nobility to conclude a peace treaty that guaranteed the Armenians the right to practice the Christian faith.

The war with Persia drew the attention of the church hierarchy away from the fifth-century debates and controversies on Christian dogma. After the council of Nicaea, two other ecumenical councils took place, one in Constantinople in 381 that clarified the doctrine of the Holy Spirit and articulated the basic Trinitarian doctrine of the orthodox church that is represented in what is now called the Nicene Creed. The fifth-century debates focused not on the Trinity

[18] See Nina Garsoïan, 1997, "The Aršakuni Dynasty," in R. G. Hovanissian, ed., *The Armenian People from Ancient to Modern Times* 1, New York: St. Martin's Press, 87.

but on the person of Christ. Disagreements about Christology—the branch of theology that studies who Christ is and how his divinity and humanity relate to each other—would tear the church apart. In 431 an ecumenical council held in Ephesus defined Christ in a way that was acceptable to most Christians but not to those who followed the teachings of the patriarch of Constantinople, Nestorius (ca. 386–450). Nestorius's Christology seemed to imply the existence of two persons in Christ: the divine Word of God and a human, Jesus. The relation of these two persons was a very close association rather than a perfect union. Those who preferred Nestorius's Christology broke off from the church and established a distinct hierarchy. At the same time, Christians who accepted the christological definition approved at Ephesus considered the Nestorians to be heretics. Along with the christological debate that was, at least in most Christians' eyes, settled at Ephesus, there was a closely related question about the status of Mary. Could we say of Mary, as some hymns already did, that she is the Mother or Bearer of God? The Greek word for this title of Mary is *theotokos*.[19] There were obvious problems with saying that the mortal human Mary gave birth to the eternal Word of God rather than just the human Jesus. The bishops assembled at Ephesus, led by the Alexandrian patriarch St. Cyril of Alexandria (ca. 375–444), affirmed the union of the divine and human in the one person of Christ. It followed that whatever one can say of Christ's humanity can equally be applied to the incarnate Word. If Mary is the mother of Jesus the human being, she is also the mother of the Word of God. Any attempt to distinguish between the human and the divine in Christ drives a wedge between the two and thus subverts the oneness of Christ's person. The Armenian church had accepted the conclusions of all three of these councils: Nicaea, Constantinople, and Ephesus. But then, in order to repair the schism with the Nestorians and to resolve some questions that emerged from Ephesus, another council was convened without Armenian participation, this time in Chalcedon, near Constantinople, in 451. This was the same year that the Armenian war with the Persians began and so no

[19] Its Armenian equivalent is *Asdvadzadzin*, literally, "the birth-giver of God."

Armenian bishops were present at Chalcedon. This council issued a new christological formula, one that the Armenian church would formally reject about a century later. I devote the next section to the specifics of the theological debate and the reasons for the Armenian church's rejection of Chalcedon. It will suffice here to note that the rejection of Chalcedon led to schism with most other churches, in particular with the sees of Rome and Constantinople. Numerous attempts during the following centuries to enact a compromise and reunite the churches failed. The Armenian church never again accepted an ecumenical council and essentially went its own way theologically, though it remained in communion with the non-Chalcedonian churches that emerged with their separate hierarchies in Syria and Egypt. Yet there were still many Chalcedonians in Armenia, including bishops. And many more bishops, priests, and monks fell under suspicion of accepting Chalcedon. Such accusations were made not only against Gregory, who may have been charged with heresy late in his life, but also his father, Khosrov, a bishop of a diocese adjoining the province in which the monastery of Narek was located, and perhaps Anania of Narek, the founding abbot of the monastery. In the cases of Gregory and Khosrov (and probably also Anania), the allegations against them were that they were covert Chalcedonians. These accusations were almost certainly unfounded, but that they were made at all indicates that the level of vehemence and outrage surrounding Chalcedon and the attendant christological conflicts had not abated even after five centuries.

As the Persian threat to Armenia waned, another nation would come to dominate Armenia politically and also influence its culture. Beginning in the middle of the seventh century, the Arabic-speaking people began to expand rapidly and were able very quickly to alter the political dynamics of the entire Mediterranean world. The Arabs succeeded in defeating the Persians at the battle of Qadisiyya in 636 and soon after that conquered Syria, Mesopotamia, and Egypt. Uniting them was not only their language and culture but also the adoption by many Arabs of the new faith of Islam, the religion that would come to dominate the region and reduce the Christian population in much of the Middle East to the status of a minority. Armenia also endured the invasions of Arab armies and came under the domination of Arab governors. While in some cases Arab rule was tolerant, the Arab governors of Armenia could also be very harsh. The first governor, Muḥammad ibn Marwān, the brother of the Umayyad caliph who appointed him, and his successor 'Abdullah are remembered in Armenian sources as especially cruel rulers. The tenth-century catholicos and historian John (Yovhannēs) of Draskhanakert calls the latter a "wicked, insolent man, extremely malicious by nature, who tortured the princes and nobles with bonds and plundered the property and possessions of the people."[20] Ibn Marwān imprisoned the Armenian catholicos, Isaac (Sahak) III, and sent him into exile in Damascus. Arab rule often imposed burdensome taxes on the Armenians, and the nobility suffered torture and executions or forced apostasy at the hands of Arab rulers. At other times, though, Arab rule was less oppressive than Byzantine rule, which could be heavy-handed in its treatment of non-Chalcedonians. For the Muslim Arabs such fine christological distinctions were not of much consequence. An Arab source, the ninth-century historian al-Balādhuri records the agreement between an Arab general and the capital Armenian city of Duin that pledged to honor the lives, possessions, and houses of worship of the Christians, Jews, and Zoroastrians living there.[21] It is not known if the general actually honored the agreement, but the fact that the Armenian church could convene councils without the interference of the Arab rulers, as occurred twice during the pontificate of John of Ōdzun (Ōdznets'i; r. 717–28), indicates the church at least during some decades was free to function autonomously.[22]

Although at first the Arab domination was primarily a military occupation and did not bring with it significant civilian Arab settlements on Armenian lands, beginning in the ninth century several Arab emirates were established in Armenia. Some of the Arab emirs married into Armenian noble families and even converted to Christianity.[23] The Arab population tended to center around the urban centers, with the Armenians mainly residing in rural areas.

[20] Armenian text in *MH* 11.1:415–16.28:35; Garsoïan 1997, 126–27.

[21] Garsoïan 1997, 121.

[22] Garsoïan 1997, 125.

[23] Garsoïan 1997, 135.

The Arab presence also had a lasting effect on Armenian culture. By the time of the invasions, Arabs had already created a rich tradition of both oral and written poetry that utilized techniques, such as end rhyme, that were previously unknown in Armenia. The Qur'an was composed in verse, and Armenians would have heard its recitation now that there was an Islamic presence in their country. Impressed as well by the captivating cadences of Arabic folk poetry and music, Armenians began to appropriate the styles of their new neighbors into their own oral poetry. The resulting cultural fusion would be momentous for Gregory's own poetic creations. He is the first Armenian writer of poetry, whether secular or sacred, to use rhyme and to attempt to conform his literary poetic style to the folk poetry of his time. His achievement is all the more notable given that his genre was sacred poetry, which tends to be more conservative and less open to adopting folk styles than secular poetry. Certainly, the poetry of the psalms was foremost in Gregory's mind, so he had an exquisite sacred poetry to draw from within his own tradition and scripture. The psalmist makes use of many of the poetic devices that Gregory exploits, including alliteration and assonance. But rhyme, which Gregory uses in some of the prayers of the *Book of Lamentation*, is not found in the psalter.

Gregory's immediate aim in writing poetry that resembled the inflections of Armenian oral poetry, now refashioned through contact with Arabic models, was to heighten its popular appeal in the same way that religious music does by mimicking the melodies and rhythms of its contemporary secular music. In this way, the Arabic influence on Gregory's poetics is indirect, mediated through Arabic-influenced Armenian folk culture. But we cannot discount direct contact with Arabic poetry and its methods. One is tempted even to consider the intriguing possibility that Gregory had the Qur'an in mind when composing his poetry. Besides the poetic commonalities, there are other similarities too. For example, almost every prayer of the *Book of Lamentation* begins with the same refrain just as each *surah*, or chapter, of the Qur'an begins "In the name of God, the compassionate, the merciful." The influence of the Qur'an and Islamic religious poetry on Gregory cannot be ruled out. We know that his near contemporary, the nobleman and prodigious scholar Gregory Magistros Pahlawuni (ca. 990–1058), produced a concise rhymed narrative of biblical events in response to a Muslim interlocutor who had boasted of the superiority of the Qur'an to the Bible because it was written entirely in verse. In composing the first extant work of completely rhymed Armenian poetry, Gregory Magistros consciously followed Arabic models, even noting that he used the Arabic *qâfiyah* rhyme scheme.[24] Gregory of Narek may not have been directly motivated to write his poetry by a polemical Islamic argument for the divine inspiration of the Qur'an, as Gregory Magistros was. But he may still have consciously desired to keep up with the latest developments in sacred poetics by composing a new book of poems that would provide a Christian alternative to the Qur'an's novel and enticing lyricism.

Gregory may have welcomed the introduction of Arabic poetry and music into his country but his attitude toward Islam was not as amiable. He makes few direct references to Islam, but when he does mention the religion he connects it with Christian heresies like Nestorianism. For example, in the commentary on the Song of Songs he equates the doctrines of the "Mohammedans" (*Mahmetakats'n*) to the thoughts of the "vile Nestorius."[25] This attitude toward Islam as equivalent to Christian heresy—based on Gregory's conflation of the Islamic belief that Christ, though a prophet, is merely a man and not the Son of God, with what he takes to be Nestorius's denial of Christ's divinity—is in basic agreement with the assessment of St. John of Damascus (ca. 676–749). The Damascene, one of the earliest Christian witnesses to the burgeoning faith, suggested that Muhammad fell under the influence of an Arian monk.[26]

[24] For the text of the poem, Grigor Magistros Pahlawuni, 1868, *Taghats'ut'iwnk'* [Odes], Venice: San Lazarro, 1–79. See also A. J. Hacikyan et al., 2002, *The Heritage of Armenian Literature: From the Sixth to the Eighteenth Century* 2, Detroit: Wayne State University, 325.

[25] *MH* 12.830.154; Ervine 2007, 157.

[26] For a provocative discussion of the different paradigms of Christian engagement with Islam, see Alain Besançon, 2002, *Trois tentations dans l'Église*, Collection Tempus 19, Paris: Perrin, especially 150–55 for discussion of the Damascene's views of Islam. For the sources, see Raymond Le Coz, 1992, *Jean Damascène, Écrits sur l'Islam*, SC 383, Paris: Cerf.

Restoration of Autonomy

By the middle of the ninth century the Arab hold over Armenia had weakened. Two of the noble houses of Armenia began to enjoy greater autonomy. In the north, the Bagratuni family emerged as the dominant political force. In 862 the Arab caliph confirmed Ashot Bagratuni as "prince of princes" of Armenia. A few years later, around 884, the Byzantine emperor recognized Ashot as the legitimate ruler in Armenia and bestowed on him the crown. Ashot thus became the first recognized king of Armenia since the demise of the Arsacid dynasty. Meanwhile, in the southern regions of Armenia around Lake Van, another noble family, the Artsruni, began to consolidate their power. With the support of one of the Muslim emirs, an Artsruni prince named Gagik declared himself king of his realm, Vaspurakan. By offering these privileges and distinctions to the rival families, the Byzantine and Arab rulers were, of course, playing a tactical game against each other as they attempted to gain the favor and military support of the Armenian nobility.

As rival royal houses, the Artsruni and Bagratuni made grandiose claims about their pedigree to bolster their standing. The Bagratids boasted of their descent from King David while the Artsruni recognized the Assyrian king Sennacherib as their ancestor.[27] They both also took great interest in the affairs of the church, and for a time the residence of the catholicos—who was considered the bishop of the Armenian royal family since the time of Tiridates—shifted back and forth between Bagratuni and Artsruni lands. Both houses also spent lavishly to build formidable palaces and churches. The pride of the Bagratuni was their capital city of Ani, today a desolate field dotted with the ruins of churches on the Turkish side of the Akhurian river that forms the border with Armenia, but once a vast metropolis. The centerpiece of Artsruni architectural achievement was the island of Aght'amar in Lake Van. There, Gagik built his palace and a uniquely magnificent palatine

[27] Gérard Dédéyan, 2010, "Princes et rois du Vaspurakan face à leur Église (VIII–XIe siècles)," in Jean-Pierre Mahé, Boghos Levon Zekiyan, and Paul Rouhana, *Saint Grégoire de Narek et la liturgie de L'Église: colloque international*. Revue théologique de Kaslik 3/4, Kaslik: Faculté pontificale de théologie, 57–72.

Cathedral of the Holy Cross. Since Narek is located on the southern shore of Lake Van in the Vaspurakan realms under Artsruni dominion and not far from Aght'amar, I will begin the next chapter by focusing on the kingdom of Vaspurakan and in particular the Artsrunis's patronage of the church and then turn to the theological background of Gregory's work.

Chapter Two
The Political and Theological Background

The Kingdom of Vaspurakan

As the two new Armenian royal families obtained some measure of sovereignty over their lands, Armenia began to experience a cultural renaissance, one in which the church would take a leading role. New monasteries and churches were established, but in addition to this flourishing of material culture, Armenia also experienced a spiritual renaissance born from a sense that the Christian faith needed to penetrate more deeply into the daily lives of the faithful in order to sustain the new church structures and monastic institutions.

The Artsruni family played a central role as patrons of this renaissance. They charged their resident historian, a priest named Thomas (T'ovma) Artsruni, with the task of glorifying the family's ancestry not only by tying the rulers of Vaspurakan to ancient Assyrian kings but also by affirming a bond with the earliest Christians in Armenia.[1] A prince of their house named Khuran is said to have been baptized at the hands of the apostle Thaddeus himself.[2] According to Thomas, it was the first Arsacid king of Armenia who conferred on the Artsruni family the lands of Vaspurakan. The

[1] *MH* 11.1:15–313. For English translation, Thomas Artsruni, 1985, *History of the House of the Artsrunik'*, trans. Robert W. Thomson, Detroit: Wayne State University Press. For further background on Thomas, see also R. W. Thomson, 2000, "Tovma Artsruni: Historian of Vaspurakan" in R. G. Hovannisian, ed., *Armenian Van/Vaspurakan*, Costa Mesa, CA: Mazda, 57–72.

[2] *MH* 11.1:91.56; Artsruni 1985, 111.

king also granted them the right to display an eagle on their coat of arms. From then on, they would be called the *Artsruni* (supposedly meaning "bearers of the eagle," from Armenian *artsiw*, "eagle").[3] Displaying the valiance of eagles, the Artsruni, Thomas impresses on us, bravely resisted even under extreme torture and threat of death any assault on their freedom and their faith. Thomas cites the examples of the princes Gregory and Koriwn Artsruni, who on refusing to pay a ransom to the Ummayyad caliphate were tortured and crucified.[4] The Arab governor of Armenia, Khouzayma, who served under the Abbasid caliph al-Hadi (r. 785–86), angered by the presence of the three Artsruni brothers—Hamazasp, Isaac (Sahak), and Meruzhan—had them imprisoned for three years, after which he demanded on pain of death that they convert to Islam. Although Meruzhan pretended to convert, his brothers were tortured, beaten, and decapitated. While being tortured, Sahak prayed to God in silence but his soul was shaken by interior sobs.[5] Even crueler acts of brutality were committed under the caliph Moutawakki (r. 847–861). These narratives of the tortures and martyrdom of the members of the Artsruni family were meant to show that their faith was no superficial pretense but a deep devotion that extended back for generations to the apostolic age and for which the family paid dearly with its own blood.

Despite this history of violent encounters with Arab governors, it was an Arab emir who granted Gagik Artsruni the coveted royal crown. The Bagratid monarch, Ashot I, had already been presented with the crown by the caliph as well as the Byzantine emperor. Gagik desired the same dignity, and the emir of Azerbaijan, Yoûsoûf, wishing to counterbalance the growing power of the Bagratid kingdom that posed a threat to him, was more than willing to oblige. Yoûsoûf sent Gagik the royal crown in 908 and the erstwhile prince now reigned as the king of Vaspurakan.

[3] Dédéyan 2010, 57–58.

[4] Dédéyan 2010, 58, who notes that the Arab sources celebrate Khouzayma as a skilled administrator while the Armenian sources excoriate him in the harshest of terms.

[5] Garsoïan 1997, 133; Dédéyan 2010, 59–60.

Gagik distinguished himself as a formidable builder. He had an impressive system of underground water pipes built between the cities of Varag and Van and also constructed palaces, fortresses, and banquet halls throughout his realm.[6] But his architectural projects on the island of Aght'amar (located about four kilometers off the southern shore of Lake Van) were his most memorable achievements. Aght'amar, with its serene beauty, attracted Gagik, who was also impressed by its strategic advantage as an island in a large sea that would afford refuge from invasions.[7] He established there a city that his chronicler described as containing many parks and gardens.[8] Having made ramparts with imposing towers to protect his island city and a port to allow for access from the mainland, he began the construction of his luxurious palace and beside it a palatine cathedral, the Church of the Holy Sign (*Nshan*) or Cross. The work on the church was assigned to a noted architect named Manuel who worked on the project from 915 to 921. According to the continuator of Thomas Artsruni's history, after Gagik had demolished a fortress of the Arab Zurarid tribe, he had the stones of the fortress transported to the island "over the waves of the lake" to form from them a "temple of glory in place of the impure houses of idolatry."[9] The cathedral is distinguished by the ornate bas-reliefs on the external walls and the murals on the interior. The church also contained in its southern apse a loggia with a balustrade reserved for the royal family. There was direct access from the palace to the loggia, so that the king would have a private "oratory where he could commune with God completely apart from men."[10]

The bas-reliefs that cover the exterior walls include depictions of Old Testament figures: Adam and Eve in the garden, Abraham's binding of Isaac, Moses receiving the tablets on Mount Sinai, David and Goliath, Daniel in the lion's den, the three youths tortured in the furnace, and the prophet Jonah cast into the mouth of

[6] Dédéyan 2010, 66.

[7] *MH* 11.1:290–92.1–18; Artsruni 1985, 355–60.

[8] Artsruni 1985, 356.

[9] Artsruni 1985, 360.

[10] Dédéyan 2010, 67.

a sea-monster.[11] While these are well-known biblical themes, at least some of them resonate with the environment and history of Vaspurakan. The three youths in the furnace, Shadrach, Meshach, and Abednego, were victims of King Nebuchadnezzar. Do they not call to mind the plight of the three Artsruni princes, Sahak, Meruzhan, and Hamazasp, tortured together by the Arab governor Khouzayma? And while the sea-monster that swallows Jonah has the scales and body of a fish, its head looks more like that of an ox. Is it a representation of the sea-monsters known as *vishap* that were believed to inhabit the waters of Lake Van?[12] Prehistoric carvings in the shape of the *vishap* monster appear on stones along the banks of the lake. They may have served as charms to ward off the monsters. Was the bizarre sea-monster carved into the wall of the cathedral a tribute to these ancient steles, a marvelous blend of pre-Christian Armenian and biblical lore?

Not only do biblical vignettes adorn the exterior, but there are also more direct references to the royal dynasty. Depicted in the center of the west façade is the king himself donating a model of his cathedral to Christ. Portraits of both real and fabulous animals are found on every wall. Among the existing animals are wild animals, such as a lion, deer, eagle, and pelican, and domesticated animals like camels and sheep. The mythical creatures include a siren and griffin. The artists may have used the ancient Greek bestiary known as the *Physiologus*, a work that existed in Armenian translation and was frequently consulted by medieval Armenian au-

[11] For description of the cathedral, see Thierry 1989, 269–284, and Sirarpie Der Nersessian, 1965, *Aght'amar: Church of the Holy Cross*, Harvard Armenian Texts and Studies 1, Cambridge, MA: Harvard University Press. See also the insightful article of Nairy Hampikian, 2000, "The Architectural Heritage of Vaspurakan and the Preservation of Memory Layers" in Hovannisian 2000, 87–117, which includes photographs and layouts of several of the notable edifices of Vaspurakan. Hampikian underscores in particular the three challenges that condition the style of building in the region: the rocky terrain, the prevalence of seismic activity, and exposure to invasion.

[12] James R. Russell, 2000, "Van and the Persistence of Memory," in Hovannisian 2000, 43–56, especially 47–48.

thors.[13] The *Physiologus* contains descriptions and allegorical interpretations of many of the beasts that appear on the walls of the cathedral.

Another distinctive feature of the cathedral are the murals on the internal walls. There are very few Armenian churches whose walls are completely covered with paintings. In its current state after years of neglect the frescoes are in poor condition and only some are discernible. On the drum are portrayals of the fall of Adam and Eve. Also depicted are the creation of Adam, Eve's creation from Adam's side, Adam's naming of the animals, and the expulsion from paradise. There are paintings of the life of Christ: the annunciation, visitation of Elizabeth, the nativity, the flight into Egypt, Christ before Pilate, and the crucifixion. The images of the twelve apostles encircle the apse of the main altar.

In describing Gagik's patronage and support of the church we would be remiss not to include his consort, Queen Mlk'ē, who was actively involved in her family's sponsorship and direction of the construction on Aght'amar and monuments elsewhere. Her name today is mainly remembered from the Queen Mlk'ē Gospel, a masterpiece of medieval art containing brilliant illuminated miniatures, produced in the 860s and in the possession of the royal family until the queen donated it to the monastery of Varag.[14]

For two decades (927–47), the catholicos of all Armenians resided at Aght'amar, a matter of prestige for the Artsruni, since the catholicos was regarded as the bishop of the Armenian king and moved with the royal retinue. Three of these catholicoi were members of the noble Rshtunik' family, vassals to the Artsruni at this time and whose estate was located in the territory south of Lake Van that also included Narek. In 947 the seat moved back to Bagratid territory, to Argina near Ani. The return of the see to the Bagratuni kingdom

[13] The English translation and study of the two Armenian recensions is Gohar Muradyan, 2005, *Physiologus*, Leuven: Peeters.

[14] Varag is famed for its relic of the True Cross, which was buried by the martyred nun Hripsimē and discovered by a hermit in the mountain (known as Mount Erek in Turkish) near Van. Thomas F. Matthews and Avedis K. Sanjian, 1991, *Armenian Gospel Iconography: The Tradition of the Glajor Gospel*, Washington, DC: Dumbarton Oaks Research Library and Collection, 52.

would be a sore point for the Artsruni and soured relations between the catholicos and the Vaspurakan rulers.

In addition to his churches, Gagik must have given considerable support to the establishment of monasteries. Among these new foundations were Narekavank' (the monastery of Narek) and farther to the south, Aparank'. These new monasteries were part of the king's program of revitalizing Christianity in his realm. They served as centers of learning and worship, and the monks formed there would subsequently educate and elevate the spiritual lives of the faithful by preaching in the churches of the surrounding towns and villages.

Gagik's reign lasted until his death in 943, when he was succeeded by his son Derenik-Ashot. The reign of the Artsruni in Vaspurakan ended in 1021, when Senek'erim-John (r. 1003–21) relinquished the throne under Byzantine and Seljuk pressure and moved to Cilicia, where emperor Basil II granted him an estate. A vestige of Artsruni rule over the church remained in the guise of the catholicate of Aght'amar, established in 1113 and at first schismatic but later subordinate to the catholicate of all Armenians. The catholicate's jurisdiction was limited primarily to the dioceses located in the former kingdom of Vaspurakan.[15]

Although the cathedral has remained in poor condition since its abandonment after the 1915 Genocide, the Turkish government authorized renovation in 2007, though its official status is as a museum rather than a house of worship. Today the cathedral is a popular tourist destination and, for many, a place of pilgrimage. In 2010 the Turkish government permitted a divine liturgy that was celebrated by the interim Armenian patriarch of Constantinople with the attendance of many Armenians as well as members of the diplomatic corps and local government officials. The government has pledged to allow the celebration of liturgy there once every year since. Gagik's cathedral remains today an imposing yet for-

[15] The Aght'amar catholicate was disbanded in 1895 during the massacres of Armenians under Sultan Abdul Hamid. See Robert H. Hewsen, 1984, "Arcrunid House of Sefedinian: Survival of a Princely Dynasty in Ecclesiastical Guise," in *JSAS* 1, 123–37.

lorn monument of a vibrant Christian culture that has almost entirely vanished from the region.

The Theological Background

"Who do people say that I am?" Jesus posed this question to his apostles in the gospels. The disciples gave different answers until Jesus asked who they thought he was. In the telling of Matthew 16:16, Peter answers for them: "You are the Christ, the Son of the living God."

Questions about Christ's nature did not end there with Peter's response. The successors of the apostles, the bishops of the church, would continue to wrestle over the implications of confessing Jesus as the Son of God. The controversies surrounding the correct way to understand how Jesus can be both God and man would threaten the stability of the church and shatter its unity. The Armenian church would establish its distinct identity as a separate communion as a result of its rejection of the doctrine of Christ propounded in middle of the fifth century and adopted by the majority of the world's Christians. Knowing the reasons behind this disagreement is essential for understanding not only the theological doctrines of the Armenian church but also many of the events and controversies surrounding the monastery of Narek. This section of the chapter provides a brief overview of those doctrines and their development in order to appreciate the theological context of Gregory's work.

It would not be inaccurate to summarize the history of the dogmatic theology of the Armenian church as a history of a struggle against dualism. The earliest surviving original theological treatise by an Armenian, the *De deo* or "On God" of Eznik, bishop of Koghb, is mostly an attempt to refute a variety of dualistic religions and philosophies thought to pose a threat to the orthodox teachings of Christianity.[16] Dualism manifests itself in two forms.

[16] The Armenian text is in *MH* 1:433–512. An English translation is by Monica J. Blanchard and Robin D. Young, 1998, *A Treatise on God written in Armenian by Eznik of Kołb: On God*, Leuven: Peeters.

There is a cosmic version in which the universe is divided into two forces or principles that are in unrelenting struggle against each other. One of these is the good principle, often associated with light. In its Zoroastrian guise, the principle is represented by the deity Ahura Mazda (hence Zoroastrianism is sometimes referred to as Mazdaism). Its countervailing evil force is Ahriman or Angra Mainyu. Likewise, in Manicheanism, another religion founded by an Iranian, there are two principles, neither of which created the other. Some of the Greek philosophies are dualistic, too, most notably Platonism at least in some of its forms.

The second kind of dualism is anthropological, a dualism of the human person: humans are a compound of two elements, a good soul and an evil body that is the source of sin and wickedness. Plato, for example, sometimes speaks of matter, and thus the human body, as inherently evil while he claims that the soul is inherently divine.[17] The life of the philosopher, according to Plato, is aimed at overcoming the burdens of the body and distancing the soul from its corporeal prison. Such a life eschews material pleasures and resembles in many ways that of a Christian ascetic. And yet there are important differences in the way that Platonic and Christian asceticism think about the body and its moral status. Although orthodox Christianity affirms a cosmic duality of the Creator and his creation and a personal duality of soul and body, it rejects the existence of two uncreated beings. God is the creator of all beings, including Satan and the fallen angels, who are by nature good but through their free will chose to reject God. Likewise, through the free choice of the first humans, humanity fell from its ideal state in Eden. In contrast to Plato's claim that the body is inherently evil, orthodox Christian theology recognizes the inherent goodness of the body and the physical realm, both of which are created by God and into which God enters in the incarnation.

But there have always been persistent dualist currents among Christians. These dualist influences were especially strong in Armenia because of its proximity to Iran and its dualist religions. But the attractions of dualism existed throughout the Christian world.

[17] Plato, 1982, *Euthyphro, Apology, Crito, Phaedo*, trans. Harold North Fowler, Cambridge, MA: Harvard University Press, 228–231, 66b–d.

That is the reason why some Christians in the earliest centuries rejected the belief that Jesus had a real body and instead argued that he only appeared to be incarnate. These Christians are sometimes called Gnostics, but the term that specifically refers to the heretical teaching that denies that Jesus had a body is Docetism (from the Greek *dokeō*, "to seem"), for Jesus only seemed to have a body. Sometimes his body is called a *phantasm* (from the Greek *phantasma*, "apparition, phantom"), as it was supposed to be ethereal and ghostlike, unlike our solid and impermeable flesh.

There is an understandable logic underlying the Docetists' teachings. If, as Christians proclaim, Jesus Christ is the Son of God, then he must appear to the world in a manner befitting God. God would dress himself not in our disgraced and demeaning clothing of flesh but in finery appropriate to his glory. Those who consider the body to be inherently wicked must diminish or deny Christ's humanity in order to preserve and uphold his divinity. Yet in orthodox—that is, non-Docetist—Christianity, Jesus Christ is fully God and fully human and thus possesses a body that is like ours. His complete humanity is essential to his role as the bridge or mediator between God and humans. In the striking proclamation of St. Athanasius of Alexandria (ca. 296–373), "God became man so that man may become God."[18] Athansius's statement of the purpose of the incarnation may seem blasphemous with its bold claim that humans are capable of becoming God. But it is the most direct and blunt statement of the doctrine of the Greek word *theosis*, sometimes translated as "divinization" or "deification," an idea that expresses the essence of the Eastern Christian understanding of the incarnation's purpose and the true end of all human existence. Without appreciating the centrality of *theosis* in Eastern Christian theology, we will understand neither the theology of the Armenian church nor Gregory's thought. Nor will we begin to comprehend why the debates on the nature of Christ were often so vitriolic, even to the point of producing inveterate schisms and, in some cases, acts of violence among the partisans of the different theological outlooks.

[18] Athanasius, 1973, *Sur l'Incarnation de Verbe*, ed. Charles Kannengiesser, SC 199, Paris: Cerf, 54.3.

Today we may look back at the polemics and animosity and wonder why the theologians were so animated by these questions concerning Christ's divinity and humanity. These disputes seem so arcane, with little direct connection to the practice of faith. Yet we should not dismiss these seemingly academic theological concerns without first asking why they were so salient to the early church and why they occupied the attention of the leading theologians of the fifth century. In trying to answer these questions, we will learn not only about the ancient Christians but also about ourselves and how much we may differ from them in our assumptions about Christianity. In viewing these theologians and disputants charitably, we do not imply that they are without fault. Many of the main figures in these debates were impetuous and unfair when presenting their opponent's arguments. But we will not understand them properly if we do not make an effort to meet them on their own ground.

One thing should be clear: for the early theologians, these questions about Christ were never merely academic debates. The questions are intimately connected to the practice of the faith and even to the vital issue of what a human being is and should be. For if Christ is the perfect human, by studying Christology we also study humanity in its most ideal and pristine form. And if one truly believes that the goal of all human life is *theosis*, then any teaching that denies that humans can unite or come to be one with God will be a barrier to the life that God intends for us and which alone can deliver supreme happiness. Anyone who has an intense desire to achieve some goal and yet reads only books that imply that this goal is unattainable will end up frustrated and disappointed. Eventually, they will abandon their pursuit. The early Christians who considered *theosis* to be the ultimate end of existence thus viewed as pernicious any Christology that implied the impossibility of genuine union with God. If Christ is divine but does not perfectly share our humanity, then a rift opens up between him and humanity that obstructs complete reconciliation with God. Conversely, there is a danger that by making Christ too human, we diminish his divinity. If, like us, he hungers and thirsts, and experiences fear and grief, in what sense is he still the almighty God who is beyond all human weakness and infirmity?

Among the most strident participants in the debates concerning Christology were the monks and ascetics. They devoted their lives entirely to the project of *theosis*. Their occupation was to come to know God and become one with him. That is why the early Desert Fathers retreated to the desert away from the distractions and disturbances of the cities and secular life. Just as astronomers build their observatories away from the artificial lights of populated areas and retreat to darkness in order to see the stars more clearly, so too the ascetics withdrew into the wilderness in order to see God better and develop a relation with him. The sole aim of their exertion was *theosis*, and thus they needed a theory that undergirded and justified their practice.

After having worked through problems about the Trinity and the relation of the three persons of God at the councils of Nicaea and Constantinople, attention turned more immediately to questions of Christology at the third ecumenical council held in Ephesus in 431. Since Christ is one person who is both divine and human, he must possess the qualities of both. Like us, Jesus had a body made of flesh and blood, but since he is also God, unlike us, he did not sin. The problem is that many human attributes are incompatible with the properties of God. God is everywhere, but humans are limited by their bodies and can only be in one place at a time. God knows everything, but humans are severely restricted in our knowledge. God is immortal, but all humans die. How can Christ, being fully God and perfect human, be both omniscient and ignorant, omnipresent and yet confined to a particular body that entered the world in Bethlehem, a person who is at the same time immortal and mortal? Perhaps Christ is really composed of two distinct elements: a divine Christ who is immortal and omnipotent, and a human Christ who is mortal and limited in power.

It is easy to see why this approach to Christology would raise objections. The Christ composed of both a divine and human element seems to imply the existence of two persons: a human Jesus and a divine Christ—two persons, not one. If there are two separate persons who simply appear to us as one, then the unity of humanity and divinity is illusory and masks a discontinuity that is never repaired. In essence, the chasm that separates us from God continues to exist within Christ and he becomes an ineffective mediator between humans and their creator.

Something like this two-person view of Christ was suggested by Nestorius, the archbishop of Constantinople from 428 until his deposition and exile in 431. The fathers at Ephesus had rejected the Christology attributed to him there. Ephesus's leading theologian was St. Cyril, the patriarch of Alexandria, who preferred to speak of Christ as the "one nature (*mia phusis*) of the incarnate Word of God," emphasizing the perfect unity of the divine and human in the one person of Christ, without any chasm or division.[19] We can appreciate why Cyril, who represented the concerns of many of the desert monks of Egypt, objected to a doctrine that would, from the monks' perspective, forestall their longing for a full union of God and humans through the one indivisible nature of Christ. But problems remained. There were serious questions about the logical coherence of Cyril's formula and whether by being so tightly bound to God, Christ's human attributes would be swallowed up or obliterated by his divinity. In that case, one could no longer speak of Christ as truly human in any form that resembled our humanity. As well, in the wake of Ephesus, the first lasting schism in the church occurred, with the so-called Nestorian Christians forming a separate church no longer in communion with the other churches that had accepted the doctrines proclaimed at Ephesus.

In an attempt to clarify some of the problems posed by the Christology of Ephesus and to mend the breach with the anti-Ephesian churches, another council was convened in 451 at Chalcedon. The bishops at Chalcedon agreed that Christ had two natures, human and divine, and that although these two natures form one person, they are not mixed or confused into one nature but maintain their identity in a union "without confusion or change, indivisibly and inseparably."[20] The first two adjectives were meant to prevent an extreme one-nature view that minimized or denied Christ's humanity in the manner of the Docetists. The latter two adjectives emphasized that the two natures were joined together in a union that was so tight that there was no gap between Christ's person that would block God's encounter with humanity. The indivisibility of the union of the two natures was intended to allay the suspicions of the adherents of Cyril's one-nature Christology that the

[19] Henry Bettenson, 1963, *Doctrines of the Christian Church*, second edition, Oxford: Oxford University Press, 47–48.

[20] Bettenson 1963, 51–52.

christological definition of Chalcedon conceded too much to the Nestorians and could be interpreted as supporting a two-person Christology.

Chalcedon was an admirable attempt at compromise, but it was a failure in the sense that it did not restore communion with the church that separated after Ephesus but instead brought about another lasting schism. That separated communion, now known as the Church of the East, still did not accept the doctrine of Ephesus and, at the same time, many of the bishops of Egypt and Syria who considered Ephesus to be the last word on Christology deemed Chalcedon an unacceptable deviation from Cyril's one-nature Christology. The Coptic Church of Egypt and the Syriac Orthodox Church, together with the Ethiopian Orthodox Church, the Eritrean Orthodox Church, and the Malankara Orthodox Syrian Church of India are the modern descendants of these non-Chalcedonian bishops and hierarchs, and these churches—usually called Oriental Orthodox to distinguish them from the Chalcedonian Eastern Orthodox churches—each have their own distinct hierarchies and rites separate from each other (though they remain in full communion with their sister Oriental Orthodox churches).

The Armenian bishops were not closely involved in the christological disputes centering around Chalcedon. As we have seen, Christianity in Armenia was facing its gravest crisis since becoming the established faith of the country. Given the Sassanian monarchy's pursuit of a vigorous policy imposing its state religion, Zoroastrianism, the Armenian nobility and bishop were preoccupied with defending their faith. Thus, the Armenian church did not take an official stand on Chalcedon for many decades.

But the church would eventually have to make a decision on which christological course to follow. There were, as there would continue to be, adherents of both the Chalcedonian and the non-Chalcedonian position in Armenia and in the neighboring countries of Georgia and Caucasian Albania.[21] Only at the First Council of Duin, held in 506 and later confirmed at the Second Council of Duin in 551, did the Armenian bishops together with their Georgian and

[21] Not to be confused with Balkan Albania, Caucasian Albania was located to the northeast of Armenia mainly in present-day Azerbaijan.

Caucasian Albanian counterparts formally reject the christological definition of Chalcedon and affirm Cyril's one-nature formula as the best expression of the orthodox teaching about Christ.[22]

If we go back to the original context that connects these christological debates with the practice of *theosis*, we can begin to understand the objections to Chalcedon. For most supporters of Cyrillian christology, which above all else focuses on the "oneness" of Christ in his divinity and humanity, any talk of two natures in Christ entailed an unacceptable imposition of a barrier or boundary that separates humanity from God. Only by speaking of the oneness of Christ in his humanity and divinity could one do justice to the firmness and immediacy of the Word's embrace of our human flesh. This extremely close relation of what were once two distinct natures into one nature is difficult to express and perhaps even

[22] Early in the seventh century, the Georgian church would accept Chalcedon and return to communion with the see of Constantinople. The Albanian church, which no longer exists, was also often led by pro-Chalcedonian bishops. As we will see, tensions between the Armenian and Albanian hierarchy on Christology would plague their relations and also implicate the school of Narek. The seminal study of the position of the Armenian church is Karekin Sarkissian, 1975, *The Council of Chalcedon and the Armenian Church*, New York: Armenian Church Prelacy, republished in 2006 by the Karekin I Theological and Armenological Studies Series with English translations of the Latin and Greek texts. The book is based on the author's thesis written at Oxford. The author later became Catholicos Karekin I of all Armenians, whose joint declaration with Pope John Paul II in 1996 affirmed that the two churches profess belief in Christ, who is "Perfect God as to his divinity, perfect man as to his humanity" and that "his divinity is united to his humanity in the Person of the Only-begotten Son of God, in a union which is real, perfect, without confusion, without alteration, without division, without any form of separation." (The full text of the declaration is at http://www.vatican.va/roman_curia/pontifical_councils/chrstuni/anc-orient-ch-docs/rc_pc_christuni_doc_19961213_jp-ii-karekin-i_en.html.) Though the two churches remain separated, the statement expresses an essential agreement between the Roman Catholic Church and the Armenian Apostolic Church on fundamental matters of Christology, even if they may use different idioms to communicate that same understanding of who Christ is. Similar statements and agreements have also been made by the Oriental Orthodox and Eastern Orthodox in numerous encounters and ecumenical meetings.

harder to comprehend. Perhaps the best way is through images and metaphor. Gregory gives one such figure in Prayer 93 of the *Book of Lamentation*. This particular prayer is about the holy oil (*muron*) used in sacramental anointing. Describing the wick that will be placed in the oil lamp and lit, he writes:

> You wove and fashioned the wick,
> A figure of the union of your impassible nature
> Intertwined with our own,
> Knit together and constructed
> Out of your love of humanity, . . .
> So that we may be illuminated with the flame of faith.[23]

This image of the wick that is woven together describes Christ's union in terms of the art of weaving, a craft that for a medieval audience would be familiar. Gregory uses the wick to illustrate how tightly bound the connection of Christ's humanity and his divinity is. Unless one looks very carefully at the wick, it looks like one uniform piece. Examined more closely, however, one makes out threads braided so tightly that it becomes difficult to distinguish one from another. That is how snug and taut the union of Christ's humanity and divinity is. No earthly image can do justice to this union, but Gregory's metaphor comes very close to representing the one-nature conception of the incarnation that would come to be characteristic of orthodox Armenian Christology. Also important is Gregory's description of the union as impassible or incapable of suffering, indicating that the Word's divine impassibility is united with our passible flesh to produce a paradoxical "impassable suffering," a characteristic feature of Cyrillian Christology.

Recently the term *miaphysitism* ("one-naturism") has been adopted to distinguish the non-Chalcedonian doctrine of the Oriental Orthodox from the heretical doctrine of *monophysitism* ("sole-naturism") as well as the Chalcedonian *dyophysitism* ("two-naturism").[24] Monophysitism is the belief that Christ has *solely* or *only* one nature, which

[23] *BL* 93.2; *MH* 12:567.4.

[24] The earliest occurrences listed in the *Oxford English Dictionary* are from the 1990s.

would comprehend the heretical Docetist position that denies full humanity to Christ, as well as the views attributed to Euthyches, an early fifth-century priest who supposedly stated that Christ's humanity "dissolved like a drop of honey in the sea."[25] That doctrine is not the same as the miaphysite position, according to which the incarnation unites Christ's divine and human natures into *one* nature, a position that all but the most recalcitrant Chalcedonians can recognize as orthodox. The position adopted by the Armenian church at the Duin councils and shared with the other Oriental Orthodox churches is this *one nature* Christology of miaphysitism. By contrast, the doctrine of Chalcedon is a *two-nature* Christology, or dyophysitism. The *two-person* doctrine, sometimes associated with Nestorius and his followers, is a heresy in the eyes of the Chalcedonians and the miaphysites, but some of the Armenian miaphysites did not recognize any difference between dyophysitism and Nestorianism. As I will try to show, Gregory does distinguish between these two doctrines and considers the Chalcedonian dyophysite position to be within the sphere of orthodoxy even while affirming the Armenian miaphysite Christology in his writings.

The Julianist Controversy

One of the best known and most moving works of religious art is Michelangelo's Pietà, a sculpture that today rests behind glass in St. Peter's Basilica. It depicts the Virgin Mary holding in her lap the body of Christ taken down from the cross. Its intent is to instill in us compassion and pity, but in studying it more carefully, we notice its anomalies. The body of Christ does not look like the body of a man who has suffered the excruciating pain of the cross after brutal torture and scourging. There are few, if any, signs of his passion. The body looks serene and ideal. It is not Christ's body that evokes pity, but Mary, the *mater dolorosa*, the sorrowful mother grieving for

[25] The image is from Eutyches's opponent, Theodoret of Cyrus. See Gérard H. Ettlinger, ed., 2003, *Eranistes*, Washington, DC: Catholic University of America Press, 123.

her son. The viewer experiences Christ's suffering mediated through the Virgin, her heart having been pierced.

Contrast the Pietà with a painting of the crucifixion by Michelangelo's contemporary, the German painter Matthias Grünewald (ca. 1470–1528), in the *Isenheim Altarpiece*. The altarpiece was made for the monastery of St. Anthony in Isenheim, known for its care of people suffering from the plague.[26] Compared with the idealized body of the Pietà, Christ's body in Grünewald's portrayal is harrowing: his flesh appears putrid, blood flows from the wound on his side, his fingers are rigid and contorted by the ravage of death. The body of Christ here is grotesque; there is no beauty or serenity. Most significantly, we can make out sores on his body that resemble those of the patients at the monastic hospital. Mary is off to the side, fainting into the arms of John, but the focus of one's pity is not on her, as with the Pietà, but on the agony exhibited in Christ's body. The intended effect on the patients is the realization that Christ shares their suffering. The Son of God endures the very same pain and anguish that they experience. Likewise, the caregivers at the monastery would be reminded to see Christ in their patients.

Some would say that Grünewald's depiction is more realistic. His depiction is a more accurate portrayal of the body of a tortured and crucified man. But whether Michelangelo's or Grünewald's depiction is more realistic depends upon what background beliefs we bring to their art. If we believe that Christ is God, we may suppose him incapable of suffering in the way that mere humans are. The body of Christ would not look not like a normal crucified human body because Jesus is not merely human. Given this assumption we may expect the crucified Christ to look like the idealized form of Michelangelo's sculpture and not the gruesome image in Grünewald's altarpiece.

Rather than asking which portrayal is more realistic, one may instead ask what effect the depictions have on the viewer. Both are masterful works of art that have a profound affective force. But one might say that Michelangelo's Jesus is remote. The pristine corpse

[26] For the Isenheim Altarpiece as a work of "hospital iconography" see Andrée Hayum, 1995, *The Isenheim Altarpiece: God's Medicine and the Painter's Vision*, Princeton, NJ: Princeton University Press.

of the Pietà is not the body of a man who has shared fully in our suffering. There is a distance between his experience of the cross and ours. On the other hand, the body of Christ on the altarpiece is all too familiar for the patients of the monastery. It is their body too, bearing the same wounds as theirs. Assuming that they do not turn away in revulsion, the patients in St. Anthony's monastery would see themselves in Christ's body. The distance that the Pietà creates is crossed, and the observers of the altarpiece come closer to Christ, comforted in the knowledge that God shares their torment.

Disputes about what Christ's crucified body looked like are not new. They were part of a controversy that emerged in the sixth century in connection with the question of whether Christ's body was corruptible. The principal interlocutors were not Armenian, but because the debate was first conducted by their fellow miaphysite theologians, Armenian theologians closely followed this mainly intramural dispute among adherents of the one-nature Christology. As with the broader christological debate connected with Chalcedon, here too the issues were not strictly theoretical but had implications for the efficacy of *theosis*. For if the body of Christ is incorruptible, like the Christ of the Pietà, then genuine union with Christ becomes impossible. He does not meet us directly in our suffering but keeps his distance from the full range of human misery. Yet if Christ suffers exactly as we do, can he still be God, a being immune to hardship and adversity? If we seek to unite ourselves to Christ, are we just uniting ourselves with another human being, perhaps more virtuous than we but nevertheless a mortal and not the almighty God? "What He has not assumed He has not healed" wrote Nazianzen in his letter against Apollinaris, a third-century bishop who denied that Christ possessed a human intellect or rational soul.[27] Nazianzen elaborates:

> If only half of Adam fell, then that which Christ assumed and saved may be half also; but if his whole nature fell, it must be united to the whole nature of the Begotten One and thus saved as a whole.[28]

[27] Paul Gallay, ed., 1974, *Grégoire de Nazianze: Lettres théologique*, SC 208, Paris: Cerf, 101.2.

[28] Gallay 1974, 101.3.

If Christ does not suffer as we suffer, can we in our afflictions truly be healed? And if he is not also God but a man, why do we need him to heal us? Can we not then heal ourselves?

These questions arose subsequent to the christological debates about the relation of the divine and the human in Christ. In particular, the debate focused on whether Christ's body was corruptible (given to the deterioration characteristic of the human body) and passable (capable of suffering the passions such as hunger, thirst, pain, grief, and fear). This subordinate controversy is not as widely studied or written about as the central debates surrounding Chalcedon in part because most of the relevant extant documents are written in Syriac, not Greek.[29] The controversy over Christ's suffering began with Julian of Halicarnassus, an early sixth-century bishop of Halicarnassus (now Bodrum in Turkey). Very little of Julian's writings has survived and that which does is presented in a distorted form in the works of his opponent, Severus, patriarch of Antioch from 512 to 518, a gifted champion of miaphysitism. The groundbreaking work of the Belgian scholar and priest René Draguet (1896–1980) has provided a more accurate perspective of the disagreement between Julian and Severus.[30] Julian proposed to Severus that Christ assumed the body of Adam before the Fall, and thus his body was incorruptible in the way human bodies were before the expulsion from paradise. Julian held that Jesus, unlike the rest of humans born after the fall, did not have a body corruptible and passable by nature because his virgin birth exempted him from the transmission of original sin. Julian agreed with the Augustinian theory that Adam's sin is transmitted to his descendants through sexual desire.[31] Consequently, Jesus' body was immune from the effects of Adam's disobedience.

[29] A brief but illuminating discussion of the context and issues involved is by Jaroslav Pelikan, 1971, *The Christian Tradition: A History of the Development of Doctrine* 1, Chicago: University of Chicago Press, 272–74.

[30] René Draguet, 1924, *Julien d'Halicarnasse et sa controverse avec Sèvère d'Antioche sur l'Incorruptibilité du corps du Christ*, Louvain: Imprimerie P. Smeesters, 1924.

[31] For the Augustinian account of the transmission of original sin, see Jaroslav Pelikan 1971, 299–301.

Nevertheless, Julian did acknowledge that Jesus suffered the nonculpable passions of hunger and thirst through an act of will rather than because his body was naturally given to such deprivations. But there could be in Christ no passions entailing some deficiency, emotions like fear or despair which only those without the virtue of hope and benefit of omniscience would experience. Even in the garden of Gethsemane and on the cross, Christ knew that he would soon rise and triumph over death. For Julian, passages in the gospels that represent Jesus in agony and despair must be interpreted differently or rejected as inauthentic.

Although Julian hoped to convince Severus that his teachings on Christ's body were correct and cohered with their shared miaphysite Christology, Severus harshly rejected Julian's views. Severus considered Julian's doctrine to be a form of Docetism called *aphthartodocetism* (from the Greek *aphthartos*, "incorruptible"). Severus's objection was that by insisting that Christ's body was free by nature of corruption and suffering, Julian had turned Christ's body into something very much unlike ours and more like the body depicted by Michelangelo, one that does not seem to bear any of the effects of torture and execution. The incorruptible body of Christ may have the appearance of our flesh, but in fact it is very different from the ordinary human body. And if the Word did not assume our flesh, how can our afflicted body be healed? Julian's doctrines, if accepted, would push miaphysite Christology, whose orthodoxy Severus steadfastly defended, in the direction of a monophysite teaching that both supporters and opponents of Chalcedon recognized as heretical.

In opposition to Julian's teachings, Severus affirmed that Christ assumed Adam's fallen body. He argued that since the prelapsarian bodies of Adam and Eve were only free of corruption through God's grace, the fall did not result in a change in the nature of human flesh but rather a withdrawal of that grace. Likewise, the assumed flesh of the incarnation is by nature corruptible and it is only after the resurrection that Christ's body acquires incorruptibility. The body remains corruptible prior to the resurrection and is not dissolved into the Word's divinity.

Although Severus resisted Julian's doctrine with its aphthartodocetic implications, Julianism persisted. Its adherents were especially vocal in Armenia.[32] Its most prominent advocate in Armenia was the controversial and charismatic cleric John (Yovhannēs) Mayragomets'i (seventh century). Because he had a large and loyal following, his writings have survived and thus give us direct insight into the thoughts of an Armenian Julianist rather than as represented through the distorted lens of an anti-Julianist. Of particular concern to Julianists like Mayragomets'i were any gospel verses that implied Christ's suffering and agony. One of the most striking of these verses is the pericope that describes Christ's bloody sweat in Gethsemane. The only occurrence of this pericope is Luke 22:43-44.[33] In the agony in the garden before his betrayal and arrest, Jesus' "sweat became like great drops of blood falling down on the ground." This unusual phenomenon is a sign of extreme distress that would seem clearly to counter the Julianists' belief that Christ did not experience anguish and despair. The pericope occurs in some early manuscripts of Luke but not in others, so it is a matter of debate among biblical scholars whether it was an anti-Docetist addition to the original text or a genuine verse in Luke that was suppressed by Docetists.[34] Mayragomets'i is understandably insistent that the pericope is extraneous, dismissing the verse in part on the basis of the impossibility of sweating blood.[35]

[32] For a comprehensive discussion of the development and interplay of this aspect of Christology in Armenia, see S. P. Cowe, 2004, "Armenian Christology in the Seventh and Eight Centuries with particular reference to contributions of Catholicos Yovhan Ōjnec'i and Xosrovik T'argmanič'," *JTS* New Series, 55 (1): 30–54. Also John Meyendorff, 1992, "L'aphthartodocetism en Arménie," *REArm* 23, 27–37.

[33] For discussion of the reception of this pericope in the Armenian tradition, see S. P. Cowe, 1994, "Christological Trends and Textual Transmission: The Pericope of the Bloody Sweat (Luke 22:43-44) in the Armenian Version," in S. Ajamian and M. E. Stone, *Text and Context: Studies in the Armenian New Testament*, Atlanta: Scholars Press, 35–48.

[34] See Bart D. Ehrman, 2005, *Misquoting Jesus: The Story Behind Who Changed the Bible and Why*. New York: HarperSanFrancisco, 139–44, for an engaging account that defends the anti-Docetist interpolation hypothesis.

[35] Relevant Armenian texts, a florilegium of patristic authors on the pericope, in *MH* 4.257-311. The seventh-century theologian T'ēodoros K'rt'enawor cited by Cowe 2004, 44, replied that the verse is to be read figuratively and

Julianism may have also affected the liturgical practices of the Armenian church, in particular the use of unleavened bread and wine unmixed with water in the Eucharist. Like the Latin rite but in contrast to most of the other Eastern rites, the Armenian church consecrates unleavened bread for communion. Unique to the Armenian rite is the unmixed chalice. Since leavened bread spoils more quickly than unleavened, the absence of yeast in the host may signify the incorruptibility of Christ's body. So too the unadulterated wine offered for consecration may be read as symbolic of Christ's unblemished flesh. But here we need to be careful since liturgical symbols, like other "texts," are ambiguous and opponents will often interpret deviant practices in malicious and unfounded ways. The Armenian use of unleavened bread became a point of contention with the Byzantine church. But the Armenian practice most likely predates the Julianist controversy and may represent the sinlessness of Christ rather than the incorruptibility of his body, symbolism that is based on Jesus' admonition in Matthew 16:11 to beware the leaven of the Pharisees and Sadducees.

The existence of a substantial faction of Julianists in the Armenian church caused tension with the Syrian miaphysites, who remained faithful to the teachings of their revered patriarch Severus. The Armenian catholicos John of Ōdzun convened the Council of Manazkert in 726 with the participation of miaphysite Syrian bishops to reconcile the Armenian and Syriac churches on the Julianist controversy. The council rejected both the Julianist and Severian positions and traced a middle position that combined elements of both extremes to define what would become the orthodox Armenian position.[36] Jesus is free of all sin but, in contrast to the stance of an extreme Julianist like Mayragomets'i, the body that he assumes is passable. At the incarnation, and not the resurrection (as Severus held), his body becomes impassable. Nevertheless,

---

refers not to literal blood but describes Christ's profuse sweat. Interestingly, there is clinical evidence in recent medical literature of people under extreme distress sweating blood (hematohidrosis). See H. R. Jerajani et al., 2009, "Hematohidrosis: A Rare Clinical Phenomenon," *Indian Journal of Dermatology*, 54 (3): 290–92.

[36] Cowe 2004, 45–47; Mahé 2000, 28.

through an act of his will, Christ accepts in his body all the sufferings and afflictions of humanity apart from sin. Because he is almighty, Christ does not have to suffer; because he is love, he freely chooses as an act of grace toward humanity to share our afflictions even to the very depths of human despair.

Let us turn our attention back to the two artworks described at the beginning of this section in order to get a better sense of the implications of the Julianist controversy on Armenian spirituality. If John Mayragomets'i were asked his preference, he would choose the serene and beautiful body of the crucified Christ free of any signs of suffering and distress. Michelangelo's work befits the majesty of the divine Christ. His opponents would be more drawn to the tormented and mutilated body of Grünewald's altarpiece. While Mayragomets'i would regard Grünewald's depiction to be an affront to Christ's divinity, John of Ōdzun and the bishops of Manazkert would see in the altarpiece's depiction God emptying himself willingly to be like us and joining us in our suffering. Christ is the suffering servant who not only participates in but also relieves our misery. By bearing our tormented flesh, he is able to heal it and lift it up to God.

Although a residual Julianism informed Armenian theology well after the Council of Manazkert,[37] Gregory and the scholars of Narekavank', as I will later show in chapter eight, explicitly rejected any theology that compromised the real humanity of Christ. We need a human Christ who lives and suffers with us to give us a connection with God. Just as the patients of the hospital of St. Anthony's monastery could see their lesions in the body of Christ, so too we can see there the marks of our wounds. A remote and distant God hinders a full engagement with a Christ who touches the heart of the faithful. Any theological doctrine that minimizes Christ's full humanity makes it more difficult for us to connect with the divine and prevents us from feeling Christ's solidarity with our suffering. And since among the primary missions of the monastery of Narek was to instill in the faithful a more profoundly emotional and personal piety, insistence on and attention to Christ's real suffering in

[37] Cowe 2004, 48.

all its intensity became a cardinal feature of their program of spiritual reform and revival.

The T'ondrakean Movement

Heresy is usually defined as a false teaching or doctrine contrary to the official creeds of the church. But it may be more helpful to think of heresies not as falsehoods but as partial truths, or at least ideas that emerge from a fixation on just some of the truths professed by the church. Such was the case with the Arian heresy that focused on Christ's humanity to the detriment of his divinity. Conversely, in their attempt to uphold Christ's divinity, Docetists negate the belief that his humanity fully shares our corporeal nature.

As early as the sixth century, a heretical movement known as Paulicianism had gained favor among various segments of the Armenian population.[38] By the middle of the eighth century, the Paulicians had become a formidable religious and political force within the Byzantine Empire.[39] Like the iconoclasts, the Paulicians rejected the use of images in worship, but they went beyond them in also rejecting monasticism and the sacraments, including the Eucharist and ordination. They thus also rejected the legitimacy of the hierarchy of the church. The Byzantine Empire conducted a harsh campaign to suppress the Paulicians, exiling many of them to the Balkans, where they may have had a role in the development of the Bogomil heresy in Bulgaria and even in the emergence of Catharism in southern France. According to some scholars, all of these heretical groups rooted their opposition to the sacraments and the church in a form of dualism and its concomitant christological doctrine of Docetism. There is however some disagreement about the philosophical underpinnings of the Paulicians' beliefs. Garsoïan argues that the earliest

[38] For a magisterial study of the Paulicians, see Nina G. Garsoïan, 1967, *The Paulician Heresy: A Study of the Origin and Development of Paulicianism in Armenia and the Eastern Provinces of the Byzantine Empire*, Berlin: De Gruyter.

[39] Leslie W. Bernard, 1977, "The Paulicians and Iconoclasm" in *Iconoclasm: papers given at the ninth spring symposium of Byzantine studies, University of Birmingham*, 75–82, esp. 77.

Armenian Paulicians were not dualists but only adopted dualism when they came into contact with Byzantine iconoclasts. Others believe the movement was from its outset a continuation of Manicheanism or the Christian Marcionite heresy that rejected the Old Testament and much of the New Testament in the belief that the God of the Old Testament was a wicked and vindictive deity distinct from the loving God who sent Christ to save humanity.[40]

One of the problems in settling these questions is that in most cases the writings of heretical movements are lost, usually because they were suppressed or destroyed by the church. The one exception in the case of the Armenian heretics is a manual known as the *Key of Truth*, a document discovered and seized by Armenian church authorities in the nineteenth century during an inquisition of suspected heretics in Akhaltsike in present-day Georgia. The origins of this book are mysterious, but some have argued that it was written by a Paulician in the middle of the ninth century.[41] The work advocates an adoptionist view of Christ in which Jesus was not born the Son of God but adopted by God at his baptism. Rather than rejecting the sacrament of baptism, the unknown author demands that baptisms be performed only after the candidate has reached the age of maturity.

While the Byzantine and Armenian authorities ruthlessly suppressed the Paulicians, a heresy that shared some of the same doctrines emerged in Armenia during the ninth century. The new heretics were known as the T'ondrakeans, probably after the town of T'ondrak, then within the jurisdiction of one of the Arab emirates where they had settled after being expelled from territory

[40] The view that Paulicianism is vestigial Marcionism is defended by R. J. Hoffmann, 1983, "The Paulician Heresy: A Reappraisal," *The Patristic and Byzantine Review* 2 (2–3): 251–63, especially 260.

[41] The Armenian text with English translation is in F. C. Conybeare, 1898, *The Key of Truth: A Manual of the Paulician Church of Armenia*, Oxford: Clarendon. See also Mesrob K. Krikorian, 2006, "The Letter of St. Gregory of Narek addressed to Thondrakean heretics: theological and sacramental aspects" in Jean-Pierre Mahé and Boghos Levon Zekiyan, eds., *Saint Grégoire De Narek, Théologien et Mystique: colloque international tenu à l'Institut Pontifical Oriental*, OCA 275, Rome: Pontificio Istituto Orientale, 169–86.

under Armenian control.[42] The exact relation between the Paulicians and the T'ondrakeans is also a matter of debate, but the sources, which include an admonitory letter written by Gregory to a monastery that had apparently been infiltrated by pro-T'ondrakean monks, indicate that the heretics adhered to antisacramental and antiecclesial views very similar to those attributed to the Paulicians. According to Gregory's letter, these doctrines included rejection of the sacraments of baptism, the Eucharist, and marriage as well as a refusal to venerate material objects such as the image of the cross.

The leader of the T'ondrakeans was a man named Smbat of Zahrehawan. He apparently attracted a wide following, especially among the more economically and socially disadvantaged classes in Armenia. His charisma was strong enough to keep his movement alive even after an Arab emir executed him when Smbat claimed to be the messiah sometime in the middle of the ninth century.[43] The movement continued to pose a serious threat to the authority of the Armenian church during Gregory's lifetime. As we will see, in addition to his anti-T'ondrakean letter, many of Gregory's other writings are at least in part directed against the teachings of this heresy. There are hints in the introduction to his commentary on the Song of Songs that concerns about T'ondrakean influence were behind an Artsruni prince's commissioning of the work. The prince may have desired Gregory to instruct the faithful in the orthodox doctrine of marriage in opposition to the alleged T'ondrakean rejection of marriage as a sacred bond instituted by God. According to the anti-T'ondrakean writings, the heretics believed that mutual love between spouses in the absence of ecclesial approbation sufficed to validate the marital bond.

Although the T'ondrakean movement may have begun as a popular lay organization among the poor and peasants alienated

[42] Terian associates the name with the Greek word *theandrikos*, "the God-man" and an extreme form of *theosis* rooted in the Hesychast movement. See Terian 2016, xxin11. For a comprehensive monograph on the T'ondrakeans, see Vrej Nersessian, 1987, *The Tondrakian Movement: Religious Movements in the Armenian Church from the Fourth to the Tenth Centuries*, London: Kahn & Averill.

[43] For details and discussion of dates, see Nersessian 1987, 39–41.

by the excesses of the nobility and the church, members of all classes, even the clergy, came to be associated with the heresy.[44] The movement was probably part of a more general dissident trend in Armenian society that comprised a diverse range of beliefs. Some of the dissenters may have rejected the Eucharist completely, but others, like the bishop Jacob of Hark', Gregory's contemporary and another highly charismatic religious leader, accepted the validity of the Eucharist but insisted that the sacrament be given sparingly, at most three times per year.[45] He also thought that mere participation in the sacrament of confession did not suffice by itself for admission to the Eucharist. With regard to penance, Jacob may have been reacting to the formulaic and mechanical approach to confession that prevailed in the tenth century and, as we will see, was also a matter of concern for the monks of Narek. Jacob also attacked the Armenian practice of *matagh*, in which an animal is ceremonially slaughtered in front of churches as an act of penance or petition to God. *Matagh* is still practiced in Armenia and the diaspora today, but Jacob, like others both within and outside the Armenian church, criticized the practice as a relic of pagan sacrifice.

Even though Jacob was critical of the church, his views do not conform exactly to the beliefs attributed to the T'ondrakeans as described in the sources written by their opponents. Nevertheless, there does seem to be some connection between Jacob's followers and the T'ondrakeans, however loose or informal it may have been. It is perhaps best to see the late ninth and early tenth century as a time of intellectual and spiritual ferment in Armenia, a consequence of the abatement of the calcifying effects of foreign occupation that limited the freedom of the church and the people. The medieval historians mention many intriguing figures who

[44] The view of the Armenian heresies as popular, economically motivated protest movements was especially prevalent among scholars during the period of Soviet rule in Armenia.

[45] The main source on Jacob is the eleventh century historian Aristakēs Lastiverts'i. Armenian text in Aristakēs Lastiverts'i, 1901, *Patmut'iwn Aristakeay Vardapeti Lastivertts'woy*, Venice: San Lazzaro Press. For Jacob's teachings, see chapter 22. See also citations and discussion in Ervine 2007, 23–24.

heralded a new asceticism and popular spirituality among the people. The tenth-century chronicler Stephen of Tarawn in his *Universal History* lists such names as Basilios the Elder, Stephen the Spiritual, and David the Lover of Poverty and Frugality.[46] With them Stephen also names the two founding monks of Narekavank'—Peter "the authoritative interpreter of holy scripture" and Anania "the great philosopher"—indicating that the establishment of Narekavank' was one of several movements unsettling the church establishment at this time. The monastery of Narek enjoyed a longer life and greater influence on the church in part because it respected and affirmed the traditional teachings and practices of the church while also calling for moderate reforms that would bring it closer to the people. Many of these other reforming or dissident leaders are remembered today if at all only as obscure names in medieval manuscripts. In contrast, the monastery of Narek would make a profound imprint on the subsequent course of Armenian Christianity, thanks mainly to the efforts and accomplishments of its greatest monk. But before we turn to Gregory and his monastery, it will be helpful to consider in greater detail the development of monasticism in Armenia.

Monasticism in Armenia

Just as Armenian Christianity in general was shaped by two major influences, the Greek influence from the west (especially Cappadocia) and the Syrian influence from the south, so too was Armenian monasticism formed from these currents. The Syrian form of monasticism entered Armenia earlier, perhaps from the very beginnings of the ascetic movement that flowered in Egypt, Palestine, Syria, and elsewhere. When Christianity became the official faith in Armenia and the favored religion in the Roman Empire, devout Christians no longer had the opportunity to prove their faith through martyrdom. Taking its place for those eager to demonstrate their commitment was the trial of retreating into the

[46] *MH* 15.2:753.50–52. Also Ervine 2007, 19.

desert or mountains and living the harsh life of a solitary monk. For others, though, the reason for withdrawing into the wilderness was simply to escape the temptations of urban life.

Unlike the later established monastic communities like Narekavank', these ascetic monks lived mostly solitary lives often in caves or other natural shelters where they practiced severe forms of deprivation in order to extinguish their worldly passions and come closer to God. Several early Armenian chronicles—the *Buzandaran*, for example, a fifth-century chronicle that provides a detailed account of events in Armenia from the later Arsacid period to Armenia's partition between Iran and the Byzantine Empire in the middle of the fourth century—depict the lives of Syrian anchorites like Shaghitay, noted for his diet of grass, his many miracles, and for living with wild animals.[47] The way of life of these Syrian ascetics was itself shaped by the stories told about the legendary Desert Fathers of Egypt, accounts of whose lives circulated throughout the Christian world and were preserved in written form in many manuscripts. These Desert Fathers developed reputations as spiritual masters who sometimes had to hide from the many admirers and pilgrims who sought them out.[48] They cultivated lives of self-control and incessant prayer. Arsenius, a Roman who retreated into the Egyptian desert toward the end of the fourth century, was noted for his prayer regimen:

> They said that on Saturday evening Arsenius used to turn his back to the setting sun and stretch out his hands toward heaven and pray until, at dawn on Sunday, the rising sun lit up his face, and then he sat down again.[49]

Their spiritual exercises, which involved compunction (the careful examination of conscience), were designed to develop in them a profound humility, selflessness, and an unwillingness to judge others:

[47] For Shaghitay's life, see Garsoïan 1989, 205–6.

[48] Benedicta Ward, 2003, *The Desert Fathers: Sayings of the Early Christian Monks*, London: Penguin, 6–7.

[49] Ward 2003, 130.

> Macarius was once returning to his cell from the marsh carrying palm leaves. The devil met him by the way, with a sickle, and wanted to run him through with it but he could not. The devil said, "Macarius, I suffer a lot of violence from you, for I can't overcome you. For whatever you do, I do also. If you fast, I eat nothing; if you keep watch, I get no sleep. There is only one quality in which you surpass me." Macarius said to him, "What is that?" The devil answered, "Your humility; that is why I cannot prevail against you."
>
> . . .
>
> Evagrius said, "To go against oneself is the beginning of salvation."
>
> . . .
>
> A brother sinned and the presbyter [elder] ordered him to go out of church. But Bessarion got up and went out with him, saying, "I, too, am a sinner."[50]

These hermits are usually called Desert Fathers, but that description neglects the existence of a significant number of women ascetics, most famously St. Mary of Egypt (ca. 344–421), and many other Desert Mothers who lived as solitaries and whose sayings and deeds exist beside those of the Fathers.[51] While the lives of these austere ascetics is of great interest in their own right, they are especially relevant for our study because, even though Gregory was primarily a cenobite rather than a hermit, meaning that he lived in an organized community with other monks in permanent buildings, he often withdrew in solitude to a cave overlooking Lake Van.[52] The solitary life modeled on the early desert ascetics had a profound effect on the course of Armenian monasticism for many centuries, and we will see how many of the features of the eremitic life, as the way of the hermit is called, influenced the practice of monasticism both at Narekavank' and the other monasteries of Armenia.

The *Buzandaran* records the names and deeds of several of these early fourth-century hermits of Armenia. One of these is Daniel, a

[50] Ward 2003, 156, 153, 84.

[51] See Benedicta Ward, 1987, *Harlots of the Desert: A Study of Repentance in Early Monastic Sources*, Kalamazoo, MI: Cistercian, as well as the numerous sayings of the Desert Mothers in Ward 2003.

[52] Mahé 2000, 44.

Syrian bishop and missionary. The author of the *Buzandaran* claims that Daniel was a disciple of the Illuminator, but Nina Garsoïan considers this a later gloss on the text intended to associate asceticism in Armenia with the established church in the northern parts of the country.[53] Renowned for his miracles, Daniel lived in isolation "in uninhabited mountains, though he was never unmindful of care for the needs of mankind. He had only a single garment of skins and wore sandals; his food was the roots of plants, and he had no occasion for a staff."[54] Daniel, who bore the title *chorepiskopos*, a kind of minor bishop with jurisdiction primarily in rural regions, appeared to have numerous anchorites as disciples, two of them named in the *Buzandaran*.[55] One was the Syrian Shaghitay, mentioned earlier, while his fellow hermit Epiphanius (*Epip'an*), described as a rather severe though charismatic leader, was Greek. The prevalence of Syrian and other non-Armenian names among the early hermits indicates that eremitism in Armenia was, at least in its origins and earliest periods, mainly a foreign and especially Syrian phenomenon that functioned apart from the ecclesial hierarchy. Brought up from an early age in the desert, Shaghitay is said to have eaten herbs or grass with the "desert-dwelling anchorites."[56] Supposedly, Shaghitay surrounded himself with lions. One anecdote recounts his healing of a lion with a wounded paw, a story familiar from the lives of other early saints.[57] Epiphanius is also depicted as a wonder-worker who, as in the popular lore surrounding St. Patrick in Ireland, drove away the snakes and other reptiles (the text specifies that they were adders, asps, and basilisks) upon his arrival on an island in Byzantine territory with his five hundred disciples. The *Buzandaran* reports that before leaving Armenia for the land of the Greeks he enacted "righteous regulations" for the ascetic communities he established in the land of Cop'k' (known to

[53] Garsoïan 1989, 367.

[54] Garsoïan 1989, 86–88.

[55] Garsoïan 1989, 205.

[56] Garsoïan 1989, 206.

[57] Most notably St. Jerome, though the story may derive from the pre-Christian fable of Androcles. See David Salter, 2002, *Holy and Noble Beasts: Encounters with Animals in Medieval Literature*, Cambridge: D. S. Brewer, 18.

the Byzantines as Sophanēnē), evidence that his presence in Armenia made a lasting impression on monastic practice.

But this profound eremitic strain in Armenian monasticism was not just the result of the influence of Syrian hermits residing in Armenia. Many of the earliest hermits whose lives are recorded were themselves Armenian. In *Spiritual Meadow*, a book in which John Moschus (ca. 550–619) describes his travels to the monastic centers throughout the Eastern Mediterranean world, the author mentions a certain Sergius the Armenian, a disciple of his namesake, Sergius the Anchorite, both active in the vicinity of the Dead Sea.[58] Other references to Armenian monks in the Judean desert are found in Theodoret of Cyrus (ca. 393–458), who mentions a certain Euthymius (377–473), an Armenian whose monastic establishment provided lodging for Armenian pilgrims. This early activity of Armenian monks and pilgrims in the Holy Land was the beginning of the Armenian presence in Jerusalem, which continues to this day in the form of the Armenian patriarchate and monastery in its own quarter of the Old City of Jerusalem.[59] That Armenian monks were to be found there and elsewhere beyond the borders of their country testifies to the impression the Syrian monks made on Armenians, many of whom were inspired to abandon their native country to tread the same ground as Christ and his disciples.

Eremitism was not isolated to southern Armenia but appears to have spread throughout the country. The practice in western Armenia was no doubt a more Greek-inflected, Cappadocian asceticism esteemed by the highest levels of church leadership, as evinced by the withdrawal of the Illuminator to a secluded cave after he relinquished his see, and that of his son Aristakēs, who according to Agathangelos lived in "the desert in his own hermitage" before his ordination as bishop and subsequent occupation of the patriarchal see as his father's successor.[60] And just as there were women

[58] For the accounts of Armenian ascetics see Ervine 2007, 9–10n13. Sergius is mentioned in John Moschus, 1863, *Pratum spirituale*, PG 87.3, 139.3001.27.

[59] Roberta R. Ervine, Michael E. Stone, and Nira Stone, eds., 2002, *The Armenians in Jerusalem and the Holy Land*, Leuven: Peeters.

[60] Robert W. Thomson, trans., 1976. *Agathangelos, History of the Armenians*, Albany: SUNY Press, 394–95.

ascetics in the Holy Land and Egyptian desert, so too there were female anchorites in Armenia. An especially notable example is the gifted hymnographer Sahakdukht of Siwnik', who lived in the early eighth century. She resided in a cave in the canyon of Garni near the current Armenian capital of Yerevan. The thirteenth-century bishop and chronicler of Siwnik', Stephen Ōrbēlean reports that Sahakdukht would teach students while seated behind a curtain.[61] The words of three of her hymns survive.[62] But for the women religious, as in the case of their male counterparts, it was communal monasticism that prevailed over eremitism as convents began to flourish throughout Armenia.[63]

Cenobitism came to dominate mainly due to the difficulty of sustaining the eremitic life, which has no organized structure and often operates outside of direct authority and without support of the church hierarchy. But there are reports of hermits in Armenia just prior to and during Gregory's life.[64] Around 923, John of Draskhanakert, the Armenian catholicos, wrote about his pilgrimage to the place of the Illuminator's retreat where a large group of hermits conglomerated at the foot of Mount Sepuh, a sacred site because it was believed to house the remains of the Illuminator. They had neither a spiritual leader nor any monastic buildings but lived separately in the rocky cavities of the mountain "dressed in hair-shirts, praying with continual groans and imploring supplications." The hermits individually provided for their own material

[61] Step'annos Ōrbēlean and Marie Félicité Brosset, trans., 1864, *Histoire de la Siounie*, St. Petersburg: Académie Impériale des sciences, 85–86.

[62] The verses of the hymns are published in *MH* 6:601–5. There is an English translation of her hymn on the nativity in Diana Der Hovanessian and Marzbed Margossian, eds., 1978, *Anthology of Armenian Poetry*, New York: Columbia University Press, though it deviates significantly from the Armenian text in *MH*.

[63] See Roberta R. Ervine, 1999, "Women Who Left the World: The Armenian Nuns of Jerusalem" in Thomas Hummel, Kevork Hintlian, and Ulf Carmesund, eds., *Patterns of the Past, Prospects for the Future: The Christian Heritage in the Holy Land*, London: Melisende, 124–34.

[64] Edward G. Matthews Jr., 2000, "Armenian Monasticism," in William M. Johnston, ed., *Encyclopedia of Monasticism*, Chicago: Fitzroy Dearborn, 85–87.

welfare "through the sweat of toilsome work."[65] The only thing that seems to have brought them together in this place was its renown as the retreat of the Illuminator after his retirement as catholicos and the place where his relics were first interred.

While eremitic monasticism spread from the south into the other parts of Armenia, cenobitic forms of monasticism, in which the monks lived in close proximity to each other and met regularly for communal prayer and meals, gradually came to dominate throughout the country. This cenobitic monasticism was based on the monastic teachings of Eusthatius (300–377), a friend of St. Basil of Caesarea. Because of Eusthatius's association with Basil, the so-called Rule of St. Basil, which was translated into Armenian at the end of the fifth century, became the inspiration for the organization and daily life of most of the monasteries in Armenia.[66] In contrast to the rule of St. Benedict of Nursia (ca. 480–543), which guided monastic discipline in the West, the "Rule" of St. Basil, which is in fact a compilation of responses to questions on the religious life, was less rigid and comprehensive. For example, Basil's rule does not contain any details about how the monks take their communal meals, while Benedict's rule devotes a chapter to this topic and even specifies who is to wash the utensils and towels. The Basilian rule also does not specify a course of studies for the monks.[67] It leaves to the discretion of the abbot or superior to set the proper course of studies.[68] As a result, the monasteries in Armenia enjoyed a great degree of freedom, and the abbot or abbess of each

[65] John of Draskhanakert, *Patmut'iwn Hayots'* [History of Armenia], *MH* 11.1:55.13. See also Mahé, 2010, "Érémitisme et cénobitisme en Arménie après l'Islam (IXe – XIIIe siècles)" in Mahé et al. 2010, 111–24, esp. 114–16.

[66] But see Ervine 2007, 11, who cautions against the inference from the use of the Basilian rule in some Armenian monasteries to a general conclusion about Armenian monasticism being structured by the rule. Perhaps the best we can say is that monasticism in Armenia was highly eclectic and not dominated by any particular method of governance.

[67] Chapter 35 of the Rule of St. Benedict states how the monks are to serve the food and clean the tables while chapters 39–41 discuss the type and quantity of food and drink and the time of meals. See Patrick Barry, trans., 2004, *Saint Benedict's Rule*, Mahwah, NJ: HiddenSpring, 101, 106–9.

[68] Mahé 2009, 123.

individual community was free to experiment and implement their own plans.

In surveying the extent and diversity of the forms of monasticism present in Armenia, one gets the impression that the country was a crucible into which were mixed various monastic influences from other lands, especially from the Desert Fathers of Syria, Egypt, and the Holy Land, and the communal monasticism of Cappadocia and the Pontus. From them were forged a distinctive form of religious life. But even though a kind of monastic syncretism formed in Armenia, the different elements that composed it are still detectable. Even in its most organized form of communal living, Armenian monasticism never lost its original flavor of desert asceticism. We sense this especially in the spirituality of Narekavank'. Not only did monks like Gregory occasionally live as hermits, but more generally the peculiar ethos of desert monasticism infused their daily lives.

Thus it seems cenobitic and eremitic lives coexisted within the same monastery and were alternatively practiced even by the same individual, if Gregory's periodic retreats from his monastery are instances of a more widespread practice. Mahé notes that in the thirteenth century, Mkhit'ar, the abbot of Ayrivank' (more commonly known as Geghardavank' or "monastery of the spear," so named because it housed a relic of the holy lance used to pierce Christ's side), without leaving his monastery's enclosure, locked himself in a cell where he continued to practice in solitary the daily office but otherwise separated himself from the communal affairs of his monastery.[69]

Even such matters as where the monks slept is unclear. The Armenian text of the Basilian rule does not provide any information. Nor does the architecture of the medieval monasteries provide much help. There do not seem to be anything resembling dormitories until the later Middle Ages. The monks at Mount Sepuh and Ayrivank' no doubt slept in artificial grottoes surrounding the monastery. In other monasteries, monks may have slept in the *gawit'* (corresponding to the narthex of a church, a courtyard that

[69] Mahé 2009, 120.

was often in open air but beginning in the eleventh century would have had a roof).[70] A monk would repose in an *ankoghin*, often translated as "bed" but more likely something like a sleeping bag or a set of blankets unfolded for the night and stored during the day in boxes.[71] There does not seem to have been anything resembling a modern fixed bed. Monks could have slept in different places from one night to the next, based on weather and other circumstances. We do not find any refectories until the thirteenth century, so even the details about where and when the monks ate is open to speculation.[72]

Unlike in the West, there were no distinct monastic orders such as the Benedictines or Carthusians that had monasteries in various locations. Each monastery functioned independently of the others, although as monks from one monastery left to establish another institution they may have taken with them some of the ethos of their former house or maintained a sense of kinship with their former brother monks. An example of this amity between monasteries is exemplified in Gregory's encomium concerning the monastery of Aparank', which was founded several years after Narekavank'. This encomium, discussed in chapter four, narrates the monastery's establishment and the story of how it received its illustrious reliquary, a gift from the Byzantine emperors.

Another important feature of Armenian monasticism is the proximity of many of the monasteries to cities and towns. Because the cenobitic monks in Armenia generally lived near secular communities, they remained in contact with the world, preaching in the churches in towns and villages near their monasteries, and also engaging in commerce with the people. Perhaps due to this proximity between the religious and secular, there was never any need for movements like the mendicant orders such as the Dominicans and Franciscans, who eschewed monastic life for an itinerant life of preaching and service in the world. In a sense, the monks in Armenia were already serving as preachers, and at least in some of the

[70] Garsoïan 1989, 526–27.

[71] Mahé 2009, 123–24.

[72] Mahé 2009, 125.

monasteries, monks were expected to serve their neighboring communities.

As in other parts of Christendom, the Armenian monasteries became the main centers of learning and the transmission of the literary heritage, both secular and sacred, and some could be considered nascent universities, most notably the eastern monasteries of Gladzor and Tat'ew. The latter was home to the prolific scholar and theologian Gregory of Tat'ew (1346–1410), who composed the *Book of Questions (Girk' hartsmants)*, a kind of theological *summa* reminiscent of the style of St. Thomas Aquinas. Narekavank' itself, as we will see, had a lofty reputation for learning and scholarship from its very founding.

The general impression left by the Armenian monastery complexes in the early Middle Ages is that of a haphazard juxtaposition of churches and other buildings constructed at different times and conditioned by the designs of the abbot at the time as well as the availability of donors. The autonomy granted to each monastery and even to the individual monastics by this loose form of Basilian rule meant that the Armenian cenobitic tradition continued to be permeated by a spirit of earlier ascetic and anchoritic traditions. This spirit of eremitism is especially visible in the monasticism of Narekavank' and, more specifically, in Gregory's spirituality. The circumstances and the ethos of the monastery of Narek and its school are the focus of the next chapter.

Chapter Three

The Monastery and School of Narek

The Monastery of Narek

Gregory's monastery was founded about a decade before his birth during the height of the renaissance of Armenian monasticism and spirituality that followed the recovery of political autonomy in the latter half of the ninth century. It was named for the town of Narek, located about five kilometers from the southern shore of Lake Van and in the principality of Ṛshtunik', which by this time was under the jurisdiction of Vaspurakan and its Artsruni princes. Its founding was most likely supported financially by the Artsruni family, especially its monarch Gagik I, who had a strong interest in reviving the church and the monastic institutions within its realm. The Artsruni may have heard of the reputation of a monk named Anania who had been active in two monasteries of Bagratid, Armenia.[1] A relative of the Artsruni, a learned patrician by the name of Khosrov Andzewats'i, whose wife was Anania's cousin, perhaps recommended Anania as a suitable abbot for the proposed new monastery at Narek. Anania together with his brother monk Peter, a noted biblical scholar, settled there and began the work of building the institution.

One might suppose that after Gregory's death around 1003 and the abdication of the last Artsruni king in 1021, Narekavank' would have entered a state of decline, especially after having lost its royal patronage. But the manuscript tradition reflects continued

[1] Lévon Pétrossian, 2010, *Commentaire sur le Cantique des Cantiques*, OCA 285. Rome: Pontifical Oriental Institute, 57.

activity even into the later Middle Ages. The art historian Thomas F. Matthews reports the discovery of a couple of pages of an illuminated vellum codex with an inscription indicating the manuscript was produced at Narekavank' in 1181. This was a century after the Seljuk invasions that, coupled with Byzantine pressure on the Armenian nobility to evacuate their lands and move westward away from the frontier, brought to an end Artsruni rule over Vaspurakan.[2] Matthews notes the artist's borrowing of Islamic themes: the dedicatory prayer written in Armenian imitates the foliate Arabic script found in contemporary manuscripts of the Qur'an. There are also a number of folios of a book produced at Narekavank' in the fifteenth century depicting Christ's miracles. The illuminations reveal the influence of the prevailing political situation at the time, with Christ wearing the fur cap of a Mongol prince while at the wedding at Cana.[3] These and other surviving manuscripts show that Narekavank' maintained an active scriptorium many centuries after its founding.

Anyone visiting Narek today (it is in the district of Gevaş, in southeastern Turkey's Van province) will find little if anything above ground that remains of the monastic complex. Starting in the 1960s, Jean-Michel and Nicole Thierry, both of them physicians and art historians, made numerous expeditions to historic Armenian lands to observe and study the state of the monuments. They noted in 1989 that almost nothing of the monastery of Narek remains.[4] The Thierrys describe the buildings that made up the

[2] T. F. Matthews, 1998, "The Genius of the Armenian Painter" in T. F. Matthews and R. S. Wieck, *Treasures in Heaven: Armenian Art, Religion, and Society*, New York: Pierpont Morgan Library, 163–175, especially 163–64.

[3] Matthews 1998, 164.

[4] J. M. Thierry, 1989, *Monuments Arméniens du Vaspurakan*, Paris: Orientaliste Paul Geuthner. The description of Narekavank' is on 327–30. Thierry states that the founding monks were fleeing Byzantine territory, where they faced Chalcedonian persecution. But if Anania was among the founders that seems unlikely given that his monasteries were within the territory of the Bagratuni and thus relatively isolated from Byzantine interference. Thierry also notes that despite the alleged origins of the monastery, there was a strong Chalcedonian influence. As we will see below, that claim needs to be at least qualified. Anania wrote a strongly worded critique of Chalcedonianism at the request of

monastery based on written accounts from the nineteenth century. At that time, the monastery consisted of two churches: the church dedicated to St. Sandukht, the princess-martyr of the first generation of Armenian Christianity, and the smaller church of the Mother of God adjoining its south wall. The former, which dates to the beginnings of the monastery, was a triconch cross-in-square while the layout of the latter included a domed nave. Gregory's mausoleum, covered by a small domed drum, was connected through a vestibule to the northern apse of the church of St. Sandukht. The tomb that was erected in 1867 had a stele with an inscription. The large *gawit'* or narthex served both churches. Relics of St. Thomas and St. James of Nisibis were housed there along with the graves of Anania and John, Gregory's brother. The churches were built at about the same time as the monastery's founding, but substantial renovations were made in the eighteenth and nineteenth centuries. A bell tower built in 1812 stood in front of the narthex. The complex also included auxiliary buildings along the courtyard wall that housed a school and rooms for monks and pilgrims, though it is not certain when these were built. Abandoned during the 1915 Genocide, the monastery was completely destroyed in 1951.[5]

The School of Narek

Gregory's achievements are unique, but they emerged against the backdrop of a vibrant intellectual and spiritual life fostered by

---

the Armenian catholicos, while, as I will argue, Gregory seems to have adopted a conciliatory stance similar to his father's that recognized the orthodoxy of both the Chalcedonian formula and the miaphysite doctrine of the Armenian church.

[5] Thierry 1989 includes a photograph (plate XLVIII.3) of the complex taken in 1910 with the domes of the two churches as well as Gregory's sepulcher clearly visible. Thierry says it is a view from the north, but Christina Maranci, 2006, "The Built World of Grigor Narekac'i," *Hask: Armenological Yearbook*, Antelias, Lebanon: Catholicosate of Cilicia, 51–58, especially 52n9 notes that it is actually taken from the south.

his abbot, Anania. As the impressive body of work produced by the late scholar Hrach'ya T'amrazyan has demonstrated, one can speak of a veritable school of Narek that comprised not only Gregory and his abbot and mentor but also the cofounder of the monastery, Peter, whose exegetical works unfortunately have not survived.[6] Though never a member of the monastery, Gregory's father, Khosrov, had a great interest in and surely contributed to the community's formation. Among Gregory's peers, there is of course his brother, John, who assisted in the compilation of the *Book of Lamentation*, and Ukht'anēs, also a student of Anania and the author of several historical works.[7] As a result of T'amrazyan's scholarship we no longer have to treat Gregory as an isolated figure but can better understand the intellectual and spiritual milieu from which he emerged.

Though we should not forget that the school of Narek consisted of many talented figures, some no doubt unknown to us, in theology, music, biblical studies, or any of the other arts studied there, our interest here is in Gregory and the major influences in his life and on his work. Thus we will focus on the two men who had the greatest effect on his development.[8] These are Khosrov, his father by birth, and Anania, his spiritual father and master. The large and interesting body of work that we have from them will help us to understand better Gregory's formation and the context in which he wrote.

Gregory's Father: Khosrov Andzewats'i

After his wife's death, Khosrov was consecrated a bishop by catholicos Anania of Mokk'. It is not known if he was already ordained as a married priest and then assumed the rank of a celibate priest when he was widowed, or if he was a layman who was

[6] Hrach'ya T'amrazyan, 2010, "L'école de Narek et la littérature arménienne du Xe siècle" in Mahé et al. 2010, 125–33.

[7] For Ukht'anēs, see *MH* 10.2:441–45.

[8] A comprehensive study of the school is: Hrach'ya T'amrazyan, 1999, *Narekyan Dprots'ě* (*The School of Narek*), Erevan: Hayastan.

ordained to the priesthood and to the episcopate concurrently.[9] There are precedents in church history for both scenarios. His extensive knowledge of the liturgy and theology would suggest that he already had clerical training, but on the other hand his aristocratic privileges would have afforded him the opportunity to acquire an education usually unavailable to laypersons and also would have made him a natural candidate to serve as bishop of his native Andzewats'ik'.

Once installed in his office as spiritual leader of his diocese, Khosrov began to meet his clergy and to assess the conditions of the churches in his jurisdiction. His writings make it very clear that he was not pleased with what he found. The married priests who served in the parish churches suffered from serious intellectual and spiritual deficiencies that prevented them from understanding the very words of the liturgy that they celebrated.[10] The situation of the laity was even worse. For many, the liturgy and the sacraments had become empty rituals that were witnessed without any sense of participation or inner transformation. Khosrov insisted that mere thoughtless mouthing of prayer had little value:

> For if the tongue strikes the air without thought following it, it produces no benefit. For God who knows the heart looks at the heart and mind, not the tongue. Therefore, let us render prayer to God with alert mind, undistracted thoughts and soul fully aware, to be of benefit to ourselves and others and thus gain from others' prayers.[11]

[9] Pétrossian 2010, 37, cites the example of catholicos Zak'aria Dzagets'i (r. 855–76), who, according to the historian of the Armenian church and patriarch of Constantinople Maghak'ia Ōrmanean (1841–1918), was a layman before being elected and consecrated catholicos. See M. Ōrmanean, 2001, *Azgapatum* [National History] 1, Antelias, Lebanon: Armenian Catholicosate of Cilcia, cols. 950–52.

[10] S. Peter Cowe, 1991, *Commentary on the Divine Liturgy*. New York: St. Vartan Press, 28–29. Cowe's book is an English translation with the Armenian text and comprehensive study of Khosrov's commentary on the liturgy of the Eucharist. As far as I know, there is no English translation of the first part of Khosrov's commentary, which is on the liturgy of the hours. See also Pétrossian 2001, 44.

[11] Khosrov Andzewats'i, *Bats'ayaytut'iwn kargats' ekeghets'woy k'arozut'eants' ew aghawt'its'* [Explanation of the Prayers and Liturgy of the Hours], in *MH* 10, 225–6.602–603; Cowe 1991, 225.

Khosrov also implies that beyond mere ignorance, there were many instances of clerical abuse and corruption, most notably the buying and selling of pardons and other ecclesial privileges. Such corrupt practices are called simony after Simon Magus of Acts 8:18-24, reproached by St. Peter for offering money to the apostles to gain the power of transmitting the Holy Spirit through the laying on of hands. Though it was recorded more than 200 years after Khosrov's death, a fable in the compendium of the priest and jurist Mkhit'ar Gosh (1130–1213) suggests that simony was neither isolated nor uncommon. According to the fable, one Easter all of the birds in a certain village gathered together before the priest to confess their sins before partaking of the Eucharist. Among the birds were a raven and a cormorant (both unclean birds according to the law of Moses) who stated that they were not aware of having committed any sins other than that they hunted and ate mice and frogs. The priest declared the two birds to be unclean, denied them the sacrament, and sent them away. They later returned with clean fledglings that they offered to the priest. Seduced by their bribe, the priest absolved them and gave them communion. Mkhit'ar ends the fable by noting that he told this tale as a parable of avaricious priests who expel prostitutes and other sinners by terrifying them, but that later when they accept their bribes, they find an excuse to allow them to receive communion.[12] This kind of corruption that Mkhit'ar's fable depicts may also have infected some of the clergy in Khosrov's diocese.

Based on his observations of the poor condition of the clergy and laity in his diocese, Khosrov concluded that he would have to write a commentary on the liturgy of the hours and the Eucharist that would be read and studied in the monasteries. The monks would then visit the parish churches of the diocese and expound the meaning of the rite for the faithful:

[12] Mkhit'ar Gosh, 1854, *Aṙakk'* (*Fables*),Venice: San Lazzaro, 122. An excerpt of a portion of this fable in French translation is in Mahé 2000, 125n406. For English translation of the fables, see Robert Bedrosian, Elise Antreassian Bayizian, and Anahid Janjigian, 1987, *The Fables of Mkhitar Gosh*, New York: Ashod Press.

> When it fell to my lot to become bishop and, on taking office, I perceived ignorance was rampant in everyone and, realizing the impossibility of communicating all this to everyone myself verbally, I deemed it appropriate to commit it to writing to alleviate the task of those eager to learn.[13]

Immediately after this, Khosrov asks those who happen to hear his commentary being read to pray for him.[14] So most likely he intended the book to be read out loud in the monastic schools of his diocese.

The guiding idea of Khosrov's commentary—that the mind and heart, the inner person and the deepest thought and feelings, must be engaged with the body in worship—is a major theme of the school of Narek. We will find it emphasized throughout the works both of Anania and Gregory. To be genuine and effective, faith must not only involve our external actions but penetrate into the deepest levels of our being. As Khosrov states in the very first sentence of the commentary, when we speak with God and about God we must consider the words that we say attentively and cautiously.[15] He presciently began his major work with the same phrase—*speaking with God*—that would begin almost every prayer of his son's *Book of Lamentation*.

Another major theme of Khosrov's work that Anania and Gregory also emphasized was the universality of the church. Commenting on a verse from the liturgical hours that speaks of the Church as "catholic and apostolic," Khosrov expounds on the meaning of *catholic*:

> What does *catholic* mean? It means *universal*. For all the orthodox churches, which exist throughout the universe, are one. There is one Christ in all the churches that are founded on the apostolic faith, which is why we also call the church *apostolic*. Although the churches are distinguished according to place, they are not separated by nationality. For from one end of the earth to the other, wherever the true faithful may arrive at an orthodox church, it is

[13] *MH* 10:36.14–15; Cowe 1991, 229.
[14] *MH* 10:227.625.
[15] *MH* 10:35.1.

> their church and neither the strangeness of the country nor the language separates it [from them], but like a mother it accepts them into its bosom with fervent love. Thus it is called *universal* everywhere because its doors are open and its bosom embraces all the faithful of the universe.[16]

This passage highlights a couple of remarkable features of Khosrov's ecclesiology. First, Khosrov must have considered the Chalcedonian churches to be orthodox. For he knew that the non-Chalcedonian churches did not extend throughout the inhabited world. And yet he exhorts his faithful to accept the embrace of the orthodox church wherever they may find themselves. It is also interesting to note his understanding of the church's apostolic character. It is not the fact that the bishops are successors of the apostles *per se* that defines the church as apostolic but that they teach the apostolic faith. Finally, the jurisdictional divisions of the church are determined not on the basis of the composition of the population that inhabits the region but by location. Khosrov thereby rejects what has more recently been termed *phyletism*, the association of a church with a particular ethnic group, a problem that continues to beset many of the Eastern churches.

Khosrov's broad-minded ecumenism and openness to the world beyond Armenia would have a profound effect on his son but it would also provoke the suspicion and anger of his superior, the catholicos Anania of Mokk'. The nature of Khosrov's offense is hidden behind a number of errors that Anania attributed to him. Khosrov's real affront was to challenge the authority of the Armenian patriarch both over neighboring sees and the Armenian episcopal college. Anania resorts to bizarre innuendos that suggest Khosrov held pro-Byzantine and Chalcedonian sympathies. The charges are provided in Anania's brief letter of explanation of the anathematization.[17]

[16] Khosrov, *Explanation*, *MH* 10:107.765–79.

[17] Anania Mokats'i, *Teaṛn Ananayi Hayots' Kat'oghikosi Patchaṛ yaghags zKhosrov Nzoveloyn zAndzewats'ioy episkoposn* [*Justification of the anathematization of Khosrov, bishop of Andzewatsik' by Lord Anania, catholicos of the Armenians*] *MH* 10:275–76. English translation in Cowe 1991, 10–13.

Anania's letter, written in 954, justifying his condemnation of Khosrov notes that he had entrusted to him the Diocese of Andzewats'ik when he was a "modest and learned man, white-haired and advanced in old age." But Khosrov suddenly began to act as though possessed by a "demonic spirit" and pronounced the words for *Sunday* and *Jerusalem* in the manner of the Greeks.[18] Moreover, Khosrov apparently ordered that the hair of youths be cut until their beards began to grow, after which they were to let their hair grow plaited down to their legs. Khosrov supposedly justified this practice through a dubious etymology of the words *ktrij'* ("brave, youth")[19] and *manuk* ("child, boy"), which he takes to be related to the verbs *ktrem* ("cut") and *manem* ("braid"). This criticism reveals two features of Khosrov's thought. One is his interest in etymology and developing arguments from what he takes to be the origins of words, a habit he shared with Anania of Narek. The other is his wish to conform the practices of the Armenian church more closely with those of the Greeks. Although Anania of Mokk' does not make it obvious, one may infer that the dictates on hairstyle were meant for monastics and not intended as a general rule of grooming for the males of his diocese. As bishop, Khosrov had direct authority over the monasteries in his diocese. Armenian monks kept their hair shorn, unlike their Byzantine counterparts who grew their hair long. Khosrov, so Anania implies, wanted the monks in his diocese to adopt something more like the Greek cus-

[18] The Armenian word for Sunday, *Kiraki,* is obviously derived from the Greek *Kuriakē* (the Lord's day), but Anania's ire was aroused by Khosrov's alleged attempt to bring the Armenian pronunciation closer to the Greek: *Kiuṛiaki,* with the Armenian diphthong *iu* corresponding to the Greek upsilon, restoring the iota lost in the Armenian spelling and pronunciation, and replacing the untrilled *r* with the trilled *ṛ*. Likewise, he said *Eṛusaghem* instead of *Erusaghem.* Although this effort at hellenizing Armenian pronunciation suggests an eccentricity of Khosrov's personality, it is otherwise consistent with the school of Narek's meticulous attention to the details of language, including phonetics and etymology.

[19] See entry in Ṛ. S. Ghazaryan and H. M. Avetisyan, 2009, *Mijin Hayereni baṛaran* [*Lexicon of Middle Armenian*], Yerevan: EPH Hratarakdzut'yun, 391.

tom.[20] Beyond his general Byzantine sympathies, though, Khosrov's interest in hairstyle provides us with evidence of the influence of the Pseudo-Dionysian writings, another feature he shares with the other members of the school of Narek. The Dionysian treatise known as the *Ecclesiastical Hierarchy* includes advice on the importance of the proper tonsuring of monks.[21]

These two accusations are consistent with Khosrov's universal vision of the church and his openness to learning from and adopting the traditions of other churches. But the third allegation at first glance appears puzzling and anomolous. Anania charged Khosrov with teaching that a cross blessed by a priest and an unblessed cross are equally worthy of veneration. The belief that a blessed cross is of equal worth as a plain piece of wood at first may seem to associate Khosrov with the T'ondrakeans, who rejected veneration of the cross.[22] Anania of Narek was accused of being a T'ondrakean and, according to some scholars, Gregory himself may also have been the object of such suspicions. But Anania of Mokk' is equivocal about whether Khosrov believed the cross generally unworthy of any veneration or instead that a priestly blessing was not necessary to make the cross an acceptable object of reverence. It is more likely that the dispute here was whether a priest had to anoint a cross before its veneration. It seems the Greeks thought it sufficient for an icon or object of veneration to bear the name of God or a saint, while the Armenians insisted on

[20] There is some confusion in the sources on the details of Khosrov's rule. See also Pétrossian 2001, 41, as well as Cowe 1991, 6, for details. Pétrossian suggests that Khosrov introduced tonsure on ordination but supported monks wearing their hair long during their novitiate. In either case, Anania's objection was to Khosrov's importation of a Byzantine custom.

[21] G. Heil and A. M. Ritter, 1999, *Corpus Dionysiacum II: Pseudo-Dionysius Areopagita. De coelesti hierarchia, de ecclesiastica hierarchia, de mystica theologia, epistulae,* Berlin: De Gruyter, 6.536A. English translation in Luibheid 1987, 536A, 247.

[22] Pétrossian 2001, 41, believes Anania of Mokk' is accusing Khosrov of T'ondrakean sympathies, but Cowe 1991, 7, is certainly correct that here too the objection is to Khosrov's affinity for the Byzantine approach to sacred objects.

anointing in order to avoid the appearance of idolatry.[23] Here too Khosrov's error was his wish to conform Armenian practice closer to that of the Byzantines.

Anania of Mokk' conceded that these three errors are relatively minor matters and says that he would be willing to ignore them but for the final affront, which he claims introduced a new schism into the church of God.[24] Anania alleges that Khosrov, basing his argument on the equal honor given to archangels and angels in the Pseudo-Dionysian writings, asserted that the catholicos and other bishops enjoy the same privileges and honors.[25] In the Pseudo-Dionysian *Celestial Hierarchy*, which describes the orders of the heavenly beings, the archangels are said to "join with the angels to form a single hierarchy and rank."[26] Furthermore, in the *Ecclesiastical Hierarchy* there are only three orders: hierarch, priest, and deacon, and the hierarchs, who are the bishops, "fully possess the power of consecration."[27] This was also another point on which the Armenian church differed from the Byzantines, for the Armenian catholicos receives a distinct anointing upon assuming office.[28] The final accusation of Anania of Mokk' coheres with the general charge against Khosrov of Hellenization, since the patriarch of Constantinople, unlike the Armenian catholicos, did not undergo a second anointing after his consecration as a bishop.

There were clear ramifications for church governance, with Khosrov advocating a decentralized administration led by the synod of bishops in Armenia, with the catholicos simply presiding rather than having sacramental powers beyond those of the other bishops. If all bishops had the right to ordain bishops without needing the approval of the catholicos, then the dioceses could function relatively independently.

[23] For the Armenian sources, see Cowe 1991, 7–8.

[24] *MH* 10:276.13–14.

[25] *MH* 10:276.17. La Porta 2010, 245, also draws this connection with the Pseudo-Dionysian corpus.

[26] Heil and Ritter 1991, 36.12–13.

[27] Luibheid 1987, 236.

[28] *MH* 10:276.17.

Anania could abide the idiosyncrasies of Khosrov's tonsure policies and prescriptions on proper diction, but he could not tolerate the challenge to his authority as catholicos. Khosrov's ecclesiological theories were not simply theoretical; they set him against Anania in a crisis in which the catholicos was concurrently embroiled. The catholicos of neighboring Caucasian Albania had been consecrated and installed in the presence of three bishops, but without Anania's approval. The ordination was consistent with the original Nicene canon, which stipulates that when it is not possible for all the bishops of a region to be present, three validly ordained bishops will suffice to consecrate the new bishop. The Armenian version of the fourth canon of Nicaea, however, specifies that the catholicos, rather than a metropolitan bishop, must ratify the installation. Anania invalidated the consecration because of this canon, but Khosrov argued that since the ordination was done in accordance with the original Greek canon it was valid.[29] This dispute about the jurisdictional authority of the Armenian catholicos over the see of the Albanians seems to have been the real source of Anania's animus and why he took particular umbrage at Khosrov's claim that patriarchs do not enjoy any special authority beyond a primacy of honor.[30] Khosrov, writing four years before being anathemized, anticipates what was to happen to him:

> When they quarrel with Christians of other nations, they justify themselves in an ignorant way as if only Armenians possess the truth . . . and they treat anyone who shows that other nations are correct

[29] For the Armenian version of canon four, see Vazgēn Hakobyan, 1964, *Kanonagirk' Hayots'* [*Armenian Book of Canons*], Yerevan: HSSṚ GA Hratarakch'ut'yun, 119. The bishop of the diocese of Siwnik' was a metropolitan, so his ratification of the consecration would have sufficed if the letter of the Greek rather than Armenian version of canon four were followed.

[30] Control of the hierarchy of the Albanian church and its Chalcedonian inclinations was a particular concern of the Armenian church, especially given the Armenians' bitter memories of the defection of the Georgian church to the Chalcedonians. At the same time as the conflict with the Albanian church, the situation of the see of Siwnik' was also in question. Siwnik' had a semiautonomous status and its incumbent bishops also often supported Chalcedon. See Mahé 2000, 34–5.

> on some matter out of love of truth as if they were heretics [*tsayt'*] deficient in their faith. They are ridiculed, persecuted, and threatened with death to the point that they escape with barely a hair.[31]

The term translated here as "heretic" is an epithet normally applied to people suspected of being Chalcedonians.[32]

If Anania's intent was to remove Khosrov from office, his anathema was a failure. Khosrov continued to serve as bishop of Andzewats'ik' for the rest of his life. The catholicos was relatively weak at this time and he had incurred the hostility of the Artsruni royalty, who resented the transfer of the patriarchal see from their capital in Aght'amar back to Bagratid territory. Furthermore, Vaspurakan was pursuing a pro-Byzantine policy and had little interest in enforcing an excommunication order against a bishop who favored reconciliation with the Chalcedonians. Nor would the Artsruni be inclined to act against their own kinsman.

In any event, Khosrov's writings reveal that his teachings were not heretical. His main offense was to carry out bold new measures to revive the spiritual life of his faithful. He was a committed reformer, and people who set out to reform the church often face the opposition of hierarchs threatened by change. But in doctrinal matters, Khosrov consistently affirmed the received Armenian teachings on all matters of theology and Christology. He clearly articulates the standard Armenian Cyrillian or miaphysite formula:

> [The Word] united with the flesh without confusion for He effected no change or diminution to either the divine or human nature. Rather he united the natures to be both God and man, so that God the Word might be flesh and that which was incarnate of the Virgin might be God, and He Himself both God and man, and Mary, who bore God the Word, might be the Mother of God and Virgin.[33]

[31] Khosrov Andzewats'i, 1840, *Meknut'iwn Zhamakargut'ean* [*Commentary on the Office*], Constantinople (Yort'agiwgh): Erits' Ordwots' Poghosi arapean apuch'ekhts'woy, 199.

[32] See James Russell, 1987, *Yovhannes T'lkuranc'i and the Medieval Armenian Lyric Tradition*, Atlanta: Scholars Press, 151n4. Thamar Dasnabedian, 1995, *Le panégyrique de la sainte Mère de Dieu de Grigor Narekac'i*, Antelias, Lebanon: Catholicosate of Cilicia, 16–17, connects the term with Arabic *ğâhid*, "renegade."

[33] *MH* 10:201.218–19; Cowe 1991, 161.

And he clearly rejects any Julianist tendencies while explicitly affirming the real suffering of Christ:

> Christ lived out his life but committed no sin, bearing all of the passions of the flesh, i.e. He was born, nourished, hungered, thirsted, grew tired, ate, drank, felt, became anxious, sorrowed, wept, and took upon himself all else entailed by flesh.[34]

While remaining faithful to the traditions of his church, he also looked for inspiration from other communions and adopted a conciliatory approach to other Christians. We cannot know for certain how often he saw Gregory after his son was dedicated to his monastery, but there is little doubt that Khosrov's teachings had a profound effect on his son. Like his father, Gregory remained committed to Armenian orthodoxy while also upholding the universality of the church and possessing a passion for a reform that would turn the hearts of the clergy and the laity from lukewarm indifference to a deep and heartfelt love of God and his church. In this program to revive spiritual life in Armenia, he was joined by another gifted clergyman, the abbot of Narekavank'.

Gregory's Abbot and Teacher: Anania of Narek

Though we cannot say anything with confidence about Gregory's relations with his father, we can be certain that Anania of Narek was with Gregory throughout his formative years as his abbot and teacher. Thanks to Hrach'ya T'amrazyan's scholarship, we now have available to us a large body of Anania's writings and we are in a position to speak confidently about his teachings and his influence on his most famous pupil.

Anania's year of birth is unknown but most likely was in the first decade of the tenth century.[35] Unlike Khosrov, he was not a native of Vaspurakan but came from northern Armenia, most likely the province of Ayrarat.[36] Of his early life we only know that he

[34] *MH* 10:201.221–223; Cowe 1991, 160–161.
[35] Hrach'ya T'amrazyan, *Anania Narekats'i* [*Anania of Narek*], *MH* 10:311.
[36] Mahé 2000, 40.

and his colleague Peter resided in Bagratid realms at the monasteries of Antak' (or Anduk) in the canton of Hawnunik', and Khawaradzor ("the dark valley") in Arsharunik'.[37] Around 935 he moved with Peter to the province of the Ṛshtunik', just to the east of Khosrov's diocese of Andzewats'ik'. The province was ruled by its eponymous noble house, vassals of the Artsruni royalty and three of whose members served as catholicoi when the patriarchal see was at Aght'amar from 927 to 947. There, in the town of Narek, with the patronage of the Artsruni king and Khosrov's intellectual support and encouragement, Anania established and was installed as abbot of a new monastery, Narekavank'.

In addition to his work founding and leading Narekavank', Anania produced an impressive body of writings. He shared with Khosrov a desire for spiritual renewal among the people. The goal of his monastery and his writings was to promote and advance that renewal. As we have seen, Khosrov was concerned about the indifference among many of the laity to the teachings of the church and their merely mechanical performance of ritual without any understanding or emotional connection to their actions. Just as Khosrov wrote his commentary on the liturgy to help instruct the faithful in proper worship, Anania too composed a series of pareneses (or treatises of exhortation and recommendation) to instill in the people a deeper and more potent piety. These were written at the behest of his relative, the catholicos Khachik I Arsharuni (r. 973–82), whom Anania had known before arriving at Narek.[38]

Central to Anania's thought is the distinction between the interior and exterior persons. The human person is in fact a compound of these two "persons" or aspects. The exterior person is the part of us that acts within the sensible world while the interior person is the heart or soul containing one's hidden thoughts and feelings. In many cases the two parts do not operate in tandem but exist in opposition to the other. While the exterior person may act in accordance with moral rules and church rituals, the interior person may be filled with base thoughts and passions instead of the virtues of piety and love. Anania recommends spiritual exercises designed to

[37] *MH* 10:312.

[38] Pétrossian 2001, 69.

purify the inner person and harmonize the two aspects of personhood into one integral whole.

This process of harmonization involves three steps: purification of one's heart through the prayer of tears and lamentation, the cultivation of the moral virtues, and finally the achievement of a mystical relation with God through ascetic practices.[39] This threefold process was inspired by the three levels of initiation in Pseudo-Dionysian mysticism. This threefold progression, leading ultimately to union with God, plays a prominent role in Gregory's writings, and its presence here in Anania's writings indicates that Gregory first learned about it from him.

The first step in this course of spiritual exercise is a retreat into the inner person, a prayerful discernment of the state of one's soul and the causes of sinfulness. Prayer accompanied with tears begins the process of purification. This prayer of tears arouses within us the love of God which begins to wash away the sins that have soiled the inner person and obscured the image of God within. Anania provides biblical support for the connection of tears and love:

[39] Some authors compare Anania's distinction between the inner and outer person to Paul's distinction between the inner and outer man. For example, Mahé 2001, 61, connects Anania's distinction to Paul's assertion in Romans 7:21-25 that there are "two laws in me," which in turn is connected to the Pauline contrast between the spirit and the flesh. But Anania's distinction is not the same as Paul's. For Paul understands the inward man to be the part of him that delights in the law of God (Rom 7:22) while the outer man holds him captive to the law of sin. That is, the inward man is by nature the part of us that loves God while the outward man is by nature that which rebels and sins against God. For Paul the struggle involves the spirit overcoming the flesh. By contrast, Anania does not see the inner and outer person necessarily in conflict with each other, nor does he think that the inner person always follows the will of God while the outer person is always at war with the law of God. Both aspects are morally neutral in themselves, but when the visible actions of the outer man do not conform to the thoughts and affections of the inner man, there can be no genuine and loving relation with God or our fellow humans. Paul desires that his spirit overcome his flesh, while Anania desires that our exterior self be harmonized with the interior self.

Now the grace of tears is a sign of loving Christ and desiring his kingdom. As the Lord said about the sinful woman, who wept tears upon his feet—*May her sins be forgiven, for she loved much* (Luke 7:47). So too the prophets revealed their love of the people through their tears, as Jeremiah said—*Who will give water to my head and a fountain of tears to my eyes that I may weep day and night for this people?* (Jeremiah 8.21). . . . And even the Lord himself revealed his love for Lazarus through his tears when he wept upon his grave. Seeing this, the people were astonished and said—*See how much he loved him!* (John 11:36)[40]

Anania's brief exhortation on prayer outlines the basic approach:

Never neglect the prescribed common prayers whether during the day or at night. Perform your required private discipline of prayers and fasting without any hindrance and keep your fasts in a state of holiness. Keep all your senses in a state of attention, especially your eyes, ears, and touch. You should eat and drink moderately. Do not give into laughter and frivolity nor be one who favors crowds or foolishness. Neither be drowsy nor dawdle in your labors and in your contemplation of the Holy Scriptures and in other good works, especially in your mercy toward the poor and needy. Be humble, compassionate, gracious, and modest, and not arrogant, proud, or weary when you do your good works. Always be engaged in dialogue with the divinely-inspired Scriptures. Keep your distance from vain and cheerless men, but ceaselessly wash away your sins with tears as much as you are able.[41]

How should one soften one's heart to allow this interior prayer of tears? Imagination and memory play an important role in Anania's exercises. Reflection on expressions of contrition can move the soul to penance:

By way of example, when people enter a house of mourning, and there, where they cry over the corpse, they let out a pitiful sound, those who hear it also grieve involuntarily and shed tears. When people enter a house in which a wedding is being celebrated and the

[40] Anania of Narek, *Khratk' ogeshah' yaghags zghjman ew artasuats'* [Useful Exhortations Concerning Penance and Tears], *MH* 10:360–61.2–8.

[41] Anania of Narek, *Bank' aghawt'its'* [*Discourse on Prayer*], *MH* 10:347.1–5.

> guests exchange frivolous pleasantries, those hearing it laugh involuntarily. So you, too, when your heart is like stone and you cannot weep should call to mind penitent words and images so that your heart is moved to penance and tears flow out from it.[42]

Anania observes here the powerful effect of sympathy. When surrounded by mourners, one naturally shares the sadness of one's companions as one also shares in merriment at times of joy. One would similarly expect that by joining a group of penitents one would be moved to penance. But Anania recognized that simply calling to mind the images and memories of mourning and penance can bring us to tears. He is also aware of the power of words and literary devices like assonance and repetition to soften the soul. To that end, he composed poetry designed to engender tenderness in hardened hearts. Accordingly, he intersperses some of his pareneses with verse. Mahé notes that Anania's poems are the first example of Armenian religious poetry not intended strictly for liturgical use.[43] As such, they had a profound influence on Gregory's poetry, though Anania's poems are simpler and more formulaic than Gregory's richer and more imaginative compositions. Here, for example, Anania reflects on the transience of earthly life:

> Come, O south wind, and arrive, O north wind,
> Blow upon the garden of my soul;
> Melt the frost of my sins,
> My Lord, make for me a spiritual spring;
> You who raised the water from the stone.
> Make my heart a vessel of tears.
> And say in your mind,
> "Do you not see the worldly,
> How they hurry about and toil in their fields?
> But you have left your spiritual field untended;
> Morning has dawned
> Yet you have not labored,
> Evening has come
> And you leave empty-handed.

[42] Anania Narekats'i, *Penance and Tears*, *MH* 10:362.21.
[43] Mahé 2000, 69.

Have you not considered
That your body dwells in an inn,
For this day passes like a dream,
And tomorrow is like a shadow of the evening?
Set your mind to this:
Yesterday our brothers were with us,
Yet today they do not appear,
They have gone to their Lord and ours."[44]

Anania has us focus on the fleeting passage of time and the evanescence of this world in order to rouse us to care for our spirit with the same urgency and diligence as the farm laborers do in tending their crops. The language is simple and direct and employs vivid imagery. We are asked to imagine a wedding, a funeral, a garden emerging from the winter's frost, a field of laborers, all part of the daily experience of the people. These images evoke memories that we all have experienced; they produce a powerful affective force on us as we contemplate them. Although he may have directed his advice primarily to his monks, his clear and accessible style and his use of events familiar from everyday life indicate that he intends his advice on spiritual life for a wider audience. Anania expects his exhortations to move all people regardless of class or status. Once the heart is moved by these images, the inner person aligns with the external acts of piety, and the total person is prepared to engage in genuine worship.

Though God created the physical world and filled it with goodness, it always falls short of absolute goodness and leaves us unsatisfied. This world, even with all its beauty and riches, is never enough for our restless souls. Reflection on the impermanence of our mundane pleasures leads us away from the goods of this world to the permanent and eternal goodness of God:

If you enter an elegant palace, painted in many colors,
And you delight in the sights,
Yet when you go out from there, it has passed.
It's as if you hadn't seen it at all,

[44] Anania of Narek, *Penance and Tears*, *MH* 10:391.213–16.

And you are in need of another sight.
For it is not only when a man dies,
When he is deprived of this life,
But even while he is alive that
Glory passes away one day to the next,
And from one hour to the next.[45]

Anania's poem on the transience of this world and its delights recalls Plato's description of the lover of sights in the *Republic*.[46] The beautiful things of this world are in the end vain, unable to satisfy our deepest longings. Elsewhere in this poem he alludes to Plato's dialogue, the *Gorgias*, and its play on the similarity of the words in Greek for body (*sōma*) and tomb (*sēma*) ("for the body becomes the tomb of the soul"),[47] but he could also have taken this from the Armenian version of David's *Prolegomena of Philosophy*,[48] which was the standard introduction to philosophy used in Armenian monastic academies as late as the eighteenth century.

Even if this allusion is not directly from Plato but mediated through a Neoplatonic commentary, Anania seems familiar with

[45] Anania Narekats'i, *Vasn ants'awor ashkharhis* [*On the Transience of This World*], *MH* 10:348.3–4.

[46] Plato, 1930, *The Republic*, Paul Shorey, ed., London: W. Heinemann, 476d–480a.

[47] *MH* 10:350.16; Plato's wordplay on the similarity of *sōma* and *sēma* occurs at *Gorgias* 493a3. See Plato, 1925, *Symposium; Gorgias; Lysis*, vol. 5, London: W. Heinemann.

[48] The Armenian edition of Arewshatyan and the English translation are in David, 1983, *Definitions and Divisions of Philosophy*, trans. Bridget Kendall and Robert W. Thomson, Chico, CA: Scholars Press, 72–73. Cowe takes this allusion to Plato's pun as evidence of Anania's familiarity with the central argument of the *Republic*, but this wordplay does not occur in the *Republic*. See S. Peter Cowe, 2006, "The Interpretation of the Divine and Human Spheres in Narekats'i' s Theology of Culture," in Mahé and Zekiyan 2006, 229–46. Better evidence of Anania's knowledge of the *Republic* is from his presentation of the transient pleasures of the sensible world, but these too could be coming to Anania through Neoplatonic texts. For a general treatment of the influence of Neoplatonic philosophy of the school of Narek, see Hrach'ya T'amrazyan, 2004, *Grigor Narekats'in ew Norplatonakanut'yunĕ* [*Gregory of Narek and Neoplatonism*], Yerevan: Nairi.

Platonic texts that were not widely studied in Armenia at this time. Anania does on occasion refer explicitly to the works of Plato. He must have been familiar with some of Plato's dialogues in the original Greek since the medieval Armenian versions of Plato's works were probably first made in the eleventh century.[49] For Plato, the lover of the sights and sounds of this world is never satisfied; only through contact with what never changes, the eternal Forms, do we find everlasting joy and satisfaction. Anania presents this same essentially Platonic philosophy but places it within a Christian context as so many Christian Platonists, most notably Augustine, had done before him:

> And there is nothing firm in this world,
> But everything is in flux,
> Like a shadow and a candle
> That is quickly extinguished;
> Such is the life of man:
> It is suddenly taken away,
> And the time of our youth is a few days,
> Then grey hairs begin to grow, the invitations of death,
> And the worn-out body loses its strength.[50]

He closes this treatise with the goal of this reflective exercise on the transience of the world:

> Now when the majesty of the world entices you, you should keep all this in mind and ask God for help and with the grace of Christ overcome the world in the glory of the Father and the Son and Holy Spirit now and forever.[51]

[49] The dating of the Armenian translations of Plato is in dispute. Some scholars believe they were done by the Hellenizing School prior to the founding of Narekavank', but others attribute them to the work of the eleventh century scholar Grigor Magistros Pahlawuni. See Valentina Calzolari, "Philosophical Literature in Ancient and Medieval Armenia," in Michael E. Stone and Valentina Calzolari, 2014, *Armenian Philology in the Modern Era: From Manuscript to Digital Text*, Leiden: Brill, 349–76, especially 350–51.

[50] Anania Narekats'i, *On Transience*, *MH* 10:355.53–54.

[51] Anania Narekats'i, *On Transience*, *MH* 10:355.63.

Reflection on the vanity of this world draws the mind's attention away from worldly glories and prepares it to give full attention to the glory of God. Central to his spiritual exercises is the cultivation of humility, which he calls "the head of the virtues" and to which topic he devotes one of his treatises.[52] The tears and prayers that purify the interior person also wash away pride and instill the virtue of humility that allows us to love our neighbors as well as God:

> Humility is when you see someone's faults and you do not speak ill of them or judge them, but instead say "If I am a sinner, how can I judge another?" This is why the Lord said—*Do not judge lest you be judged.* (Matt 7:1)
> Humility is also loving one's brother. For these are the commandments of love: to humble oneself before one's companions, to share their pain when they are sick, to comfort them when they mourn, to give yourself in service to them.[53]

In contrast, the proud are incapable of loving anyone besides themselves:

> The proud person does not do these things and does not regard his brother worthy of his humility but regards himself superior to all.[54]

The purified and humbled soul experiences an inner peace and tranquility; consequently it can love both its neighbor and Christ. The inner and outer persons unite so that external acts of love emanate from the internal states of purity and peace. The whole person is now filled with the love of God rather than remaining in discord by acting in one way while thinking and feeling in another way.

In achieving this internal peace and personal integrity, one is prepared to love God and to enter into union with him. Anania sees his spiritual exercises as preparation for receiving the Holy Spirit within us:

[52] Anania Narekats'i, *Khrat vasn khonarhut'ean* [*Parenesis on Humility*], *MH* 10:345.60.

[53] Anania Narekats'i, *On Humility*, *MH* 10:343.16–18.

[54] Anania Narekats'i, *On Humility*, *MH* 10:343.19.

> As long as the enemy is outside the fortress, it is easy to guard against him. But if he engages in battle and captures and enters the fortress, then it is difficult to expel him. Likewise, you should be on your guard when you battle the thoughts outside the fortress of your mind. For if they attack and enter inside, you will have to prepare for greater toil. This is why you should always be fortifying your thoughts and keeping them pleasing to God so that you will become a temple of the Holy Spirit.[55]

In contrast to the pareneses, which are written in a clear and lively style, Anania's doctrinal and polemical writings are often dense and arcane. His anti-Chalcedonian treatise is also at odds with the more irenic tenor of the school of Narek, and with positions that Anania himself accepted in his other writings. The anti-dyophysite treatise was commissioned by catholicos Khachik. Anania may have felt compelled to assume a more combative approach to defend the harsher policies that Khachik had imposed, including the requirement of rebaptism of Chalcedonians. Some scholars have also argued that the arguments for rebaptism are an extraneous addition to the text.[56] In any event, by the time of Khachik's order, the period of rapprochement between the Byzantines and the Armenian churches was over. Both sides repudiated the other's orthodoxy and moved to create rival hierarchies in the same dioceses, something that they had previously refrained from doing. Anania's hostile tone, more critical of the Chalcedonians than his other writings, may have been a concession to the new, more bitter ecclesial reality. The work was completed sometime in the 980s, when Anania personally handed the work to Khachik at the patriarchal see in Argina.

Anania's treatise against the T'ondrakeans was commissioned by Khachik's predecessor, catholicos Anania of Mokk' and is, with the exception of a fragment preserved in a fourteenth-century

[55] Anania Narekats'i, *Yaghags khorhrdots' zgushut'ean* [*On Guarding One's Thoughts*], *MH* 10:368–69.

[56] See Pétrossian 2001, 66. Pétrossian also notes that Anania focuses in this treatise more on defending the orthodoxy of the Armenian church's Christology rather than trying to establish the heterodoxy of the Chalcedonian formula. The text of the anti-Chalcedonian treatise is in *MH* 10:480–598.

manuscript, no longer extant.[57] This portion of the treatise is too short to enable reconstruction of the work's overall argument with any certainty. It is a general exposition of the universality of the church in which Anania displays the same flair for fanciful etymologies and linguistic analysis found in Khosrov's writings. Anania goes as far as to relate the Armenian word for catholic, *kat'oghikē* to *kat'* ("milk") and its verbal cognate *kat'im* ("to flow drop by drop") in order to illustrate that the universal church distributes the milk of doctrine to all.[58] The general thrust of the analysis of the words *catholic* and *church* in the fragment is to affirm the uniqueness and universality of the church and to establish that the T'ondrakeans, being a sect limited to a particular geographical region, cannot constitute the true church.[59]

Despite these efforts in defense of Armenian orthodoxy, Anania, like Khosrov, faced accusations of heresy. The circumstances surrounding his removal as abbot are more mysterious than those of Khosrov's excommunication. Anania of Mokk''s irritation at Khosrov's perceived insubordination through his support of the validity of the Albanian patriarch's installation, though not explicitly stated in the Armenian catholicos's letter, is rather transparent. The charge against Anania of Narek, by contrast, was that he was a T'ondrakean, and at least according to one tradition he was exiled to another monastery, Kchaw, where he was required to do penance. It was his relative and former colleague, catholicos Khachik,

[57] The manuscript is housed in the Matenadaran manuscript library in Yerevan, Armenia, and is catalogued as Matendaran 2173. For details, see H. H. T'amrazyan, "Hakacharut'iwn ěnddēm T'ondrakets'iots' " ["Dispuation against the T'ondrakians"] in *MH* 10:434–35. There is a French translation of the treatise in Mahé 2000, 783–86, appendix 2. See also Mahé 2000, 54.

[58] Given Anania's apparent familiarity with the Platonic corpus, it may not be farfetched to suppose that he read and was inspired by Plato's *Cratylus*, itself filled with many such absurd etymologies.

[59] It is precisely this affirmation of the universality of the church that scholars have noted to be incongruous with Anania's defense of rebaptism of Chalcedonians in his antidyophysite treatise. But since the anti-T'ondrakean work is earlier, the difference in attitude in the two works may be a reflection of the increasing antagonism between Chalcedonians and non-Chalcedonians toward the end of the tenth century.

who made the accusation.[60] The motive for the accusation remains unclear. It may be due to Anania's focus on the interior spiritual life that appeared to align him with the T'ondrakeans, for whom faith is an entirely internal condition unencumbered by sacraments and sacred objects. There may also have been a more diffuse suspicion of his attempts at reform and perhaps even envy from other monasteries at the rapid success and fame that his monastery enjoyed. In any event, Anania accepted the catholicos's verdict and resigned as Narek's abbot. It is natural to wonder why Anania accepted his punishment while Khosrov continued to function as bishop with impunity. Anania, of course, lacked the family connection to the royal house of Vaspurakan that furnished Khosrov with a good measure of immunity from maltreatment. But it may have also been due to personality: the aristocratic bishop had fewer scruples about ignoring the commands of his superior, whom he did not acknowledge as having juridical authority over him anyway, in contrast to the obedient monastic who extolled the virtues of humility and obedience. Anania may have willingly accepted his punishment out of his respect for the authority of the catholicos. The former abbot of Narekavank' composed one last work, a confessional letter in which he expresses his equanimity and peace with God:

> Blessed be the name of the Lord and glory be to God for all things. We must give thanks to the Lord in all things . . . for it is good to hope in the Lord throughout one's life, in happiness and in adversity, in times of abundance and poverty, in times of exaltation and in dishonor, in tranquility and in agitation, in glory and in humiliation. . . . If anyone has been persuaded and believes in what I have written, let them give thanks to God, and I will say, "Cursed is the one who places his hope in man and not in the Lord God of heaven and earth, and cursed is the one who places his hope in the strength of his own arm." [Jer 17:5][61]

[60] Mahé 2000, 54.

[61] Anania Narekats'i, *Eraneloy hor Ananayi gir khostovanut'ean yaghags sut kartseats'n or vasn nora* [*Letter of confession of the blessed father Anania concerning false beliefs about him*], *MH* 10:656.83–84 and 657.92.

Apart from their fondness for etymological arguments, Anania and Khosrov share many features that would come to inform Gregory's own thinking and his literary works. Anania and Khosrov both affirm the universality of the church and recognize the orthodoxy of both the Chalcedonian and miaphysite churches—though in Anania's case, this recognition is qualified by the harsher tone taken in his late treatise against the dyophysites.[62] Khosrov in particular is eager to learn from and borrow practices from other rites, and he chafes against what he deems narrow-minded and xenophobic suspicion of his interest in other traditions.

Both also see themselves as reformers of a church that has lost touch with many of its people. The problem is the lack of harmony between the inner and the outer person: priests simply mouth the words of the breviary without an understanding of the significance of the prayers and sacraments. The laypeople witness the services without an accompanying sense of awe and mystery at the divine sacrifice that takes places in their midst. Anania and Khosrov were united in the desire to revitalize the church so that both clergy and laypeople would participate fully in the gifts of the Holy Spirit that flow through the church and its sacraments. One should therefore see Narekavank' and its adherents not simply as a school but as part of a reform movement within the Armenian church, one with a definite and coherent program to restore the spiritual life of a church and its people who had suffered the damaging effects of external invasion and internal indifference and ignorance.

This reform movement was in several respects a popular one. Although the monks would take a leading role in implementing the reforms, it is clear that both Anania and Khosrov wanted their reforms to touch the lives of all the members of the church. While Anania's treatises and Khosrov's liturgical commentaries were intended primarily for educated monks, it was understood that their content would be transmitted to laypeople for their edification and

[62] A work generally attributed to Khosrov, the *Discourse to the Clergy* is uncharacteristically polemical toward Chalcedonians. Pétrossian challenges its attribution to Khosrov because of its xenophobic content. See Pétrossian 2001, 48.

spiritual growth. One part of this populism is reflected in the focus on the affective components of worship. Their program was not simply an intellectual one. It is not enough simply to understand the articles of faith. The Christian must also sense the depth of God's love and the need for his forgiveness. That is why Anania used rich and vivid images in his writings, above all in his poems that utilize the devices of meter and repetition to impress themselves on the minds of the listener. And it also explains Khosrov's desire to reform the liturgy to make it more accessible to the people.

Given their different roles in the church, one should expect to find some notable differences between the two figures. Khosrov's focus is on the liturgy and communal prayer, which befits his role as a diocesan bishop managing the affairs of parish churches. Anania was more interested in personal devotion and spiritual exercises, as is appropriate for a monastic who devoted his life to prayer and meditation. Together, though, they constitute the cornerstones or foundations of Narekavank', and it is Gregory who will be foremost in building upon this foundation and linking together both its liturgical and ecclesial aspects, as well as its personal and devotional dimensions through his extraordinary poetry, hymns, encomia, and other works.

Chapter Four
Gregory's Life and Prose Works

Gregory's Life and Legends

One occasionally reads comparisons made between Gregory and other medieval authors. For example, Gregory has been called Armenia's version of Dante or Augustine. But these comparisons do not do justice to any of these writers. There are of course some superficial similarities. Dante wrote an epic poem in three parts describing the successive stages of his journey from hell to paradise, culminating in the beatific vision of God. Gregory's great poem also appears to have a tripartite structure describing his journey toward God. Beyond these common features, though, there are significant differences. Dante is a secular poet engrossed in the political and ecclesial intrigues of his time, and these worldly concerns pervade the *Divine Comedy*.

Augustine seems closer to Gregory, since he is also a cleric and, although not himself devoted to a cloistered life, he admired and influenced monasticism and asceticism. Comparisons between Augustine and Gregory focus on Augustine's *Confessions*, which is in part an autobiographical account of Augustine's conversion to Christianity.[1] A self-reflective attention to the soul's condition and the struggle against sin runs throughout both Augustine's *Confessions* and Gregory's *Book of Lamentation*, but here again there are signficant differences. Augustine narrates for us very exacting

[1] See, for example, N. Kebranian, 2016, "Armenian Poetry and Poetics," in Roland Greene and Stephen Cushman, eds, *Princeton Handbook of World Poetries*, Princeton, NJ: Princeton University Press, 34–38.

details of his life. The reader learns about the famous episode of the stolen pears, mirroring in Augustine's own life the primal sin that also involved the stolen fruit of a tree, and his relations with his mother St. Monica as well as his concubine and his son. After reading the *Confessions* we feel that we have come to know its author very well.

Gregory's *Book of Lamentation* is also very personal and expresses a deep contrition and desire to know God and seek God's love, but autobiographical details are brief and elusive. Gregory seems not to want the personal details of his life to distract us from the purpose of his work, which is to guide his readers to pray for God's forgiveness and proceed on the path of reconciliation and union with God. While Gregory gives some hints in the *Book of Lamentation* about his life, we must turn elsewhere to learn more about him.

Our main sources on his life, in addition to the few autobiographical references in his works, are the colophons (a typically brief statement at the end of a manuscript giving details of its production) of his works, a short biography written by St. Nersēs of Lambron (1153–98), the twelfth-century bishop of Tarsus and a gifted scholar and ecumenist, the Armenian synaxarion or collection of the lives of the saints, and a rich tradition of folklore surrounding the saint.

Two of our sources identify Gregory's father as Khosrov. In the colophon to his commentary on the Song of Songs, Gregory states that the bishop of Andzewats'ik was his father. Saint Nersēs also identifies Gregory's father as Khosrov, adding that Gregory's mother, whose name does not appear in any of our sources, was the first cousin of Anania, whom Nersēs calls "the diligent tutor and abbot of the monastery of Narek."[2] Gregory does not mention his father in the colophon to the *Book of Lamentation*, an omission that has induced some scholars to question whether Gregory was Khosrov's son. These doubts were first raised by the Armenian

[2] An English translation of Nersēs's biography is in Terian 2016, 373–74. Terian's translation is ultimately based on the oldest extant manuscript of the *BL* copied in 1173 with Gregory's biography written in Nersēs's hand. Terian notes that over time the biography was augmented and became the basis for the account in the synaxarion.

Catholic priest Kiwregh K'iparean,[3] who argued that the omission of Khosrov from the colophon suggests that Khosrov's son must have been another Gregory, perhaps a parish priest of Narek who copied Khosrov's commentary on the liturgy and also authored the commentary on the Song of Songs.[4] In the colophon to the Canticle commentary, the author identifies himself as "Gregory, a priest (*k'ahanay*) of Narek," which need not imply that he was a monk of Narekavank', since Narek was the name of the town where the monastery was located. In contemporary Armenian usage the term *k'ahanay* is usually applied only to married priests. K'iparean also notes an age discrepancy based on Khosrov's description in Anania of Mokk''s letter of excommunication. The letter, composed in 954, describes Khosrov as already white-haired and advanced in age, which would make him too old to be the husband of Anania of Narek's cousin. Apart from these personal details, the supposed "pedantic" style of the commentary in contrast to the brilliance of the later *Book of Lamentation* suggests different authorship.

These objections to Gregory's authorship are not compelling. It is true that in modern Armenian the word *k'ahanay* refers to a married priest, but the premodern usage is generic and may refer to celibate priests as well. Indeed, in his colophon to the *Book of Lamentation* Gregory says that he is a *k'ahanay*, albeit a religious (*krawnawor*) one. Pétrossian proposes also that Anania's letter of anathema was written later than 954, perhaps as late the early 960s, which would significantly reduce the age difference between Khosrov and Gregory's mother.[5] Finally, the commentary on the Canticle is a work of Gregory's youth, perhaps written while still in his twenties. Though obviously the work of a gifted scholar, Gregory's commentary need

[3] K. K'iparean 1961, "S[ourb] Grigor Narekat'si ew Erg-Ergots'i Meknut'iwnĕ [St. Gregory of Narek and the commentary on the *Song of Songs*]," in *Bamzavēp* 1–2, 1–10.

[4] See discussion in Pétrossian 2010, 121–26.

[5] Pétrossian 2010, 125. Further support for this dating is provided by Gregory's reference in the *Book of Lamentation* (51.1; *MH* 12:325.11–12) to his father's age and failing health. Gregory must have written this verse much later than 954.

not possess the same spiritual depth as his *Book of Lamentation*, which received its final form just prior to his death. As well, the commentary genre places limitations on the author; even the best of exegetes at least occasionally falls into pedantry. By contrast, the poetic medium of the *Book of Lamentation* gives the author greater freedom to express his genius. The commentary on the Canticle should be read along with the rest of Gregory's work to reveal how it coheres with the general tenor of Gregory's mystical theology. For now, though, we can conclude in agreement with the overwhelming majority of scholars that the commentary on the Canticle and the *Book of Lamentation* are the products of one author, Gregory of Narek, the monastic priest and son of Khosrov Andzewats'i.

The precise year of Gregory's birth is unknown but it must have been sometime during the 940s. Khosrov had three sons. The eldest, Sahak (Isaac), remained with his father and appears to have served him as a secretary. At any rate, he is the scribe of the first copy of his father's liturgical commentary, completed in 950.[6] After their mother's death, John, the middle brother, and Gregory were entrusted to the care of Narekavank', where they would remain for the rest of their lives. The circumstances and date of their mother's death are unknown. One may suppose that she died after complications from giving birth to the youngest child, Gregory, but the one reference to her in the *Book of Lamentation* suggests that Gregory has memories of her. There, he writes of "my mother, who suffered labor pains [and whose] compassion declined as her life receded."[7] The mention of her labor pains implies that her death was connected to her pregnancy, though it need not have been a complication of Gregory's birth but a later stillbirth. In any event, her death must predate 950, when Khosrov was ordained a bishop. At Narekavank', Gregory came under Anania's tutelage and distinguished himself promptly as a gifted and pious student. He and his brother excelled in particular in the study of the Bible. Anania's colleague, Peter, known for his biblical studies, must have been their instructor in scripture. Unfortunately, none of Peter's writings

[6] *MH* 10:227n1. There is an English translation of the colophon in Terian 2016, 365, appendix A.

[7] *BL* 51.1; *MH* 12:325.13–14 .

have survived. If they had, they would doubtless have provided important insights on the formation of Gregory's thoughts on biblical interpretation. Gregory must already have been recognized for his exegetical abilities, for he was commissioned by an Artsruni prince to compose the commentary on the Canticle. One might have thought that Peter, as the monastery's senior biblical scholar, would have been the prince's first choice, but he must have either died or been too infirm to write by this time. Gregory completed the commentary in 977. It would be the first of many works of poetry, hymns, encomia, and theological treatises, all culminating in his masterpiece, the *Book of Lamentation*.

Nersēs of Lambron says that John predeceased Gregory, but the colophon to the *Book of Lamentation* states that John, who succeeded Anania as abbot, assisted Gregory in the book's compilation toward the end of Gregory's life. Nersēs notes that Gregory died while still young, not having completed the course of life. If he died soon after the compilation of the *Book of Lamentation*, his death would have occurred around 1003, so he may still have been in his fifties, well short of his biblical allotment of three score and ten as stated in Psalm 90:10, if that is what Nersēs means by the "course of life."

Gregory divided his time between the monastery and his retreat overlooking Lake Van where he led the life of a hermit, undergoing the rigorous spiritual exercises that Anania taught. It was in this cave that one of the many miracles ascribed to him occurred. According to various accounts, Gregory had a vision of the Virgin Mary standing above an island in the lake, enthroned in the clouds, and holding the infant Christ. She spoke to Gregory, saying, "Gregory, come to the Lord (aṛ Tēṛ)." On hearing these words, Gregory ran along the waves of the lake to this island where he venerated the Mother of God. The island, located about four kilometers to the northwest of Aght'amar island, was from then on known as Aṛtēṛ.[8]

[8] Mahé 2000, 41. According to Thierry 1989, 292, a monastery was later built on the island to commemorate Gregory's vision and miracle. Thierry reports that at the time of his visit only the walls of the monastery and one of the original two churches on the island were still standing. In modern Armenian the island is called *Arti* (see R. H. Hewsen, 2001, *Armenia: A Historical Atlas*, Chicago: University of Chicago Press, 57).

Given Gregory's renown, it is not surprising that there are a host of stories and legends about him and his miracles. James Russell enumerates some of these in his monograph on the fourteenth-century lyric poet John (Yovhannēs) T'lkurats'i.[9] One legend states that Gregory herded sheep for seven years to provide for the children of a deceased shepherd. In another story, he helps a villager in the city of Mush who had incurred an onerous debt by working for him for free as long as the debtor agreed to attend church regularly. While visiting another village, he supposedly resurrected a groom who had died on his wedding day. A curious poem recounts the visit of two priests to Narek. When they requested water from the monk, Gregory made the sign of the cross and, like Moses, struck a dry rock from which water proceeded to flow. This was not ordinary water but a fountain of youth, for the poet recounts that "[the priests'] old white beards became young . . . they became immortal there."[10]

Tales of visiting priests occur in a number of sources. The Armenian synaxarion may be the source of all these tales, since it begins with the credible claim that Gregory was accused of heresy, as both his biological and spiritual fathers were. But unlike in their cases, Gregory was able to acquit himself of the charges by performing a miracle in the presence of the monks ordered to bring him to trial. The synaxarion for February 27 reports that when Gregory occupied himself with the task of reforming the institutions and rituals of the church that had fallen out of use, several jealous people accused him in front of the bishops and prince, saying that he was a heretic and a schismatic. The term translated as heretic here is *tsayt'*, the very same word that Khosrov says is the epithet used for those who show an interest in learning from other Christian traditions. Because the term is normally applied to those suspected of Chalcedonian sympathies, if Gregory was accused of heresy, he was most likely charged with dyophysitism. When the monks ar-

[9] For these legends see Russell, 1987, 149–50, and Aram Ghanalanyan, 1969, *Avandapatum* [*Armenian Traditions*], Yerevan: Haykakan SSH GA Hratarakch'ut'iwn, 306–20.

[10] Russell 1987, 150.

rived at his cell, Gregory requested that they eat something together before embarking on the journey. After he brought out two doves and began to roast them, his would-be captors protested and said, "Teacher (*vardapet*), isn't it Friday?" a day of fasting and abstinence from the consumption of animal products. The saint responded, "I beg your forgiveness, my brothers, I acted out of ignorance." Then he spoke to the doves: "Arise and return to your nest and your flock, for today is a day of abstinence." Immediately the birds came back to life, flapped their wings, and flew away. The men were astonished; they threw themselves at Gregory's feet and asked for forgiveness. Later they returned to the bishop without Gregory and recounted what they had witnessed. Gregory's accusers, seized with fear, no longer spoke out against him.[11]

Was Gregory actually accused of heresy? He prays that God forgive his accusers in Prayer 83 of the *Book of Lamentation*, asking that God not be angry at them for his sake but "forgive their sins/as though they rebuke my evil deeds/ and rightly reproach me."[12] Apart from appealing to the veracity of the miracle, though, how can we explain his ability to escape excommunication and punishment? This episode most likely occurred late in Gregory's life when the catholicos was Sergius (Sargis) of Sewan (r. 992–1019). Sargis favored asceticism and most likely admired Gregory. He would have been loath to prosecute Gregory and probably dismissed the charges against him quickly.[13]

These fanciful tales that have entered into Armenian folklore reveal the extent to which Gregory's person and reputation for piety had penetrated the Armenian collective imagination. Gregory's

[11] G. Bayan, 1980, *Le synaxaire arménien de Tēr Israyēl*, Patrologia Orientalis 106, Turnhout: Brepols, 110, and Ghanalanyan 1969, 318. The miracle of the revived birds recalls the miracle of the clay pigeons attributed to Christ in the apocryphal Infancy Gospel. See Abraham Terian, 2008, *The Armenian Gospel of the Infancy: With Three Early Versions of the Protevangelium of James*, Oxford: Oxford University Press, 88. Also, Gregory's feigned ignorance of the day of abstinence is reminiscent of the accounts of Desert Fathers who disregarded the fasting disciplines in deference to hospitality toward guests. See Ward 2003, 134.

[12] *BL* 83.1; *MH* 12:515–16.18.

[13] Pétrossian 2010, 84.

place in Armenian popular piety is not just a medieval phenomenon but has persisted to the present. Prayer 18 of the *Book of Lamentation* is a popular prayer read still today over those who are ill, and the entire book, even if not regularly read or studied, occupies a place of honor in most devout Armenian homes. Even during the period of Soviet repression, Armenians looked to Gregory for comfort and spiritual nurture. Armenuhi Drost-Abgarjan cites the example of a woman named Margarit Alexanian, living in Shushi, at the time part of Soviet Azerbaijan but today in the disputed region of Nagorno-Karabakh under Armenian control. Alexanian produced an illuminated gospel with depictions of Gregory and his vision of Christ at the beginning of each gospel book. An unnamed woman attributed her survival through the hardship of the gulag to her activity of transcribing Gregory's words during her imprisonment.[14] Through all the tragedies and disruptions that the nation suffered, Gregory's life and works remained an inspiration and consolation for his people.

The Prose Works

Though best known for his *Book of Lamentation*, Gregory expressed himself in a variety of formats and genres not only through his poetry and hymns but also encomia, biblical commentaries, and theological treatises.[15] Here, I will provide a survey of his prose literary corpus before turning to his better known poetic works in the next chapter.

[14] Armenuhi Drost-Abgarjan, 2006, "Veneration and Reception of Surb Grigor Narekac'i in Armenian Culture and Spirituality," in Mahé and Zekiyan 2006, 57–66, esp. 64.

[15] Besides the commentary on Song of Songs, the only other strictly exegetical work attributed to Gregory is a brief commentary on chapters 38 and 39 of the book of Job (*MH* 12:884–910). It survives in a single damaged manuscript housed in the library of the Mkhit'arean congregation in Venice. The attribution of this work to Gregory has been questioned, though a cursory study of its contents and language suggests to me that Gregory's authorship is plausible. Job was a favorite book of the early Armenian commentators, as we have today fragments of the commentary of the eighth-century bishop Stephen of Siwnik' as well as the commentary on Job 38–39 by the obscure ninth-century author Hamam Arewelts'i.

The Commentary on the Song of Songs

In the colophon to the commentary, Gregory reports that the Artsruni prince, Gurgēn—one of the three sons of Abusahl Hamazasp (king of Vaspurakan, r. 953–72)[16] and who, after Abusahl's death, reigned in the principality of Andzewats'ik'—commanded him to compose a commentary on the "awesome words of Solomon and to make clear the things hidden deep within it."[17] Gregory provides some clues for the prince's interest in the Canticle. He notes the erotically charged nature of the book, which never mentions God but does praise the "breasts and reddened lips, the beautiful cheeks and desirable eyes" of the bride. Gregory observes that when people "with uncomprehending minds" hear these words, they fail to comprehend the spiritual dimension of the book.[18] To correct this tendency for people to focus on the literal and carnal sense of these romantic verses, Gurgēn asked the young monk to write a commentary. The people who do not understand the book properly may include the T'ondrakeans with their dissident views on marriage and sexuality. The T'ondrakeans may have pointed to the Song's lack of any explicit mention of God as evidence for their belief that marriage was not a sacrament nor did it require the blessing of the church, but that the physical bond of love between the couple was enough to validate their marital relation. The Artsruni rulers were always solicitous of the church, seeing its health as essential to the stability of their state, and so concerns about the threat posed by T'ondrakism would be reason enough for Gurgēn to order the young monk to compose a commentary that would affirm the church's teachings on marriage.

Although the T'ondrakean crisis may have precipitated Gurgēn's behest, the scope of the commentary goes well beyond the threat that the heresy posed. Gregory's work is not merely a defense of the church's teachings on marriage. Although it may have been

[16] It is not certain if Gurgēn at this time was considered a king or simply a prince, as his domain was restricted to the province of Andzewats'ik' and not all of Vaspurakan. Gregory refers to him in the colophon as both *ark'ay* ("ruler") and also *t'agawor* ("king").

[17] *MH* 12:760–883. The excellent English translation is Ervine 2007. The French translation with extensive and illuminating introductions is Pétrossian 2010.

[18] *MH* 12:882–3.2; Ervine 2007, 209.

occasioned by Gurgēn's interests in suppressing T'ondrakism, in Gregory's hands the commentary becomes much more. Keeping with the traditional Christian allegorical approach to the book, Gregory interprets the expressions of erotic desire between the bride and the groom as symbols of the love of God that impels the individual soul to union with Christ as well as the love between Christ and his church that Paul in Ephesians 5:32 already understood as the model and archetype of all earthly love. Accordingly, the commentary is especially relevant to the pursuits of the monks and ascetics who devote themselves to spiritual exercises of purification and illumination, leading ultimately to a union with Christ.[19] But the commentary also pertains to the lives of the faithful and presents the sacraments, especially the Eucharist, as foretastes of the heavenly and eternal union of the soul with God. In this way, the book is a defense of the necessity of the church and its sacraments for salvation.

With characteristic modesty, Gregory initially demurred from accepting Gurgēn's request, considering it beyond his abilities and entailing a boldness on his part that would expose him not only to ridicule from his fellow monks but even to God's punishment for his pride. But alluding to Romans 13:1, he says that Christ enjoined obedience to kings as well as to God, and so he must comply with Gurgēn's order. In composing the work, he made use of and sometimes explicitly refers to previous commentaries on the Song, most frequently Nyssen's commentary.[20] Occasionally he will refer the reader to Nyssen's commentary for further elaboration. He is well aware that Nyssen did not complete his homiletic commentary on the Song and despairs of finishing the work himself, for compared

[19] Dom Jean Leclerq has highlighted the significance of the Song of Songs in the Western monastic tradition and noted it was the biblical book most frequently read and commented on in the cloisters. The book's theme of "searching and hiding" and the dragging out of the quest for God seem to LeClerq to be apt descriptions of a monk's life. See Jean Leclercq, 1982, *The Love of Learning and the Desire for God: A Study of Monastic Culture*, New York: Fordham University Press, 84–85.

[20] For the parallels with Nyssen's commentary, see Robert W. Thomson, 1983, "Gregory of Narek's *Commentary on the Song of Songs*," *JTS* New Series 34 (2): 453–96.

to the Cappadocian father, who was "a perfect teacher . . . in whom the Spirit dwelt," he is ignorant and devoid of grace.[21]

For Gregory and all who adopt the allegorical approach to reading scripture, not only is the written word a symbol of a higher reality, but all of creation is saturated with meaning. Everything in the physical world proclaims the glory of its creator, and the skilled interpreter uncovers all the splendor hidden within even the most mundane of things. Taking the author of the Canticle to be Solomon, Gregory writes:

> Solomon, wishing to relate the ineffable, did it by means of an allegory in carnal form, that is, by means of a groom and bride, nephew and maiden, daughter and dove, breasts and myrrh, and oil poured out, apples and mountain goats, Solomon, a king, Jerusalem, a garden, and all such things that the eyes desire to see, the ears enjoy, and the mind longs for.[22]

These images and figures all point to something greater:

> All this the Song of Songs recounts: the splendid adornment of the Church with the cross and altar, with the flesh and blood of the Lord, the holy font and holy oil, the Old and New Testaments, the apostles, prophets, and teachers, priests and ascetics, virgins and martyrs, Christian kings, and all of the people of purity planted in the Church.[23]

The very name of the book reveals its rank and importance in the biblical canon:

> Now first it is worthy to say how "Song of Songs" is interpreted and thereby learn about its endless dignity. The song of songs is a blessing of blessings. In the same way, we call the holy apse where the holy altar stands the *holy of holies*, as the apostle says [Hebrews 9:3]. That is, if the church is holy, then the altar is doubly holy. So too this book is above and beyond all songs and blessings. Just as the Gospel is holier than the other books of the New Testament, so too this book

[21] *MH* 12:760.2; Ervine 2007, 77.
[22] *MH* 12:763.19; Ervine 2007, 79.
[23] *MH* 12:764.27; Ervine 2007, 80.

> is holier than [the other books of the Old Testament]. About it one should know that it was sung aloud in the temple with greater suitability and prophetic spirit than David's psalms, for the mystery concealed within its awesome words is beyond words. None of the carnal beings can understand it except those who are in spirit like Paul . . . for our ears cannot bear to hear the mysteries of God, just as our eyes cannot bear to see God [2 Corinthians 12:3-4].[24]

Gregory here follows Origen of Alexandria, the great Christian biblical scholar of the third century, in reading the title "Song of Songs" as a superlative that expresses the superiority of the Song to the other songs of scripture. Origen himself lists the subordinate songs of the Bible in his commentary and explains why the Song of Songs is greater than them.[25] But Gregory says he does not want to prolong his commentary by filling it with such detail. He goes on to the expression *holy of holies* and compares the book to the holiest part of the temple and by extension to the altar of the church. This comparison of a book to the structure of a church is a characteristic feature of Gregory's writings. We will see it again in the *Book of Lamentation*. Gregory's interest in structuring his literary works in the architectural form of a church is in part a response to the T'ondrakean rejection of the physical or incarnate church and preference for worship in private houses or outdoors. In his commentary on Song 6:8, he cites Psalm 57:4—"sinners are alienated from their mother; from the womb they are led astray"—as a reference to the church and those estranged from it.[26] Gregory writes:

> They detested and removed themselves from the confession of faith and oath they took at their birth at the font to love God the Father and their Mother Church. For Satan, like a slave merchant who

[24] *MH* 127:62.13–18; Ervine 78–79.

[25] Extant in the Latin translation of Rufinus, W. A Baehrens, 1925, *Origenes Werke* 8, GCS, Leipzig: J.C. Hinrichs, 78–79. English translation in Rowan A. Greer, 1979, *Origen, An Exhortation to Martyrdom, Prayer, and Selected Works*, Classics of Western Spirituality, New York: Paulist Press, 236–39.

[26] The wording of the psalm in Gregory's Armenian version differs from the NRSV, which reads, "The wicked go astray from the womb; they err from their birth, speaking lies."

> steals children whom he finds separated from their parents, imprisons anyone whom he finds estranged from their mother, the Church. One must make prayers in the church before the altar where the Holy Trinity dwells, but they [the T'ondrakeans] make their offerings in the roads and marketplaces and profane places; they give the honor due to the church over to the vulgar and the streets. They will find not mercy but condemnation because of this sin of holding the church in contempt and worshipping outside her.[27]

The T'ondrakean practice of worshipping outside the church was based on their belief that worship is a private matter and may be conducted anywhere.[28] In contrast, Gregory continually reminds us of the importance of sacred spaces. He compares books and prayers in their construction and form to the built and established structures of the church. In the *Book of Lamentation*, he asks God to grant him strength that he may "construct an edifice of faith" through his book of prayers.[29] He intends by this analogy between linguistic and architectural structures to illustrate the essential connection of prayer to the house of prayer and to emphasize that proper worship is always conducted within the confines and maternal care of the church. The point is not just that one must worship indoors in a sacred space to shield oneself from the profanity of the streets, but that the church building is itself symbolic of something greater, the one holy catholic and apostolic church of Christ that is the foundation of proper worship of God and the source through which all graces flow. The heretics have separated themselves from the house of God and to them, Gregory says, "we must offer words of lamentation and grief."[30]

But it is not only the physical structure of the church that points to something that transcends its constituents of stone and wood. The richness of the Song's images provides Gregory with an abundance of opportunities to display his allegorical imagination. All the elements of creation offer themselves up to interpretation. The

[27] *MH* 12:842–43.77–79; Ervine 2007, 169.

[28] See Garsoïan 1967, 162.

[29] *BL* 10.2; *MH* 12:104.24.

[30] *MH* 12:843.80; Ervine 2007, 169.

pomegranate is a fruit but also an emblem of the hardships and reward of virtue. Commenting on the groom's words to the bride in Song 4:3—"As the rind of a pomegranate are your cheeks behind your veil," Gregory writes:

> In their visible nature, pomegranates are unpleasant, but their invisible natures are appetizing and the cause of health. Now the Bride of Christ, which is the Church, has hidden her face behind a veil of virtuous habits and a rough and tired manner; these are on the outside like a pomegranate's skin. But what is stored up inside is hope, faith, and love (1 Cor 13:13) toward God. It is through this hope that she endures all things. For just as the things stored up in the pomegranate can be very desirable to eat, in the same way the works of virtue are filled with sweat and with great labor but the fruit of virtue is extolled in all its glory. As the prophet has said—*all her glory as the king's daughter is within* (Ps 44:14).[31]

Here, Gregory follows Nyssen and uses the pomegranate to illustrate the difficult process of cultivating the virtues.[32] Anyone who has tried to cut apart the rough outer shell of a pomegranate will appreciate the analogy. But once the difficult task is complete, one can enjoy the fruits of one's efforts, the sweetness of the three theological virtues of faith, hope, and love. In expectation of this reward we persist in our labors.

Even the parts of the lovers' bodies possess meaning, sometimes even multiple meanings. The bride's breasts are interpreted not only as the two testaments of scripture, which nourish the faithful with spiritual food (commentary on Song 6:9, "my dove is one, she is perfect") but also the bride's purity of heart, which is all that God seeks from humans (commentary on Song 4:5, "The bride says to the groom, there I will give my breasts to you") as well as the soul and the mind which are "perpetually attached to the heart, where the breasts are located" (commentary on Song 7:4, "your two breasts are like two fawns of a gazelle"). Gregory explains that

[31] *MH* 12:800.23–25; Ervine 2007, 126.

[32] Gregory of Nyssa, 2012, *Homilies on the Song of Songs*, ed. Richard A. Norris, Atlanta: Society of Biblical Literature, 240–43.

gazelles possess keen sight that enables them to avoid hunters' traps, just as the vigilant soul and mind evade Satan's snares.

These readings of the pomegranate and breasts are not original and follow the same lines of interpretation found in the earlier commentary tradition. But there are some peculiarities in Gregory's commentary that set it apart from the rest of the tradition. The most glaring of these is that the Armenian text of the Song of Songs has six extra verses that are not found either in the Hebrew text or the Septuagint or in any other translation of the Old Testament. In most versions of the Armenian Bible these six verses are appended to the end of the book. But Gregory comments on these verses at the beginning of his commentary and gives them the title "Ecclesiastes" (*Eklesiatēs*), indicating by this perhaps that he thought them to be part of the second book of the Solomonic trilogy comprised of Proverbs, Ecclesiastes, and the Song of Songs.[33] The expression *blessing of blessings*, which Gregory offers in his introduction as an alternative title for the Song, is in fact found in one of these additional verses as it appears in the commentary:

> The Lord made you and established you; he prepared you from the womb; your mother is most beautiful among women; a body will be born for him without fault or blemish from another providence, for He has prepared such, and it was the blessing of blessing.[34]

Gregory takes this verse to be a reference to baptism, through which fallen humanity is restored to the original state of paradise from the font represented here as the womb of the church, the

[33] Treating these books together and in this order as well as attributing the works to Solomon is ancient and based on Origen's interpretation. On the connection between Origen's ordering of the three Solomonic books and Dionysian initiation, see Andrew Louth, 1981, *The Origins of the Christian Mystical Tradition: From Plato to Denys*, Oxford: Clarendon Press, 54–61.

[34] This is the last verse of the Armenian version of the Song of Songs (in the Zohrapean edition it is Song 9:6), but for Gregory it is the last verse of the preface to the Song. *MH* 12:771.43–52; Ervine 2007, 88–89. For the Armenian Bible, see Yōhannēs Zohrapean, 1805, *Astuatsashunch' Matean Hin ew Nor Ktakaranats'* [*Old and New Testaments of Holy Scripture*], Venice: San Lazzaro, reprinted 1984, Delmar, NY: Caravan.

bride of Christ. Through the Holy Spirit, the "other providence" whom God will provide (John 14:16), humanity is granted a new and glorified body. Gregory may have placed these extraneous verses at the beginning of the Song rather than at the end where the Armenian Bible normally locates them because he thought this reference to rebirth through the baptismal font served as a kind of verbal vestibule where the body is purified through baptism before entering into the Song of Songs (or holy of holies) where the soul is ready to seek communion with Christ. The presence of these uncanonical verses in the Armenian version of the Canticle is a mystery.[35] Gregory gives no indication that he thinks they are uncanonical or that he even knows that they do not appear in the Septuagint. But he recognizes that they are not strictly part of the Song since he partitions them from the rest of the commentary and places them under a separate heading.

Another distinctive feature of Gregory's commentary is his use of uniquely Armenian sources. His main Armenian patristic source are the homilies recorded in the *Teaching of Saint Gregory* and the accounts of the Illuminator's tortures described by Agathangelos. Commenting on Song 3:11—"Love from the daughters of Jerusalem. Arise and let us look, daughters of Jerusalem, at King Solomon with the crown with which his mother crowned him on the day of his wedding, on the day of his happiness"—Gregory remarks that the Illuminator sees Solomon's crown as a type of the crown of thorns placed on the head of Christ, thus placing on his own head the curse of Adam—"thorns and thistles shall it bring forth for you" (Gen 3:18). He also remarks that Nyssen interprets the crown differently. For Nyssen, the crown represents the Church

[35] The only extended scholarly treatment of these verses that I am aware of is Sebastian Euringer, 1913, "Ein unkanonischer Text des Hohenliedes (Canticle 8:15-20) in der armenischen Bibel," *Zeitschrift für die alttestamentliche Wissenschaft* 33 (4): 272–94. Euringer compiles the variants of these verses, including those in Gregory's lemmas, and proposes tentatively that the verses are a remnant either of the opening of the apocryphal *Odes of Solomon* or a preface to that book that at one time was considered canonical and placed after the Song. For some reason, these extraneous verses were never expunged from the Armenian text of the Song.

and the jewels are the virtues of the saints adorning it.[36] Gregory does not give any details about Nyssen's interpretation but simply remarks that he cites Nyssen more often and so presumably thinks it fitting to report the Illuminator's interpretation here instead.[37] The Illuminator's trials and tortures are mentioned several times. In one passage, Gregory plays on the meaning of the name he shares with the apostle of the Armenians. Commenting on Song 5:2—"I sleep yet my heart is awake"—he notes that the ascetic fathers remained alert and vigilant through all their hardships, and that "our Illuminator," beaten with sticks by ten men for seven days, nevertheless remained *awake* and *alert* with his mind lifted up and ceaselessly praying to God.[38] In a motif that recurs in his other writings, the poet ties his name to its origin from the Greek adjective *grēgorikos*, meaning "watchful, awake." In his own case, though, he notes the inappropriateness of his given name:

> From the font, I have been called "Awake,"
> And yet I sleep in death's slumber;
> On the day of salvation, I was named "Watcher,"
> But I shut my eyes to vigilance.[39]

Gregory's wordplay does not work in Armenian since the word for *awake* (*art'un*) and its synonyms are unrelated to the Greek word for alertness. Readers would have to know Greek to catch Gregory's puns. However, since *Art'un* is a masculine Armenian given name and its name day is celebrated on the feast days of the Illuminator, even Armenians ignorant of Greek may have some awareness of this connection in meaning.[40]

Gregory also makes use of Armenian apocryphal writings. In explaining why Solomon portrays the love of God in terms of romantic

[36] Gregory of Nyssa 2012, 224–25.

[37] *MH* 12:797.65–66; Ervine 2007, 121. Ervine notes that Thomson 1983 gives *Teaching* §348 as the relevant passage, but she considers that passage to be too general to be Gregory's source.

[38] *MH* 12:815.32–33; Ervine 2007, 141.

[39] *BL* 72.4; *MH* 12:447.71–74.

[40] Hrach'ya Acharean, 1942, *Hayots' andzanunneri bararan* [*Dictionary of Armenian names*], Yerevan: Yerevan State University, 276.

love, Gregory says that of all the forms of earthly love, it is the love of a married couple that most resembles the love of God. This is because of all lovers, it is spouses who are most willing to sacrifice themselves for their partners:

> Adam, out of love for his wife, gave up paradise and the light of glory and fell outside it not because he wanted to become God, but because it seemed to him too unbearable to be separated from [Eve]. He knew very well that God would punish him, for he was not ignorant but filled with prophetic spirit, and he had not yet fallen away from the graces of the Spirit because he had not yet transgressed the commandment. . . . Even now, out of love for their wives, men obey their commands, knowing that their will can be very wicked or that what they want is improper, but still they are constrained by love. Now Solomon understood that in humans this love is greater than any other love, and so he allegorized it to the love of Christ and the Church for each other.[41]

This particular explanation of the resemblance of marital and divine love draws from the lore surrounding the first couple recorded in what is known as the Armenian Apocryphal Adam literature. The account of Adam's motives for eating of the fruit stems from the short narrative known as the *History of the Creation and Transgression of Adam*, or *Transgression* for short. The *Transgression* portrays Adam encountering Eve after she ate the fruit:

> When Adam came and saw his wife stripped of the light, he grieved and said, "Why have you eaten of the fruit?"
>
> Eve said, "Because the fruit is very sweet. Taste and see how sweet the fruit is!"[42]
>
> Adam said, "I cannot eat it and become like you."
>
> Eve said, "I ate too much and was stripped because of that. Just taste a little."
>
> Adam said, "I cannot taste it and be stripped like you."

[41] *MH* 12:766–67.42, 49; Ervine 2007, 82–83.

[42] Eve's words mimic Ps 33:8 in its Armenian version: "Taste and see that the Lord is sweet."

> Eve said, "Even if you eat it, God won't get mad at you because he really loves you very much."
>
> Adam took the fruit and examined it, but he was afraid he would be stripped like the woman. If he did not taste it, the woman would cry and beg him, saying, " Let us die together or live together. Don't leave me!" But when Adam looked upon the beauty of the woman, he lost his mind. Even though she had been stripped of the light, she was still beautiful, her flesh dazzling white like a pearl since God had just recently created her and adorned her with his own hands. Adam gave it much thought and said, "Maybe God will have mercy on me and won't strip me? When would I be stripped? It would be better for me to die than to be separated and be away from this woman."
>
> For Adam did not realize that if he kept the commandment, God would have been able to create a woman even more beautiful. He studied the fruit in his hand for three hours and said, "I can't live without this woman." So he ignored God's decree and listening to the woman's words, he ate the fruit and was stripped of the light."[43]

Gregory must have been familiar with this apocryphal tale and uses the story to explain the special status of marital love that leads the lover to sacrifice his own good for the good of his beloved. Although the story is quaint and problematic in a number of ways, Gregory's use of it is interesting for reasons that go beyond just his willingness to bring in noncanonical texts to aid in the interpretation of scripture. Gregory's discussion of Adam's motives and the nature of his love clarifies some points on a topic that has been widely discussed by theologians and scholars since the publication by the twentieth-century Swedish Lutheran bishop and theologian Anders Nygren of the book *Agape and Eros.*[44]

According to Nygren, there is a stark difference between these two loves. *Eros* is a passionate desire and longing for the object of one's love. God's love is *agapē*, a sacrificial love that does not seek its own, while *eros* is the human, acquisitive form of love. Although

[43] The Armenian text is in W. L. Lipscomb, 1990, *The Armenian Apocryphal Adam Literature*, Atlanta: Scholars Press, 108–17, followed by English translation, 118–27. I have made some minor revisions in the translation to better capture the colloquial style of the dialogue.

[44] Anders Nygren, 1957, *Agape and Eros*, London: SPCK.

Nygren draws a sharp distinction between these two loves, Gregory indicates that the romantic love of a married couple, based as it is on erotic desire, is nevertheless the closest human equivalent to God's love. Gregory's example shows that Adam's erotic arousal on seeing Eve's flesh in its still pristine form moves him against his better judgment to sacrifice what he knew to be his own good. Gregory does warn us that not every sacrifice for love of one's spouse is commendable. Alluding to the contemporary reality of forced apostasy to Islam, he reminds his readers that in times of persecution many have fallen away from Christ out of their love for their family members. What appears to be a noble choice by Adam actually brought about the cataclysmic downfall of the human race, henceforth tainted by his disobedience. So sacrificial love need not be a virtue. It is only virtuous if it is done in accordance with the will of God and out of love for him.

Eros and *agapē* are Greek words and have no exact correlate in either English or Armenian. Gregory's terms *love of God* (*Astutsoy sēr*) and *conjugal love* (*amusnut'ean sēr*) do not correspond exactly to *agapē* and *eros*. Conjugal love need not be exclusively erotic. Adam's love for Eve, as Gregory shows, is at least in part sacrificial or kenotic. Likewise, Christ's love for the church, as described in the Song of Songs is not purely agapic. It resembles and can be understood in the language of a human romantic relationship, as is made clear in the highly erotic descriptions of the groom's desire for the bride.[45]

In place of Nygren's stark dichotomy of erotic and divine love, Gregory's interpretation of the Song connects carnal love with the love of God. Such a reading is already present in Origen and reaches Gregory through Nyssen. It is a clear break from a dualistic approach that separates the two loves and sees physical love as operating in a different realm. Instead, physical love is itself a reflection of and a way toward the higher love of God. The things of this world are signposts to the divine. As such the Song of Songs is a powerful reply to the T'ondrakeans who seem to have accepted

[45] For an insightful discussion of love in Gregory's work from the perspective of modern theology, see Lévon Petrossian, 2012, "Gregory of Narek and the Narekian Fathers: The mystery of love from the Commentary on the Song of Songs to the Book of Lamentations," *JSAS* 21, 27–51.

some of the dualist precepts of earlier heresies and therefore do not see any point in the sanctification of marriage. For them conjugal love is not a sign of some higher reality but is nothing more than the interior feelings and passions experienced by human lovers. For Gregory, though, marriage elevates and sanctifies carnal love, turning it into an earthly image of God's love. Gregory affirms the value of marriage: "there is nothing greater and more honorable on earth than the love of man and woman. . . . Those who approach marriage in a pure and undefiled manner and who are united together by the ineffable love of the Holy Spirit are blessed with the same blessing by which Adam and Eve were blessedly united."[46] The groom and bride are figures of the mystery of Christ and the church, and since in our fallen state the eyes of our hearts have been blinded to the higher spiritual mysteries, we must approach the spiritual through the physical—that is, through the marital love that resembles it.[47]

Besides being a defense of sacramental marriage, Gregory's commentary is also an account of the monastic life, restoration of which was crucial for the vitality of the church. The early commentaries on the Song tend to focus either on the union of the individual soul with Christ or the love of Christ for his church. Gregory does not see these two interpretations as at odds with each other. The individual souls of the faithful seeking the love of Christ are all collectively part of the church, which is the body of Christ, so it is one love that all the members of the church experience in their union in the body of Christ. When the groom praises the different parts of the bride's body, he is expressing his love for all the members of the church with their distinct roles and graces, just as Paul compared the members of the church to the parts of the body (1 Cor 12:12-26). Gregory writes:

> One can understand the eyes to be the prophets, who acquired foresight through this grace, as Solomon and those like him did. The neck, on which the head remains fastened, and which joins all life from above and below with all the senses, and which was compared

[46] *MH* 12:766.37–39; Ervine 2007, 82.

[47] *MH* 12:765.31; Ervine 2007, 81.

> to David's tower that he built in Talpiot for the adminstration of warriors, is the great Paul and those like him upon whom Christ stood and from whom all life is distributed to the Church. And the belly are men like our holy Illuminator and John and those like him about whom the Lord testifies when he says *out of his heart will flow rivers of living water* (John 7.38), that is, the grace of the Spirit. Likewise also the teeth with the reddened lips bring up the words of scripture from the belly and ruminate on them finely, making what is unclear clear and making it understandable to men, and illuminating the other modest members of the body, that is, the Church. By this the whole man becomes the bride of Christ.[48]

The Song describes encounters with Christ that are fleeting and elusive. As such it is an especially apt description of the life of the Christian on earth who is given only a brief foretaste of the presence of God through the Eucharist. This point comes to the fore in the commentary on Song 5:5-6, whose lemma (the section heading that presents the verses commented on) reads:

> I rose to open to my nephew.[49] My hands dripped with myrrh and my fingers filled with myrrh were upon the handles of the lock. . . . I opened it for my nephew, but my nephew passed by, and my soul went after him with his word. . . . I searched for him and did not find him. I called for him, but he did not respond.[50]

Gregory, speaking in the person of the bride, remarks on this verse:

> When I lifted the eyes of my mind to the mind of scripture in order to see the unfathomable depth of its understanding of grace, and I opened my heart to gather within it the brief glimpse and to examine and be instructed in and attain an understanding of his depths,

[48] *MH* 12:801–2.39–42; Ervine 2007, 128.

[49] "Nephew," or more precisely, "brother's son," is the translation of the Armenian word *eghbōrordi* that renders the Greek of the Septuagint, *adelphidos*, which can mean either nephew or beloved. Gregory, following Nyssen, makes sense of this appellation through the allegory of the bride as the church, the younger sister of the synagogue and by extension the Jews, from whom Christ came into the world as a son.

[50] *MH* 12:819.65–66, 822.86, 88, 823.93; Ervine 2007, 146, 148, 149.

> what remained outside the grasp of my weak mind so astonished me that in desiring it I forget what knowledge I had received when I opened. This is why she says *my nephew passed by*. It is as if while seeing him, he suddenly went away like swift lightning. *And my soul went after him with his word*. That is, though I received but a small ray of his word, my soul left me and I went to his word. It is as if I recognized him and united in his love, ebullient with his commandments. And in supposing that I had reached him, I recognized myself to be even more removed from understanding. For in seeing the true sun, I recognized by the light how far I was from knowledge, I recalled the saying of the divine Solomon elsewhere—*he who increases knowledge will increase suffering* [Eccl 1:18].[51]

The desire for God is never satiated, but these brief encounters impel the soul to long for more. Gregory describes here an aspect of Nyssen's mystical theology, which is called *epektasis* (from the Greek, literally, a "reaching out after").[52] The food of Christ fills us but also leaves us hungry and ever more desirous of him. The person yearning for knowledge of God is like a drunkard who cannot stop drinking.[53] Those who taste the love of Christ become drunk with his love and come to despise all other loves, including the love of spouse and children.[54] Gregory implies that however exalted marital love may be, at least some Christians, such as the monks committed to celibacy, are able to transcend the desire of earthly love and seek only the perfect and endless love of God. It is a frenzied madness that impels the soul out of itself, but it is the madness of divine love.

In addition to the interpretations that see the bride as emblematic of the soul and the Church, there is also a Marian interpretation that treats the bride as a figure of the Virgin Mary. While this Marian interpretation only became prominent in the exegetical traditions of the West with the Song commentary of the Benedictine theologian Rupert of Deutz (ca. 1075–1129), the connections between the bride and the Virgin run throughout ancient patristic

[51] *MH* 12.822.87–90; Ervine 2007, 148.

[52] For Nyssen on *epektasis*, see Andrew Louth 1981, 88–89.

[53] *MH* 12.822.92; Ervine 2007, 149.

[54] *MH* 12.864.12; Ervine 2007, 190.

commentary.[55] In Gregory's commentary the Marian aspect is present but does not have the same prominence as the individual or ecclesial readings of the bride. The focus on the ecclesial reading is the most salient, given Gregory's intent to respond to the T'ondrakean rejection of the church. But the Marian reading does have a minor role in the commentary. In one instance, Gregory identifies Mary with the bride when the daughters of Jerusalem remark, "our sister is small and does not have breasts; what will we do for our sister on the day she is spoken for?" (Song 8:8).[56] After giving the ecclesial reading of this verse according to which the daughters, who are the angelic powers, are speaking about the new church of the gentiles, Gregory notes that the sister may also be the *Theotokos* at the annunciation. The mortal young girl is to all appearances too weak to bear the incarnate Lord in her womb, but when the bride hears the doubts of the angels, she is emboldened and responds to their bewilderment, "I am a wall, and my breasts are as towers; I was in his eyes as one who has found peace."[57] In chapter nine on Gregory's Mariology, I will discuss how even though the Marian reading is suppressed in the commentary, it is clearly on Gregory's mind and becomes more pronounced in one of his hymns.

The Song of Songs presents us with a glimpse of the holy of holies, the summit of human happiness when the individual soul together with the church pursues and unites with Christ, but that happiness is described in erotic language comprehensible for our carnal minds. As such, the work is relevant to Gregory's mystical theology. Writing the commentary may also have inspired Gregory's idea of constructing a book in the form of a church. Realizing that the Song serves as a figure of the holy of holies, the altar of the church, Gregory may have conceived of composing a longer song that would represent the entire journey of the faithful through the church to God. The commentary even suggests that the noncanonical verses placed at the front of the Song serve as a kind of a nar-

[55] Rupert of Deutz, 1974, *Rupert Tuitiensis Commentaria in Canticum Canticorum*, Turnhaut: Brepols.

[56] *MH* 12.870.76; Ervine 2007, 196.

[57] *MH* 12.872.97, 101; Ervine 2007, 199.

thex before the sanctuary. Those verses, which invoke baptism, served as a kind of baptistry to prepare the reader prior to entering the sanctuary. The thought of conceiving the sections of a book like the chambers of a building, as we will see, guided his later construction of the *Book of Lamentation*. But already in his commentary on the Canticle, Gregory appears to have implemented this concept on a smaller scale.

We do not know if Gurgēn was pleased with the results of the commission he had given Gregory, but given the monk's burgeoning reputation, we may suppose that it was another distinction that conferred upon the new monastery of Narek even greater prestige and prominence as a center of learning and creativity.

The Encomia

In the case of his encomia or panegyrics—formal literary expressions of praise—Gregory was adding to a long tradition in Armenian literature, dating back to the fifth century, beginning with Koriwn's biography of his teacher, Mashtots', the inventor of the Armenian alphabet.[58] Gregory's encomia, as befits the genre, are written in an elevated, highly ornate literary style. He wrote the *History of the Holy Cross of Aparank'* for Stephen (Step'anos), the bishop of Mokk', probably in 983 just after the donation of the relic of the True Cross to the monastery of Aparank', about 40 kilometers southwest of Narekavank' and located in Stephen's diocese. Although there is a tradition that the Illuminator established a monastery at Aparank', the earliest written record of the monastery is Gregory's encomium. It was there in the tenth century that a bishop named David built the church of St. John the Baptist.[59] Even if there were religious communities at this location prior to David's

[58] For Koriwn's work as an encomium, see Abraham Terian, "Koriwn's *Life of Mashtots'* as an Encomium," *JSAS* 3, 1–14, reprinted in Terian, 2008, *Opera Select Teriana: A Scholarly Retrospective*, New Rochelle, NY: St. Nersess Armenian Seminary, 91–106. For the tradition of panegyrics on the Illuminator, see also Terian, 2005, *Patriotism and Piety in Armenian Christianity: The Early Panegyrics*, Crestwood, NY: St. Vladimir's Seminary Press.

[59] For details on the site and its structures, see Thierry 1989, 424. Thierry bases his description on the reports of Armenians who visited the site in 1972.

building efforts, the establishment of a formal monastery probably came later in the middle of the tenth century, part of the general flowering of monasteries and convents throughout Armenia and especially in Vaspurakan and the Lake Van basin. As a monk of a monastery that had been established just a couple of decades before Aparank', Gregory's affinity for the monks of Aparank' may have motivated him to accept Stephen's request to compose the encomium. Aparank' monastery had achieved renown as a result of David's remains buried there. His tomb, under the "solid vault of the altar" became a place of pilgrimage where "amazing and remarkable healing miracles" were reported.[60] According to one account, Stephen, who succeeded David as bishop of Mokk', sold the soil surrounding the tomb in an effort to finance his project of building a church dedicated to the Virgin there. As word reached Constantinople, the Byzantine emperors, Basil II (r. 976–1025) and his younger brother Constantine VIII, who officially shared the throne but did not reign until after Basil's death, became interested in financing the construction.[61]

Gregory's history expressly denies that Stephen had any desire or need to sell the miraculous soil. In Gregory's account, Stephen's unnamed uncle decided of his own accord to renounce his family inheritance and journey to Constantinople to pursue a military career in the imperial court. He took with him some of the miraculous earth from David's tomb as a memento of his native land. The emperors, impressed with the abilities of Stephen's uncle as well as the miraculous powers of the soil, pledged their support to the bishop's construction projects at Aparank'. Stephen politely declined any material assistance and instead asked for a spiritual gift, which turned out to be a piece of the relic of the True Cross. Honoring the request, the emperors ordered an elaborate reliquary be built to house the sacred wood, "a four-winged artifact cast in gold, in the shape of the divine cross, and placed in it a piece cut

[60] *MH* 12:917.36–37; Terian 229–30.

[61] Or so the account given in Thierry 1989, 424. According to Thierry, the monastery of the Holy Cross of Aparank' was located on the southwestern slope of Vankin dağ (Sarixač') towering over Namran çay (stream), a tributary of the Müküs çay.

from the life-giving Wood which held the glorious Lord."[62] To it they added other relics of Christ's crucifixion: the sponge soaked in vinegar, the towel by which he was girded, thorns from the crown, one of the nails that pierced his body, and one relic of the nativity: the swaddling cloth with which the infant Jesus was wrapped "like a homeless being on the day of his birth." Stephen's uncle returned to his native land with the reliquary, which was received with ceremonious solemnity and placed "under covers made of precious and golden threads" next to David's tomb. Stephen had built elaborate and imposing buildings on the site, with altars "replicating in a most attractive way the seraph-inhabited courts at Zion."[63] Gregory's encomium lavishes its praise not only on Stephen and his uncle but also on the emperors Basil and Constantine, who ruled "with dignity, peace, and tranquility, extending their own most-trusted progeny, high and marvelous branches stemming from the lordly, royal, and well-rooted tree."[64] Gregory's praise of the emperors is in part due to Basil's pursuit of a policy of peaceful coexistence with the non-Chalcedonian Armenians. But beyond any religious motives he may have had, there were compelling political and military reasons for Basil to maintain warm relations with the Artsruni house. The gift of the reliquary to a monastery in Vaspurakan would go far in cultivating goodwill.

The *History of the Holy Cross of Aparank'* formed part of a triptych of encomia, all written at the behest of Stephen of Mokk'. The other two panels of the triptych are the *Encomium on the Holy Cross* and the *Encomium on the Holy Virgin Mother of God*. Both of these works exist in two different recensions.[65] There was already a tradition in

[62] *MH* 12:920.58–63; Terian 2016, 232–233.

[63] *MH* 12:921.71; Terian 2016, 233.

[64] *MH* 12:913–14.5; Terian 2016, 225.

[65] Recension A of the *Encomium on the Holy Cross* is in *MH* 12:930–41, with English translation in Terian 2016, 244–65. The second recension is in *MH* 12:942–52 and the translation is 266–87 in Terian 2016. The first recension of the *Encomium on the Holy Virgin* is in *MH* 12:953–63 with the second rescension following at 965–75. English translations of both recensions are again available in Terian 2016, 288–325. There is a French translation and instructive theological study of the encomium on the Virgin in Dasnabedian 1995.

Armenian theological literature of writing encomia on the Holy Cross, beginning in the seventh century with David of Nergin's panegyric on the God-receiving cross, a work often wrongly attributed to David the Neoplatonic philosopher.[66] Gregory adds to this tradition, mindful also of the importance of extolling the cross in the context of T'ondrakean rejection of its veneration. He sets the cross before us as a fitting object of our reverence, for it is a sign of Christ's redemption:

> You are praised, O redemptive sign of the glory of Jesus. You hold the gift of life in the form of death. The wise man, the author of the Songs, observed ahead of time your amazing mystery which he expressed with the flow of the Spirit, saying with gratitude—*blessed is the wood by which righteousness comes* [Wisdom of Solomon 14:7].[67]

At first glance, an encomium to the Virgin Mary does not seem to fit in with the other two panels of Gregory's triptych. But just as the cross bore Christ's body at his death, so too Mary bore his body at his birth. Because both Mary and the cross are life-giving "bearers of God" the inclusion of an encomium of the *theotokos* in the trilogy is entirely appropriate and lends Gregory's triptych a congenial symmetry. Gregory himself makes the connection of the Virgin and the cross explicit in his litany for the feast of the Assumption.[68] There, he describes the word of God being nailed to Mary's body in the incarnation. We will study this encomium on the Virgin in detail in chapter nine.

Two other encomia are devoted to St. James (Yakob) of Nisibis and the Apostles. St. James, a Syrian who served as bishop of Nisibis (modern-day Nusaybin in southeastern Turkey, straddling the border with Syria) in the early years of the fourth century, was a popular saint whose cult was especially observed in southern Armenia. The saint had a particular significance for the monks of

[66] The Armenian text of David's encomium is in *MH* 6:1020–29. An English translation by Hagop Nersoyan is in Avedis K. Sanjian, ed., 1986, *David Anhaght', the 'Invincible Philosopher'*, Atlanta: Scholars Press, 81–100.

[67] *MH* 12:947.56; Terian 2016, 276.

[68] *MH* 12:708.45–48; Terian 2016, 148–49.

Narek since their monastery housed his relics. James was a contemporary and, according to the Armenian tradition, a cousin of the Illuminator. He took part in the Council of Nicaea and was a noted miracle worker. Apparently James had a fondness for mountain climbing; during his climb to the top of Mount Sararad, he believed that he recovered a piece of Noah's ark.[69] Sararad should not be confused with Mount Ararat or Ağri Dağ farther to the north and currently on the Turkish side of the border with Armenia. Ararat is associated in more recent times with the ark. Mount Sararad is most likely Mount Judi, near the point where Turkey, Syria, and Iraq meet, where the early Armenian tradition together with the Syriac and Qur'anic traditions locate the ark's resting place.[70] In the course of praising James's works of piety, Gregory expounds on the significance of his discovery:

> By remembering Noah's wooden ark, a means of salvation for a few out of countless many, he brought its mystery to attention. . . . The preeminently honorable Saint James longed to have a blessed piece of a plank from the old ark, which became a refuge for clean and unclean animals, as a reminder of the experiences of past generations. For there were those in his days who, having shut the eye of faith, considered the stories and acts of old ages to be fables and deduced that certain events never happened. Thus they considered these accounts useless and laughable, born of the pangs of mental blabber. For among the pagans the story bears the name of Deucalion instead of Noah, and the ark was purportedly made by him. Because of this misleading hearsay, and to straighten out unbelievers, he displayed the slice of wood granted him from the ark, and this shattered the misconceptions and doubts.[71]

In Greek mythology, Deucalion built a boat to save himself and his wife Pyrrha from the deluge unleashed by Zeus's wrath. Those who questioned the biblical account may have pointed to parallel

[69] The Armenian text is in *MH* 12:990–1005. An English translation of the hagiographical account is Garsoïan 1989, 77–80; see also Garsoïan's comments on 431 and 489.

[70] Surah 11:44 of the Qur'an states that the ark landed on Mount Judi.

[71] *MH* 12:996.44, 998.58–60; Terian 2016, 351, 354.

flood myths in other cultures and written off the Genesis story as one more fiction. So at least in Gregory's mind James's discovery served to disabuse the skeptics of their doubts. But beyond that, the relic was a symbol of the church, the New Ark "that carries all" safely along the "tempestuous sea, upset not by turbulent waves but by various happenings and violent passions."[72]

The encomium on the apostles affords Gregory the opportunity to display some of the numerological skills learned from Anania and that were part of the broader Neoplatonic patrimony of the school of Narek.[73] The number of apostles, three times four, symbolizes the "praiseworthy goodness" of the "daring preachers" who proclaimed the Trinitarian God to the four corners of the earth.[74] Foremost among the apostles is Peter,

> first in number and primacy, the solid Rock, the seven-word confession to his credit, the chosen and glorified in harmony with the mystical cycle of this world's beginning and end, is Cephas, who was pronounced blessed by the lips of the Giver of Life, was inspired by the Father's benevolence, and made wise. Moved by the Spirit of Wisdom to confess rightly, having discerned the eternal purpose for the inscrutable birth, he was deservedly blessed by the statement of the uncreated One, "Blessed are you, Simon, heir to Jonah" [Matt 16:17].[75]

Gregory achieves dubious success in making Peter's confession, "You are the Christ, the Son of the Living God," have seven words in Armenian by treating the definite article—which is in fact a demonstrative suffix appended to the modified word "Christ"—as though it is a separate word. The seven words harmonize both with the six days of creation followed by the seventh day of the Sabbath, and the seven millennia of the world's existence before Christ's second coming.[76]

[72] *MH* 12:999.63; 12:996.44; Terian 2016, 354; 351.

[73] A treatise on the meaning of numbers that was once thought to be the work of the seventh century Armenian mathematician and geographer Anania of Shirak has been shown to be by Anania of Narek. See *MH* 10:439–55.

[74] *MH* 12:978.25; Terian 2016, 329.

[75] *MH* 12:981.45–46; Terian 2016, 332–33.

[76] For Gregory's belief that seven millennia would elapse before Christ's coming, see Ervine 2007, 122–23n151 and n166.

Alluding to the apostolic succession, Gregory praises the apostles not only for their own deeds, but for those done by their disciples whom they ordained to carry on the mission of the church. Including Paul among the apostles, Gregory notes that two of the evangelists were disciples of the apostles—Mark, a disciple of Peter, and Luke, of Paul:

> Mark, the saintly youth who was named High Wall, a disciple of the Rock; Luke, the bearer of the resplendent Resurrection, teller of the story of the Ascension, an Antiochian young man, a master healer of souls rather than of bodies; others from among you were shepherds and teachers.[77]

Here again, Gregory is influenced by both Anania and Khosrov's penchant for etymology, interpreting Mark (*Markos*) in the sense of "boundary" or "wall" (as in English "march"). Presumably Gregory is connecting the apostle's name with the unrelated Armenian word *marz* ("border"). He is correct, though, in associating *Luke* with light.

In keeping with the school of Narek's broad ecumenical convictions, Gregory ends this encomium by lauding the universal range of the apostles' preaching, which resulted in producing disciples of the Gospel throughout the world: from the "famed regions of Kedar" to the "islands of the Cretans descended from Canaan," "the easternmost regions of the Parthians and Persian hordes," Libya and Ethiopia, "Tyre with the Phoenicians," and the Latins and Romans where "their message was well received."[78]

Advice on the Orthodox Faith and the Pure and Virtuous Life

This treatise is among the least known and studied of Gregory's works but it offers important insights into his doctrinal beliefs as well as moral teachings. As far as I know it has not been translated into English or any other Western language, but it deserves wider exposure because it serves as a kind of summula (mini-summary) of Gregory's theological doctrines and ethical advice, not unlike the *Sentences* of Peter Lombard (1096–1160) in the Western Christian

[77] *MH* 12:982.60; Terian 2016, 334.
[78] *MH* 12:987.101–4; Terian 2016, 340–41.

tradition. Gregory's work consists of seventy-six "sentences." Much of this material is repeated elsewhere in his writings, but the Advice is a convenient compendium of his teachings.

Gregory begins with his doctrine of the Trinity and the incarnation. God the Father is "true essence, perfect, uncreated, without beginning, eternal, uncaused, incomprehensible, invisible, ineffable."[79] But in addition to these attributes of the Father, Gregory also lists terms that indicate God's transcendence of all our descriptions: God is *superessential*, *superexistent*, *superlight*, and *superineffable*. Gregory again shows the influence of Pseudo-Dionysius. The Greek equivalent to "superineffable"[80] occurs in several places in the Pseudo-Dionysius corpus—twice in the *Divine Names*, in particular—so Gregory must have been familiar with this work and been influenced by its approach to mysticism.[81] The negation of all the names of God requires that we negate even the negated names (like *un*created and *in*effable) that deny affirmative properties. To say that God is ineffable is to define him with our own concepts, but his ineffability is such that it even evades our ability to describe it with our word "ineffable." His ineffability is itself ineffable. We will say more in chapter eight about the role of these names and descriptions in Gregory's mystical theology.

The Son of God is the very form and brilliance of the Father, expressing his image (Heb 1:3) and sharing his essence. He is God from God, uncreated from uncreated, eternity from eternity, life from life, light from light. Though he is the Son of the Father, he is not younger than the Father but they are coexistent. For without the Son, the Father is not the Father, nor without the Father can the Son be the Son.

The Holy Spirit flows from the Father ineffably. He is not begotten with the Son but proceeds from the divine essence, in support of which Gregory cites John 15:26—"the Spirit of truth proceeds

[79] *MH* 12:1024.20–22.

[80] *huperarrētos*. The Armenian calque of the Greek word is *geranjaṛ*.

[81] B. R. Suchla, 1990, *Corpus Dionysiacum I: Pseudo-Dionysius Areopagita. De divinis nominibus*, Berlin: De Gruyter, 115.11 and 126.9. Retrieved from http://stephanus.tlg.uci.edu/Iris/Cite?2798:004:22679.

from the Father." The Spirit shares the essence of the Father and the glory of the Son.[82]

At the annunciation, the Word came to dwell in the womb of the all-holy Virgin Mary, purified by the Spirit. He is perfect man and true God, mixed with what cannot be mixed in an unconfused union, in a new and miraculous composition. Gregory affirms that Christ suffered all the human passions except for sin. Paradoxically, the one who feeds all living things experienced hunger, and the one who grants the water of life to all his faithful thirsted. He who gives rest to all the afflicted wearied; the ever-vigilant guardian of Israel slept. And the one who removed every tear from each face himself wept.[83]

Concerning ethics and proper conduct, Gregory cites James 2:26—"faith without works is dead"—to support his claim that salvation cannot be achieved without virtuous works. Faith is not sufficient since even the demons believe in and tremble before God (James 2:19). The law and prophets and the Gospel together teach that in all things we must love.[84] Jesus said that he recognizes his disciples by their love for one another (John 13:35), not through their healing the sick or exorcising demons. He knows that when we truly love God and our fellow humans, we will perform all the other commandments. Virtuous living requires that we close the eyes of both our body and mind to the temptations of lust, envy, and all other sins but open them to the beauty of creation. We ought to marvel at the miraculous works of God, as David did—"I look at your heavens, the work of your fingers, the moon and the stars that you have established" (Ps 8:3).[85] We must hasten in pursuit of this life of Christian virtue so that like the wise virgins we may be found pleasing by the heavenly groom and may with lit lamps enter the heavenly bridal chamber (Matt 25:1-13).

Against the T'ondrakeans

Kchaw must have been a forbidding monastery, a place of exile and penance for wayward and troublesome monks. Centuries earlier

[82] *MH* 12:1025.26–30.
[83] *MH* 12:1026-7.42–46.
[84] *MH* 12:1041–42.157–60.
[85] *MH* 12:1049–50.226–28.

before Christianity became the established religion in Armenia, according to the region's folklore, malignant demons inhabited the place. When the nuns who were fleeing Rome, Gayanē, Hripsimē, and their companions, arrived they exorcized the demons and planted a cross on the site where the monastery was later built.[86]

Though he was one of the monks of Kchaw in Gregory's day, Mushegh was not contrite. After arriving at Kchaw he began to preach T'ondrakean doctrines and turned the monastery into a haven for the heretics. Or at least that is what the reports that reached Narek stated, and Gregory considered these accounts trustworthy and free of malicious intent. Gregory's concern about T'ondrakean heresy runs throughout his works. In the commentary on the Song of Songs, he upholds marriage as the most honorable and greatest of earthly things, and criticizes those to whom it "does not appear of great value or importance," among them the T'ondrakeans. Gregory's emphasis on the material character of the sacraments and worship is a pervasive theme of the *Book of Lamentation*. Examples include his celebration in Prayer 92 of the wooden semantron, a percussion instrument struck with a mallet to call monks to prayer, and of the sacramental holy oil in Prayer 93. While Gregory is presenting a constructive sacramental theology in his writings, his focus on the physical dimension of worship is also intended to counter the T'ondrakean's rejection of the sacraments. His encomium on the Holy Cross, as well as his history of the Holy Cross of Aparank', while commemorating and honoring the relations between Byzantium and Vaspurakan, emphasize the importance of the veneration of the cross in opposition to the T'ondrakean contempt for material veneration. But it is in his letter in response to the situation at Kchaw that Gregory provides the most sustained and explicit treatment of the heresy. His letter to the monks there was not written at anyone's request but was composed only through his desire to "free them from their evil ideas."[87]

[86] The legend of the nuns expelling the demons of Kchaw is found in the *History of the Hripsimeants' Saints* attributed to Moses of Khorēn and recounted in Thierry 1989, 420.

[87] *MH* 12:1087–89. There is an English translation in Conybeare 1898, a German translation in Karapet Tēr-Mkrtschean 1893, *Die Paulikaner im byzantischen*

Gregory lists the ideas that Mushegh propagated and that his brother monks at Kchaw did not consider "foreign to the apostolic faith." The list reveals the antisacramental and antimaterial nature of T'ondrakean teachings and practice. Ordination was inefficacious. Communion did not transform the elements of bread and wine into the body and blood of Christ but is merely a "common meal." The water of baptism was nothing more than "bath water" with no higher spiritual significance.[88] They disparaged marriage as well, refusing to acknowledge, Gregory writes, that marriage was "blessed by the Lord himself, honored by his miracles and the presence of his mother, the *Theotokos*." Nor do they regard Sunday as a special day set apart for the Lord and his worship, even though it is "the image of the blessed day on which God created the first light, perfected the light of His Resurrection, and dispensed the life-giving light of the Advent." They rejected the veneration of the cross, the "sign that the Incarnate God lifted up and carried on his shoulders." And the leader of their sect, Smbat of Zahrehawan, blasphemously declared himself to be a Christ, though he was in truth, Gregory says, one of those about whom "Christ had earlier testified when he said that false messiahs and prophets would arise" (Mark 13:22).[89]

Gregory refers to the treatise against the T'ondrakeans by Anania of Narek, whom he identifies here as his teacher and uncle, a wise champion of the orthodox faith, who had examined the false teachings of Mushegh and "demolished the fanciful blasphemy of the iniquitous heretics."[90] But in contrast to the remnant of Anania's treatise with its ponderous arguments and contrived etymologies,

---

Kaiserreiche, Leipzig: J.C. Hinrichs, and a French translation in Mahé 2000, 787–93. Conybeare believes that Gregory at one point accepted T'ondrakean doctrines and that his tone in this letter reflected his conflicted relation with them. But nothing in Gregory's writings indicates any T'ondrakean tendencies but rather only shows his opposition to their teachings. If Gregory was ever charged with T'ondrakism, this would surely have been for the same reason that Anania was.

[88] *MH* 12:1087.6–7.

[89] *MH* 12:1088.19.

[90] Gregory refers at *MH* 12:1088.21 to Anania as his *horeghbayr*, which literally means "father's brother," but Gregory was related to his teacher through

Gregory's letter is direct and personal. He even employs stylistic devices like alliteration. This is my attempt to reproduce his alliterative denunciation of the heretics:

> They are a drove of dogs, a throng of thieves, a welter of wolves, a den of demons, an assembly of assassins, a collection of crucifiers . . . a society of sorcerers, contemptible not only to the clergy but even to the pagans!

The pagans, offended by the T'ondrakeans, are in fact Muslims and, in particular, the Arab emir Abu'l-Ward, who executed Smbat and massacred many of his followers. Though considering him a pagan, Gregory is content to recognize God's hand in the emir's persecution of heretics: "the avenging heathen emir Apl-Vard has justly become the rod of the Lord Jesus' wrath."[91] In Gregory's account, Abu'l-Ward taunted Smbat and expressed his desire to test his claim to be a Christ. If after being put to death and buried, Smbat rises from the dead like the true Christ, Abu'l-Ward pledged to recognize him as Christ. Gregory praises these words, stating that "God, and not something of this world, had planted this thought in the [emir]." God's providence acts even through Muslims so that "evil may be reprimanded or killed through evil, just as the monstrous Indian dragon feeds."[92]

Mushegh had asked by what authority Gregory chastised him and which scripture permittted him to condemn a fellow monk. Gregory responded by noting that Paul was not ashamed even to

---

his mother. Perhaps Gregory was speaking figuratively, regarding Anania as his own father's spiritual brother.

[91] *MH* 12:1087.1.

[92] Tēr-Mkrtchean sees an allusion to a passage in Job here, but Gregory is more likely referring to the Indian dragon mentioned by Philo of Alexandria in *de Aeternitate Mundi* 128. See F. H. Colson and G. H. Whitaker, trans., 1929, *Philo*, vol. 9, London: W. Heinemann. Though a large number of Philo's works were translated into Armenian, this particular work does not appear on lists of Armenian versions of Philo.Yet it is the probable source of Gregory's simile, especially since the example of the Indian dragon draining the blood of elephants is a more appropriate image here than any of the beasts mentioned in Job.

condemn twice an angel who preaches an alien gospel (Gal 1:8). And the church condemns those whose teachings deviate even in part from orthodoxy. These include the Arians condemned in the anathema of the Council of Nicaea, as well as the Nestorians repudiated by Cyril of Alexandria.[93] If these reprimands directed at those who deviate only in part from orthodoxy are proper, then we are even more justified, Gregory argues, in denouncing those who are "much more separated from us, and [who] have cut themselves off from Christ and bound themselves to Satan!"

Gregory ends by asking the abbot of Kchaw not to be offended nor to presume that his words of chastisement are motivated by hate rather than by love. He asks that the abbot order the copying of Anania's "wisdom-filled books against the heretics." Ironically, the monastery of Kchaw's most prized relic was the autographed manuscript of Gregory's letter. At the time of the Thierrys' visit in the 1970s, Kchaw's monastic church was still partially standing, although its narthex had been leveled. [94]

[93] This anathema remains to this day a part of the Armenian divine liturgy, recited by the deacon immediately after the Nicene creed.

[94] Thierry 1989, 420.

Chapter Five

A New Song to the Lord: Gregory's Hymns and Poetry

Hymns and Liturgical Poetry

Gurgēn, the prince who had commissioned Gregory to compose his commentary on the Song of Songs was perhaps drawn to the monk because he had already made a name for himself through his innovative composition of hymns. Gregory's desire to adorn the liturgy with new melodies and words was no doubt inspired by his father's efforts at liturgical reform.

Khosrov's main concern was to reform the liturgy and make it more accessible to the people.[1] Gregory shared his father's desire to enrich the liturgy so that it would more effectively touch the hearts of the faithful. He understood the power of music to stir people's sentiments. His own experience of the church's rich hymnody would have impressed this on him, but also as a young student in the academy of Narekavank' he must have read books like the textbook of the Neoplatonic philosopher David that provided theoretical support for what he also perceived from direct experience:

[1] Pétrossian notes that Khosrov's interest was in standardizing the liturgy rather than changing it, but Gregory's goal was to reform it, most notably through his new hymns. Instead of standardization, Gregory was interested in "personalization" of the liturgy. See Pétrossian 2001, 44 and 86n336. But while Khosrov was clearly concerned by the lack of uniformity and discipline in the celebration of the liturgy, he also reveals an openness to reform and innovation based on practices in other rites.

> Music possesses great power, for it can plunge the soul into various states and restore it to good humor, to which laments (*oghb*) and elegies bear witness, for these can dispose the soul accordingly. Thus some people tell the tale of how when at a feast Alexander [the Great] heard a musician play a war song, at which he instantly took up arms and departed. But when a musician began to play a festive tune he returned to join his fellow guests.[2]

This passage may have planted in his mind the seed of the idea of composing not only hymns but a book of lamentation (*oghbergut'iwn*). Anania may have encouraged Gregory's main poetic innovation, the genre of sacred litanies called *gandz*, which means "treasure." Later Armenian sacred composers would add to Gregory's treasures to produce an impressive anthology known as the *gandzaran* or "treasury." Each of these "treasure-hymns" begins with the word "treasure." An example is the treasure-hymn for the nativity and baptism of Christ, which are celebrated in the Armenian church on the same day, January 6. Although dedicated to the nativity of Christ, this treasure-hymn is addressed to the Virgin Mary, as is common for hymns celebrating this feast:

> Treasure incorruptible, greatness concealed,
> Awe-inspiring, ineffable mystery that appeared on earth,
> Holy Bearer of God—
> The unfathomable God the Word
> Whom you bore physically within you and gave birth to the Savior of the world,
> Lifting him up into your bosom to suckle,
> The One who was revealed today for the rejoicing of the human race,
> To deliver the first Adam from the former curses,
> Also to erase the seal of condemnation placed upon the foremother Eve
>
> By giving birth to the Only-Begotten Son.
> Please intercede with Christ the King
> To come to our help; we plead.[3]

[2] David 1983, 134–35.

[3] *MH* 12:627–32; 13:100–105; Terian 2016, 8–15.

A treasure-hymn is often paired with a *tagh*, or ode, a celebration of the event with a responsorial in the form of a refrain. In his Ode for the Holy Cross, Gregory symbolically transforms the sacrificed lamb into the resurrected and triumphant lion. The imagery of Christ as lion is already familiar from the Old Testament, as in Hosea 5:14: "for I will be like a lion to Ephraim, and like a young lion to the house of Judah." Terian also mentions the Aramaic Targum to Isaiah 53, which explicitly transforms the lamb into a defiant lion. Remarkably, Gregory's ode is sung from the perspective of a soul held captive in the depths of the earth, in Hell, who expects to be released from the bonds by Christ's harrowing. Perhaps it is Adam himself who sings. Also notable is that the last word of each line is repeated at the start of the next verse. This verbal linking together of the verses is a poetic figure of the chains binding the soul in Hades. The only break in the chain occurs between the penultimate and last lines, signifying Christ's undoing of the bonds of captivity as he descends into Hell:

> I speak of the Lion's roar,
> crying on the four-winged cross,
> On the four-winged cross, crying,
> calling to the depths of the earth,
> The depths of the earth trembled,
> they shook beneath his mighty voice.
> This mighty voice I heard
> loosens the bonds I'm in,
> He longs to loosen my bonds,
> to reverse the captivity of the captives.
> I say, "Blessed are the captives
> whom the Lion raised."
> Those raised by the Lion
> expect no further suffering;
> They expect no suffering,
> they await the wreaths that wither not.
> They receive the braided wreaths
> from the Lion, the immortal King.
> Let us give glory to the Redeemer
> who rescued the captives from prison.[4]

[4] *MH* 12:721; Terian 2016, 170–71.

One other genre of sacred poetry that Gregory composed is the *meghedi*, or "melody," a type of ode that is usually sung during the preparation of the gifts.[5] One example is this melody on the raising of Lazarus:

> Good news to Mary
> And also to Martha, beloved sisters.
> Sister following sister approached the Savior with the request:
> "Savior, Lord Jesus Christ, had you been here
> Our brother would not have died."
> The Giver of Life cried out with a loud voice,
> "Lazarus, come forth."[6]

Gregory's hymnodic creations spread from his monastery throughout Armenia and became part of the rich liturgical heritage of the rite. Unfortunately, the treasure-hymns and odes were assembled in separate collections, so the continuity between the two was mostly forgotten. The original intent was for the treasure-hymn commemorating the feast for the day to be paired with a corresponding ode. In this way, the faithful would acquire both an understanding of the meaning of the feast and an emotional attachment through the music and evocative imagery of the lyrics. For the exaltation of the Holy Cross, one may begin with the treasure-hymn proper for the day:

> Treasure ineffable, greatness concealed,
> Mighty, awe-inspiring, always good,
> Thrice-holy, unbounded, blessed, living Name,
> Indescribable reality, shut beyond sense perception, altogether inexplicable,
> Transcendent, beyond reach, yet accessibly near, eternal King,
> Behold, our petitions rise like incense before you, Almighty; we plead.
> . . .
> Forecaster of spring and upward flights,
> Example of your will upheld for the world,

[5] See Terian 2016, xxviii.

[6] *MH* 12:643; Terian 2016, 37.

To adhere to the light, to Noah's ark
Image of redemption, representation of miracles, refuge of hope,
By covenant you interceded for a new people, above those in heaven,
Drawing them to you by the wing of your cross.
Behold, our petitions rise like incense before you, Almighty; we
plead.[7]

This treasure-hymn for the Holy Cross would then be followed with an ode for the cross. One such ode imagines a visitor to Jerusalem addressing a bird that has perched on one of the wings of the cross. Terian compares the structure of this ode to the medieval Italian *canzone*, a poem resembling sonnets but with greater flexibility in terms of meter and number of stanzas. The visitor informs the bird that the Good News of Christ's resurrection is addressed to it too, indicating that Christ came to redeem not only all of humanity but also all of creation. The bird also symbolizes the resurrection. Like the cross, it has two wings, and in spreading its wings and flying from the site of the crucifixion, the bird represents the new life that emanates from the cross:

I go up to Jerusalem,
To that city built by God,
To that beautifully built temple,
To that lily-like Zion.
Who is like the one unlike others?
O unlike One![8]

A bright bird perched
On that wing of the cross.
It had a silver-plated wing,
Like the rays of the sun.
Who is like the one unlike all others?
O unlike One!

[7] *MH* 12:717–20; Terian 164–69.

[8] My translation of the refrain differs from Terian in order to make more evident what seems to me an allusion to Wisdom 2:15—"because his manner of life is unlike that of others"—referring to the righteous man who is, in Christian exegesis, a foreshadowing of Christ.

It let out a fine sound
Like Gabriel's trumpet,
Filled its eyes with tears
Like the morning dew.
Who is like the one unlike all others?
O unlike One!

O most beautiful bird,
Perched on that wing of the Cross:
How do you produce that melodious sound
Like Gabriel's trumpet?
How do you fill your eyes with tears
Like the morning dew?
Who is like the one unlike all others?
O unlike One!

O most beautiful bird:
The summons of the good news is addressed to you.
Keep rejoicing with your superb song.
Who is like the one unlike all others?
O unlike One![9]

The text of fifteen of these festal collections or cycles survives in manuscript collection, although the original music for most of the hymns has been lost.[10] In some cases, later composers have written new melodies or arrangements for the lyrics.[11] Since hymns have an important and even fundamental role as a source of theology in the churches of the East, I will in the subsequent discussion of Gregory's theology draw from his hymnography, as well as his other works.

[9] *MH* 12:735–36; 14:1228–29; Terian 197–98. Terian notes that the image of the bird alighting on the cross is found in Armenian iconography but rarely in Gregory's works.

[10] Mahé 2000, 47.

[11] Some of the modern arrangements of Gregory's poetry are available in recordings. The Ode for the Holy Cross addressed to the bird appears as one of several tracks of Gregory's songs performed with instrumental accompaniment: Grigor Narekatsi, "Havik—Little Bird," track 7 of Sharakan Early Music Ensemble, *The Music of Armenia*, volume 2, Celestial Harmonies 13116–2, CD, 1996.

The Book of Lamentation

A Cathedral of Words

While his other poetic works display his brilliance and creativity, Gregory's crowning achievement is the *Book of Lamentation*, also sometimes given the title *Speaking with God* as almost all of its prayers begin with the prelude: "Speech with God from the depths of my heart." Expressing even more the intimacy felt toward this work, Armenians often just call it the *Narek*. For many Armenians, it has assumed the role of a second Bible. Some Armenians even attribute to it magical powers. The prayers comprising the work were recited, placed under pillows, even eaten for good luck.[12]

The opening of the poem, bearing the title *Threshold* or *Tenets*, states that the words of the book are intended to provide help for the afflicted by providing rules for living the penitential life and confessing one's sins.[13] The book is a "salve for incurable wounds/ effective potions for unseen pains/remedies for multifaceted life-threatening throes."[14] It is meant to move the reader or listener to tears and motivate them to pray. Gregory says that he composed the poem at the request of "the monastic fathers and many hermits." At the end of the work is his colophon in which Gregory adds that he compiled the poems in the years 1001–2 during the reign of Basil II, three years after the emperor had arrived and subsequently subdued the "enemies of the church" in Bulgaria. During

[12] See Sergio La Porta, 2007, "Translation and Transformation: Armenian Meditations on the Metamorphic Power of Language" in Sergio La Porta and D. Shulman, *The Poetics of Grammar and the Metaphysics of Sound and Sign*, Leiden: Brill, 360n39.

[13] "Threshold" is the translation in Mahé 2001; "tenets" is that of Samuelian 2001. The word in Armenian is *drut'iwnk'*, whose literal meaning of *theses* or *positions* is perhaps better captured by Samuelian's translation. The Mahés, however, plausibly connect *drut'iwnk'* to *duṛn*, "door" in order to yield *threshold*. This translation is supported also by their architectural reading of the book, which they see as having the structure of a church. According to them this opening poem is like the door of the narthex or the vestibule of the invisible church that the entire poem resembles. See Mahé 2001, 32.

[14] *MH* 12:49.10. The word here is *erkants'*, literally "labor pains," a word that recurs throughout Gregory's works.

this time, the poet "planned, structured, arranged, collected, inscribed, compiled, amplified, established in detail, and assembled into one the many facets of this sacred book" with the assistance of his brother John. His claim to have spent this time collecting and compiling the various individual poems into one structure is consistent with the hints in some of the poems that they were originally written much earlier. Thus, in Prayer 51, Gregory speaks of his "earthly father, whose care diminishes in his waning days" as though he were still alive.[15] By 1001 Khosrov would surely have been dead for at least two decades. It is plausible that Gregory began to write some of these poems as early as the 970s when his father was still alive and then added to them over the years until finally toward the end of their own lives he and his brother assembled them in their present form.

The format and style of composition is remarkable in many ways. I will mention here some of the most striking features. The book consists of ninety-five "words" or "discourses." The Armenian word is *ban*, which corresponds to the Greek word *logos* and shares much of its ambiguity and range of meaning. I follow Samuelian, though, in translating *ban* as "prayer." Perhaps a more apt translation would be "prayerful words," since in Gregory's mystical understanding, the prayer of words will one day be supplanted with a prayer of utter silence and stillness in God, the Word who is beyond all words. But since in our ordinary experience prayers are verbal, "prayer" will do as a translation of Gregory's *ban*. Although in the manuscript tradition the prayers are written as if they were prose, it is clear that Gregory intended them as verse.[16] The meter is fairly flexible; mostly Gregory favors groupings of five syllables. More striking is his extensive use of various poetic devices including alliteration, assonance, repetition, and rhyme to heighten the emotional effect of his prayers. Gregory is the first known Armenian to write poems using both internal and external rhyme, all of which were already present in oral folk poetry influenced by Arabic models. In some cases, the repetition and rhyme are intended to bring about an incantatory effect in the listener, as in the following

[15] *MH* 12:325.11–12.

[16] Mahé 2001, 163.

verses where each line begins and ends with the words *I have sinned*, which in Armenian is one word (*meghay*):

> I have sinned against your beneficence, in my worthlessness I have sinned,
> I have sinned against your ray of dawn, in my darkness I have sinned,
> I have sinned against your countless kind graces, truly I have sinned. . . .[17]

The repetitive rhythm of this prayer makes it suitable for the kind of ceaseless prayer counseled by Paul and which also accords with Anania's teaching on prayer as a spiritual exercise. It also has obvious connections with the Byzantine hesychast practice of prayer of the heart involving repetition of the phrase "Lord Jesus, have mercy on me," or the repetition of single words in the Western work *The Cloud of Unknowing*, written by an anonymous author.[18]

Some of the poems contain end rhymes. The value of the vowel of the rhyme may have some hidden significance, something that Gregory playfully suggests at one point. Prayer 26.2 ends every verse with the Armenian vowel *i*, the letter that also represents the numeral 20 in Armenian notation. Here, I take a few minor liberties in order to maintain a rhyme:

> I will affix my lamentations here in a different way,
> I will alter my bitter tears with this sound that I say,
> I will state the very same condition by way of wordplay,
> With the indivisible, mystical number ten and two convey.[19]

[17] *BL* 27.2; *MH* 12:189.11–13.

[18] The relation may be traced back to the influence of Evagrius of Pontus (345–99), who had a significant influence on the development of Armenian monasticism. Such prayer techniques were also advocated by Gregory's contemporary St. Symeon the New Theologian (949–1021), who shared with him a call for tearful prayers. There is no evidence that they knew of each other, but given the relaxation in Greek-Armenian ecclesial relations in their lifetimes and Khosrov's avowed interest in the currents of Byzantine thought, we cannot exclude such familiarity.

[19] *BL* 26.2; *MH* 185–86.

The significance of the number 20 here is unclear, and commentators continue to speculate over its meaning.[20] There is much more that should be said about Gregory's impressive use of language and rhetoric, a topic that would easily fill many books. But our focus in this book is more on the content of Gregory's works, so we should turn to another difficult question: Is there any guiding principle of the organization of the prayers?

Given that Gregory and John worked together to compile the book, it is natural to suppose some overarching logic to the organization of the ninety-five prayers. The Mahés have put forward the convincing thesis that the prayers are partitioned into three unequal parts.[21] Noticing that some of the prayers are much longer than others, they propose that these longer prayers were not extraneous insertions but serve as the boundaries or vestibules between the chambers of a church. For example, Prayer 34, which is a profession of faith in the Trinity and prayer to the Holy Spirit, is approximately twice the length of the immediately preceding and following prayers. So too is Prayer 75, an extended creed that focuses on the church. Then there is the diptych formed by Prayers 92 and 93, the former a meditation on the semantron and the latter on the holy oil or *muron* used in chrismation and ordination. Because these prayers are more traditionally theological than the other prayers, some scholars have deemed them extraneous to the book and have even excluded them from their editions. But the Mahés believe that the differences are deliberate and serve as markers of "monumental porticos" that partition the three chambers of the church. They were not the first to recognize the tripartite structure of the book, but they are the first I know of to read the architecture of a church in the book. The first part of the book, Prayers 1 to 32, constitutes the *gawit*, or narthex, of the church. The narthex served as a place for the gathering of the penitents and unbaptized who were not permitted in the sanctuary during the

[20] For example, Samuelian 2000, 197 and 744n61, who notes that twenty is the number of talents returned by the industrious servant in the parable of the three servants, specifically the version given in Luke 19:11-27 rather than Matthew 25:14-30.

[21] Mahé 2001, 168–69.

liturgy of the Eucharist. The order of dismissal of the catechumens right before eucharistic celebration remains a part of the Armenian divine liturgy, though it is rarely enforced today.[22] With the profession of faith in Prayer 34, Gregory indicates that the reader who has made it to this point is entering the nave of the church from the narthex. The focus of the previous prayers was on confession of sin and penance. Now that the faithful are prepared to enter the nave after having been baptized, they are ready to receive communion after professing the creed.[23] Although they have received the initial sacramental grace of the Eucharist, the faithful must still work to receive the supplementary graces that allow them to grow in virtue. Strengthened through participation in the sacraments, they can now pray for their enemies and discern those sins that have evaded the initial examination of their conscience. With the meditation on the church in Prayer 75 they pass into the tabernacle or sanctuary where the church is revealed as not only a visible edifice but also a spiritual temple that bridges heaven and earth. The foretaste of the kingdom and union of God that the communicants receive from the Eucharist is consummated in the last judgment. Gregory prays for the intercession of all the saints, apostles, martyrs, and angels, and especially the Mother of God, who is the focus of Prayer 80. Prayer 91 is the compline prayer as Gregory retires to sleep, followed by his awakening at the sounding of the semantron, on which the following prayer is a meditation, and his anointing of immortality with the holy chrism in Prayer 93, and ending with the dawn of the new life in Christ in Prayer 95.

While some details of the Mahés' analysis of the poem are questionable, I think that they are fundamentally correct that Gregory sees himself constructing a poem in the form of a church and that the different sections represent the different parts of the church structure, as well as the life of the faithful in the journey toward God. Gregory himself compares the words of his poem to stones

[22] Mahé 2001, 169–71. The Mahés note that there is a similar dismissal of the catechumens in Prayer 34.9—"we close the doors of life before them, the narthex of our churches"—but in fact this is a command to expel the Arian and Macedonian heretics from the narthex of the church.

[23] Mahé 2001, 173.

used to build churches, although they are, at least at first, stones that he uses to torment his sinful soul:

> And because I have made of you a target
> In front of my mind's eye,
> O my worthless soul,
> I mercilessly cast these stones
> Like pillars of words at you
> As if you were some untamed wild beast.[24]

Yet those same stones can be used to construct a building:

> May I, a sinner, afflicted, mortal,
> Receive from the beneficent Heavenly Father
> The fruit of salvation and healing
> That I may at the outset of this
> Book of lamentation and prayers
> Construct an edifice of faith.[25]

Building on the Mahé thesis of the architectural structure of the poem, I want to propose that the church of poems that Gregory has assembled is not just any church but the majestic cathedral standing on the island within view of his cave and which he must have visited on numerous occasions: the Cathedral of the Holy Cross of Aght'amar. This unique and majestic architectural achievement, the palatine cathedral of King Gagik, is alluded to at least once in his poem:

> Will I see again your holy temple,
> I who cry out with the prophet's voice,
> From the belly of the sea-monster?[26]

The reference to Jonah and the sea-monster calls to mind the relief on the cathedral's exterior wall of the prophet being thrown from the ship into the mouth of a fantastic scaly sea creature. Just as the

[24] *BL* 9.3; *MH* 12:97.47–52.
[25] *BL* 10.2; *MH* 12:101.20–24.
[26] *BL* 25.4; *MH* 12:181.79–80.

exterior walls of the cathedral are covered with bas-reliefs depicting biblical scenes and the interior walls with brilliant frescoes, so too Gregory's poem is dotted with biblical vignettes with just enough detail for anyone versed in scripture to appreciate.[27] Jonah and the sea creature make a fleeting appearance, as do Adam and Eve tempted by the serpent and eating the forbidden fruit. In Prayer 71 he writes, "I abandoned the Lord's commandment and followed the serpent's suggestion."[28] Likewise, the depiction of Isaac being bound by his father (Gen 22):

> As the first scripture gives a subtle figure
> Of a vow at the altar,
> An offering of the blood of the slaughtered,
> In the allegory of Abraham's sacrifice,
> Revealing in advance your will, O giver of life,
> To save the wretched.[29]

Like the relief on the cathedral wall of David with the Philistine giant towering over him, Gregory's prayer sings the praise of Christ's victory through the cross over Satan, prefigured by the king of Israel slaying his foe: "You unleashed the stones against Goliath with your slingshot of wood."[30]

So, too, the three youths in the furnace of Daniel 3, who appear on the southern façade of the cathedral, are celebrated in the poem:

> Like the three blessed youths,
> Who were tested in the blazing fire
> In Babylon and were not harmed,
> I sigh their song of grief.[31]

These vignettes are meant to evoke an emotional and personal connection with the biblical stories. Gregory sees himself in the

[27] For a description of the reliefs and frescoes as well as the architecture of the cathedral, see Thierry 1989, 269–84.

[28] *BL* 71.3; *MH* 12:439.97.

[29] *BL* 44.2; *MH* 12:284.31–36.

[30] *BL* 92.4; *MH* 12:555.1.

[31] *BL* 20.1; *MH* 12:152.6–9.

plight of the three young men just as he expects us to share in their experiences and aspire to their faith. His brief references to the biblical figures are glimpses of the narratives that make the depicted events as concrete and personal as the reliefs on the exterior of the cathedral.

Just as the Artsruni king envisioned his cathedral as the crown jewel of his plan to glorify God and revitalize the church, so too this great poem of lamentation represents Gregory's design to offer to God a sacrifice of prayer for the edification not only of his brother monks at Narekavank' but for "every race of rational beings/wherever they may be planted on earth."[32] It is therefore fitting that Gregory's universal poem be likened to a cathedral, especially one so prominent and within Gregory's visual field. In Armenian, cathedrals are often called catholic or universal (*kat'oghikē*) churches.[33] Gregory's poem aspires to be the literary equivalent of this architectural achievement, a canticle built in words of stone, a cathedral of poetry and song.

The Journey to God

The tripartite structure of the book not only gives it the form of a church, but each of the parts represents a stage in the development of the Christian faithful in the journey toward union with God. This connection between the three sections of the poem and the ascent to God is an insight of Sergio La Porta, who explores the relation between the structure of the poem and the three Dionysian levels of initiation: purification, illumination, and perfection.[34] Combining the insights of both the Mahés and La Porta on the significance of the tripartite structure of the *Book of Lamentation*, I devote the next three chapters to the three chambers of the cathedral, each corresponding to the three stages of spiritual development as delineated in the Pseudo-Dionysian writings. Beginning with

[32] *BL* 3.2; *MH* 12: 65.47–48.

[33] *NBHL*, second entry for *kat'oghikē*, 1032.

[34] Sergio La Porta, 2010, "Two Visions of Mysticism: The Corpus Dionysiacum and the Book of Lamentation," in Mahé et al. 2010, 243–57.

purification, I develop Gregory's theology of sin and confession in the next chapter. Then we will explore Gregory's understanding of the next stage in Christian life—illumination through the sacraments (above all, baptism and the Eucharist)—and the spiritual exercises that instill the virtues, especially the theological virtues of faith, hope, and love. The third chapter will focus on union with God. There, I will discuss Gregory's doctrine of God, specifically the Trinity and his Christology, as well as his pronouncements on *theosis* and the distinctive features of Gregory's conception of the divine. But my discussion in each of the next three chapters does not just draw from its corresponding section of the *Book of Lamentation*, for Gregory meditates on sin and confession throughout the book, although the prayers of the first part of the book especially emphasize the purification of the soul. The persistence and interweaving of these themes throughout the book are consistent with Dionysian theology. The dominant themes of one stage of Christian formation are never completely discarded or neglected in the later stages. The effects of the three levels of progression subsist in and flow from each of the three sacraments. While baptism represents the washing away of sin, it also bestows illumination on the baptized, and through the anointing with holy oil at the conclusion of baptism, the sacrament is tied to perfection and union with God.[35] Even after illumination through baptism, the baptized Christian still stands in need of penance and confession. And at the very outset during the enumeration of sins that one has committed, the penitent must keep in mind the ultimate goal of penance, which is salvation and eventual union with God. The act of penance would be a futile and perverse exercise in self-flagellation if the penitent lacked any hope of redemption. So none of the three levels of Christian formation are ever completely separated from the rest. Nevertheless, each of the parts of the poem has a discernible theme of Christian formation on which it dwells. Thus, the lengthy meditations and confessions of sin are mostly in the first

[35] Luibheid, 1987, *Ecclesiastical Hierarchy* 393A–D and 504B, where Pseudo-Dionysius states that *divine birth*—the term used for the complete rite of baptism including chrismation, a practice still observed in the Eastern churches—is called both a rite of purification and the mystery of illumination.

part of Gregory's book. And the later prayers focus more on the theme of union with God, with Prayer 93 devoted to the holy oil that in Dionysian spirituality signifies perfection and union with God.[36]

In discussing these themes, I will not only draw from the *Book of Lamentation* but from Gregory's other writings when relevant to shed light on the theological ideas underlying his poem and to show a consistency of thought that runs throughout his writings. Gregory is not a systematic theologian as traditionally conceived. He is not like Aquinas or other schoolmen, laying out clear theses backed by arguments using precise and exacting logic. But he is still a theologian, albeit a poetic theologian in the manner of Ephrem the Syrian and even St. Anselm who composed theology in the form of prayer. It will fall to us to extract the theology that underlies his poetic prayers. With these caveats in mind, let us, the unbaptized but repentant sinners, enter the narthex of Gregory's cathedral.

[36] Luibheid 1987, 224 (472D), where Pseudo-Dionysius refers to the sacrament of ointment as a "rite of perfection."

Chapter Six

Gregory's Theology of Sin and Penance

For whom does Gregory write his great poem? In the opening of the *Book of Lamentation*, he makes clear that he prepared his prayers at the request of the "hermit fathers and the multitude in the desert." Who are these hermits wandering through the wilderness? Although Gregory on occasion retreated to his grotto to seek solitude, he was foremost a cenobite dedicated to the communal life of his monastery. When he writes at greater length about his book's intended audience, it becomes evident that the wilderness is a metaphor and that it is we, his readers and hearers, who are the solitaries wandering and lost in the desert of sin. Responding to the command to compose an icon of words,[1] a new book of psalms and lamentations, he says that his poem is for all the members of the universal church, and from all the ranks and stations of society and at every stage of life:

> For those in the first hour of their lives,
> And for those called to the second,
> Having reached the age of marriage,
> And those at the end of their days,
> Frail from their advanced age.
> To both sinners and the righteous,
> To the arrogant infatuated with themselves,
> And to those reproaching themselves in self-examination,

[1] The Armenian word is *nkaragir*, which can simply mean "descriptive" but which I translate to reflect its status as a calque of the Greek word *eikonographē*, "iconograph."

To the good and the wicked,
The contemptible and the valiant,
To slaves and subordinates,
To nobles and the supernal,
To the middle class and aristocracy,
To peasants and patricians,
Men and women,
Rulers and subjects,
The elevated and the humble,
The majestic and the small,
The venerable and the commoners,
The cavaliers and infantry,
For city-dwellers and villagers,
For those subdued by the cruel bridle of insolent kings,
To hermits who converse with higher beings,
To the chaste with God-given temperance,
To the priests, chosen for their blessed piety,
To the bishops, vested in their good stewardship,
To the primates, granted the sacred duty of supervision.[2]

Following the architectural reading, here in the first part of the poem all of us stand in the narthex in preparation for the sacrament of baptism. We are gathered as unreconciled sinners together with all of the unbaptized not yet ready to enter the nave. It follows that Gregory addresses his poem to all, not only baptized Christians, but those who are not yet baptized, infants in the first hours of their lives, and all else who are candidates for baptism. Understood in this way, the church comprises all of humanity, since God seeks reconciliation and union with all people. So Gregory directs his poem to the entire world that it may satisfy the spiritual needs of all:

May this book in the form of prayers
Dispense prayers of supplication to some,
Good counsel for others;
Through the power of Your Spirit,
I have endeavored to compose these multifaceted entreaties,

[2] *BL* 3.2; *MH* 12:65–66.52–76.

And to present the petitions of all for whom I intercede
That through this book they may each day
Stand in the presence of your great compassion.[3]

His prayer intercedes for all. Although he presents his prayer in his own person, as a priest he stands before God offering the petitions and requests for remission of sins given by all people. He stresses in the later prayers that he is taking on this universal intercessory role:

I hold within myself every one of the earth,
I am an emissary offering prayers for the whole world.[4]

Addressing his monastic brothers in Prayer 72, Gregory remarks that he bears witness to and willingly assigns guilt to himself for the myriad incurable sins committed by humanity, from Adam, the first father, extending even into the future "to the end of his generations."[5] Gregory is exercising his sacerdotal authority as an intercessor between humanity and God, praying to God and asking forgiveness for the entire world.

Uncountable Sins

Concerning the question of the origin and nature of sin, Gregory expresses confusion. He understands that the primordial disobedience of Adam and Eve produced a fallen world prone to sin and rejection of God. But it is a mystery how that sin came about and why we are implicated in that first transgression. Gregory speaks of the "dark origins of the first sins."[6] The poet does not offer any precise theories on the origin or propagation of sin, as did the Julianists who believed that original sin is transmitted through sexual relations. Perhaps Gregory is trying to distance himself here

[3] *BL* 3.2; *MH* 12:66.77–82.
[4] *BL* 28.2; *MH* 12:199.52–53.
[5] *BL* 72.1; *MH* 12:445.21–25.
[6] *BL* 38.1; *MH* 12.266.3.

from Julianism, which continued in his own day to influence Armenian theology:

> In attempting to measure the depth of my perdition
> I was never able to discover its quantity;
> I strove to display it in determined words
> With the hurried beating of my mind's wings
> But I did not even comprehend its shadow.[7]

Sin itself has enervated his mind; he can no longer think clearly about how he has fallen prey to it. Even Solomon, with his legendary wisdom and comprehensive knowledge of the law, sinned:

> If Solomon stumbled this much, what will happen to me . . . ?
> From where did his love of idols come?
> Why this longing for augury?
> Didn't he remember Samuel's scolding of Saul?
> Sorcery is a sin, he said, and idols
> Only bring grief and pain [1 Sam 15:23].[8]

We cannot eradicate sin through learning and knowledge; if that were possible, the wise Solomon would not have sinned. Rather than resulting from ignorance, sin is a product of a disobedient will. We cannot understand why our will does not conform to reason but somehow as a consequence of the fall we exist in a state of obstinate insubordination to what we know to be right. Gregory's approach to sin is based on Paul's understanding of disobedience arising from the will of the flesh that is corrupt and resistant to the will of the spirit—"for I do not do the good that I want, but the evil I do not want is what I do" (Rom 7:19).

Although the origins of this disobedient will within me may be a mystery, Gregory insists that the attempt to number and identify one's sins can still be a valuable exercise. It may be bound to fail in the end, but such self-examination will bring to light many sins that previously had gone undetected. He is aware of various

[7] *BL* 26.3; *MH* 12:187.58–60.
[8] *BL* 48.3; *MH* 12:305–6.66, 85–88.

efforts to categorize the species of sin, going back to the fourth century and the work of the monastic theorist Evagrius of Pontus. Instead of Evagrius's division of sinful thoughts into eight kinds, Gregory seems to acknowledge the existence of seven sins, the number familiar to Western theology.[9] Yet these seven species of sins are compounded further into innumerable subspecies too large for the mind to consider. Ultimately the sins are too massive and unruly to enumerate. When we try to identify our sins, our exercise in compunction unveils ever more sins that had until then been hidden:

> For as many little things become immense
> Like sand amassed on the water's edge,
> Each distinct and singular in growth and origin,
> So too are my sins and transgressions countless,
> Impossible to comprehend:
> One with its progeny,
> The other with its sprouts;
> One with its blemishes,
> The other with its dangers;
> One with its thorns,
> The other with its roots.[10]

Even the effort to assign a finite number to our sins is an exercise in pride and self-deceit, a futile attempt to minimize the true extent of our culpability. The individual sins we amass within the storehouse of our souls resemble the dust from which our bodies are formed, but these grains of sin are a disordered and indefinable accretion of particles like a cancer malignantly growing out of control. This frenetic disorder within us is the reverse of the image of the triune God, serene and still, and thus reveals the extent to which we have effaced God's pristine image in us and turned it into a disordered blur. As depressing as it may be, this practice of looking within and examining one's sin is not useless. Realizing

[9] The eight "bad thoughts" of Evagrius are found in his *Practical Treatise*. See John E. Bamberger, 1981, *Evagrius Ponticus: The Praktikos, Chapters on Prayer*, Kalamazoo, MI: Cistercian Publications.

[10] *BL* 6.4; *MH* 12:36–46.

that our sins are countless, we can begin to get a sense of how sick we are and how desperately we need God's healing mercy:

> Now these are just the supreme sins,
> The corrupters of all souls;
> Arrayed under them are the subordinate parts,
> Each one of them myriads upon myriads,
> Thousands upon thousands,
> The total number of only He knows
> Who sees as deeds that have been done
> What to us seem nonexistent. . . .
>
> These I did not write in vain,
> Though I could not define the true essence of
> The diverse failings swirling within our nature.
> But I have revealed at least to an extent
> The myriads of the fruits of evil
> So that you may then contemplate the rest,
> Even if that too will be without end.[11]

Gregory makes clear that sin is a disease and God is the only effective physician. The first step of therapy is to recognize the gravity of our illness and to ask for help. That is why it is important to become aware of the extent of sin:

> Look with mercy, Lord, on this figure of bitter distress,
> The many lethal afflictions and suffering
> That I lay out before you;
> Be my companion like a physician;
> Don't summon me to court like a judge.[12]

Appropriately, God is not a stern judge but a "physician to the suffering,"[13] because sin is a spiritual disease that distorts and corrupts the soul in such a way that the image of God in which we are created is barely perceptible and made hideous:

[11] *BL* 6.5; *MH* 12:86.119–24.

[12] *BL* 23.2; *MH* 12:167.12–15.

[13] *BL* 29.1; *MH* 12:206.6.

> If I could see my soul,
> Ugly, lethargic, completely exhausted,
> I would be to the end in a state of embarrassment.[14]

The glorious human image that once resembled God has sunk not just to the state of a thoughtless brute, but even worse, into a senseless plant or stone:

> How will I say to myself that I am human
> When I esteem myself among the inhuman?
> How will I name myself a rational being
> When I consort in the foolishness of the irrational . . . ?
> Indeed, I cannot even call myself a moving or ensouled being,
> Much less one that admits of a spirit and mind.[15]

The wages of sin are themselves the twins of the sins. They are not punishments that are arbitrarily attached by God to our transgressions but reflect the nature of our actions:

> The punishments are genuine likenesses
> Of the sins whose nature they share,
> Co-images, two of a kind,
> Converging along the same path,
> Both signifying the same idea.
>
> Because I did not comfort
> My companion with the warmth of love,
> Now I am frozen with anguish
> At the first sign of danger.
>
> Because I did not rein in
> My insolent appetite,
> I rightly suffer this miserable
> Unquenchable burning [Luke 16.24].
>
> Because I did not love
> The good news of your light,
> I am justly condemned to grope about

[14] *BL* 21.3; *MH* 12:160.40–44.
[15] *BL* 21.4; *MH* 12:160.48–55.

Errantly in the snares of darkness,
In the fog of destruction.[16]

There is a logic and symmetry to the penalties for sins. If we walk away from the warmth of God by failing to warm the hearts of those who need our comfort, then neither will we be protected from the frigid indifference of others in our times of need. If we do not moderate our passions, we will be consumed with desires that can never be assuaged. And if we fail to love the light, who is Christ, the light of the gospel (John 8:12), we should not be surprised to find ourselves in darkness. Gregory asks us to see the punishments for sin as self-inflicted; they are afflictions we impose on ourselves rather than sentences handed down by God for our misdeeds. Again, Gregory rejects a juridical model of sin and instead understands it as a disease, though one that we suffer through our neglect and rejection of the physician.

Further evidence for Gregory's understanding of our sufferings not as punishments exacted in response to sin but as a natural outflowing of our wrongdoing is provided in his treatment of the Flood. In contrast to a traditional allegorical reading of the waters of the deluge as a punishment that cleanses the world of iniquity and thus prefigures the purifying water of the baptismal font, Gregory compares the flood waters to the accumulation of sins:

All the mass of torrential waters, the inundation of every sea,
That submerges even the mountaintops.
Only breathe your wind of sweetness [Gen 8:1],
As in the time of Noah,
And your power melts the mountains,
And dries the multitudes of billowing waves,
As well as my world-destroying debts,
And the towering height of my sins.[17]

God's purification of the inundated world occurs not through the water but by the Spirit that breathes upon it and dries the world of

[16] *BL* 19.3; *MH* 12:149.57–60, 63–69.

[17] *BL* 15.3; *MH* 12:128.65–71.

the overflow of sin. If we live in a world of death and desolation, it is not God's doing but rather a result of our own failure to love God. Alluding to Wisdom 1:13—"because God did not make death, and he does not delight in the death of the living"—Gregory notes that death is not a creature of God:

> You did not create death,
> Nor rejoice at our destruction,
> As David and Solomon testify.[18]

Death is a result of our own will; it is "the mature offspring of sin" (Jas 1:15).

This ruinous state into which we have willingly thrown ourselves is dire. But as burdensome and unyielding as this mass of sin seems to us in our weakness, it is a drop of rain in the eyes of God:

> How does the sin piled up throughout the world
> Appear to your eyes, Almighty, in your generosity?
> Is it not but a lump of clay, easy to crush?
> With a swift blow it is dispelled.
> Is it not but a drop of rain,
> Burst asunder and vanished at once through your will?[19]

Though it is impossible for us to heal ourselves, God willingly and with ease relieves us of the burden of sin and begins to restore us to our original state. Once we realize the seriousness of our plight and our utter dependence on God for the cure, we can begin to seek forgiveness through the confession of our sins. But the confession must be sincere and come from our hearts. It must not be merely an outward act based on fear of God's wrath. Sin penetrates into the very depth of the inner person; it is not a superficial wound. Gregory writes that "an imperceptible furnace of vehement heat burns unquenchably/an invisible crucible boiling violently, inextinguishable/piercing the depths of my heart like poisoned darts."[20]

[18] *BL* 15.4; *MH* 12:129.85–87.
[19] *BL* 74.4; *MH* 12:458.86–91.
[20] *BL* 26.3; *MH* 12:187.64–66.

Since sin permeates deeply in us, confession itself must not be a superficial act. The cure must penetrate our hearts to root out the malady there. It must not be insincere like the contrition of Achan, who confessed only after he was caught stealing money and clothing from Jericho (Josh 7:16), or Saul, whose confession Samuel rejects because it is not heartfelt (1 Kgs 15:24-26). These Old Testament examples of inauthentic confession foreshadow Judas, remorseful over his betrayal of Jesus, but only after he realized that he was condemned (Matt 27:3-4). Their forced confessions were not made, Gregory says, from perfect love and thus they were unworthy of "complete salvation."[21] Basing his thought on Anania's distinction between the inner and outer person, and the need for the two to operate in harmony, Gregory decries the emptiness of an outward act of confession, the bare utterance of the words "I have sinned" that does not flow from love.

Moreover, one must approach confession in humility and not compare oneself favorably to other sinners, as the Pharisee does with the publican of Luke 18:9-14. The penitent must genuinely believe, as Gregory asserts, that "no one is as sinful as I."[22] Addressing the monks in Prayer 72, Gregory recalls hearing one of his brother monks boast:

> I heard someone say he was not guilty;
> I was not pleased by his inappropriate speech to him
> Before whom no earthly flesh is justified,
> "I have never committed adultery,
> Nor have I ever fornicated,
> Nor tasted any of the mortal flavors of this world."[23]

Monastics, who set themselves apart from the world, are especially in danger of acquiring a sense of superiority, an arrogance

[21] *BL* 27.4; *MH* 12:191.50–54. Cf. the contrast Augustine draws between Saul and David's confessions—"while to human ears their words were the same, the divine eye saw a difference in their hearts." The passage is from Roland J. Teske and Boniface Ramsey, 2007, *Answer to Faustus, a Manichean: Contra Faustum Manichaeum*, Hyde Park, NY: New City Press, 22.67.

[22] *BL* 72.3; *MH* 12:446.50.

[23] *BL* 72.2; *MH* 12:445.26–30.

that must be vigorously resisted. Gregory intends to disabuse the monk of his conceit:

> But he was no different in his iniquity.
> May God grant him forgiveness for this.
> Even if what he had written were true,
> He did not walk but stumbled
> When he spoke the unbecoming words of Zechariah
> before the people of Israel:
> "Blessed be the Lord, for I have grown rich" [Zech 11:5],
> A foreshadowing of the Pharisee's voice.[24]

Prayer of Tears

In contrast to these inauthentic confessions, Gregory puts forward as his model of genuine contrition the sinful woman of chapter seven of Luke's gospel. She did not say a word but stood at Jesus' feet and wept behind him (7:38), washing his feet with her tears and anointing his head (7:44-46). Her example shows that it is not even necessary to utter a word to be forgiven. Gregory asks that his tears may be equally acceptable to God:

> And accept this dew of lamentation,
> The tearful weeping of my lustful eyes
> On the immaculate feet of your Incarnation, O Christ,
> My turning back to you and my confession of faith
> Prefigured by the symbol of the sinful woman's hair.[25]

But while holding the sinful woman as an ideal model for their own contrition, the penitents must also acknowledge that their love falls far short of the love that saved the woman. The virtue of humility above all is essential to proper confession. Whatever sins the woman committed, the poet's transgressions must be worse as he is not bold enough to stand near the Lord as she did:

[24] *BL* 72.2; *MH* 12:445.31–37.
[25] *BL* 32.4; *MH* 12:228.80–83.

As one who am condemned,
I cannot approach the life-giving sole of your feet
To anoint them with oil as the sinful woman
Nor to offer the drops of my eyes and hair.[26]

Once more the influence of Gregory's teacher comes out very clearly. The prayer of tears plays a central role in both Anania and Gregory's penitential exercises. Tearful prayer is, however, by no means original to the school of Narek but has a long tradition in Christian spirituality. Tears and weeping play a prominent role in Augustine's writings, most notably in the *Confessions*. The famous scene of his conversion is preceded by a "mighty storm" within the depths of his soul "accompanied by a mighty shower of tears" brought about by the sight of his accumulated miseries.[27] In Western Christianity, the gift of tears has a prominent place in the spiritual exercises of the Basque mystic St. Ignatius Loyola (1491–1556), founder of the Society of Jesus. In his second exercise, Ignatius asks for "a great and intense sorrow and tears for [his] sins."[28]

Though most likely not familiar with the *Confessions*, Anania and Gregory are probably aware of Evagrius's *On Prayer* and its call for prayer with tears. Evagrius's advice on prayer is to ask for the gift of tears in order to tame what is savage in the soul.[29] There are also numerous biblical examples of tearful supplication that inspired the two monks of Narek. Anania too presented the sorrowful penance of the sinful woman of Luke as his ideal of contrite piety and love of God.[30]

The prayer of tears has several functions in the school of Narek's spirituality. Since the tears and sighs are expressions of emotions emanating from the heart, they help to connect the external acts of penitence with an internal ardor and affection. The prayer of tears

[26] *BL* 18.5; *MH* 12:141.46–48.

[27] Augustine, 2014, *Confessions*, Carolyn J. B. Hammond, ed., Loeb Classical Library, vol. 26–27. Cambridge, MA: Harvard University Press, 8.12.28.

[28] George E. Ganss, 1991, *Ignatius of Loyola: The Spiritual Exercises and Selected Works*, Classics of Western Spirituality, New York: Paulist Press.

[29] Robert E. Sinkewicz, 2006, *Evagrius of Pontus: The Greek Ascetic Corpus*, Oxford: Oxford University Press, esp. 26–27.

[30] *MH* 10:360.3.

is not simply an external act but the manifestation of an intensely passionate affection for God. The human person is a union of both soul and body. Accordingly, there are both physical tears and also spiritual tears. It is easy to shed physical tears simply by feigning sadness or distress. But the tears that Gregory seeks to instill are deeper; they have their source in the heart. The physical tears are signs of the spiritual tears that come not from the physical eyes but from the eyes of the soul. To shed these spiritual tears, it helps to meditate on the accounts of God's mercy and love in Gregory's poem. That is why he calls his prayers "occasions for tears."[31] The exercise of reciting these prayers can assist the penitent to shed these spiritual tears.

In addition, the tears, like a powerful disinfectant, can ward off the hidden assaults unleashed on us by Satan:

> A few teardrops from the eyes
> Suffice to wither away the whole company,
> The evil hosts of the accuser,
> Like the creeping vermin, the millipedes
> oozing out faintly from the earth's miasma,
> On which a drop of oil or
> A pinch of some fatal poison falls.
>
> A slight sigh of lament rising from the soul,
> Like the blowing of the warm south wind[32]
> Mingled with the sun,
> Melts away the harshness of the frost.
> For easily born are these things,
> And easily killed are those that oppose them.[33]

The tears also have a purifying effect on the soul, washing away the accumulated dross of sin that has polluted the soul and

[31] *BL* Introduction; *MH* 12:49.15.

[32] Cf. commentary on Song 4:16—*Arise, O north one, and come, O south one*: "Now he commanded the south wind, that is the grace of the Holy Spirit, to come to the garden and melt the works of Satan. . . . [The south one] . . . is the Holy Spirit and His warm wind which melts the winter" (*MH* 12:810.120; Ervine 2007, 136).

[33] *BL* 7.1; *MH* 12.87–88.12–21.

deformed the divine image: "Accept me, Lord, and fashion me once more in the image of the Spirit/I who am unworthy of life, deserving of death, a malefactor."[34] In this sense the prayer of tears serves as a preliminary washing of sin that is consummated in baptism, preparing the soul to receive even more grace from God and to live a life of holiness. Our tears are an image of the tears that Christ himself shed in mourning the death of Lazarus (John 11.1-44):

> O beneficent Son of God,
> Restore me to life
> With the blessed dewdrops of your eyes,
> As you did your beloved friend
> From breathless death.[35]

Not only are Christ's tears a sign of his sadness at the death of his friend, but they are also dewdrops that raise Lazarus from the grave, an allegory of the morning dew that awakens the earth each day from the slumber of night. Gregory employs this image of salvific dewdrops in his commentary on the Song, where it is connected not only with the tears of Christ but also his sweat in the garden of Gethsemane. Commenting on Song 5:2—"Open to me, my sister, my neighbor, my dove, my perfect one, for my head is wet with dew and my hair with the raindrops of the night"—he writes:

> [The groom] says, "Through my sweat you have put on this purity of the dove and perfection, and have become my sister and bride. It was through my sweat that I in that night removed the sweat of the curse; and suffering with you, I endured my sweat. Now guard what you have received, that is the innocence of the dove and your perfection, and do not lose it again, for there is no second cross nor will I die a second time for you."[36]

[34] *BL* 20.7; *MH* 12:156.94–95.
[35] *BL* 18.8; *MH* 12:143.70–75.
[36] *MH* 12:817.50; Ervine 2007, 143.

This imagery has an interesting parallel in the poetry of the Carmelite doctor St. Thérèse de Lisieux (1873–97), who often uses the figure of dew to symbolize Christ's passion and sacrifice, and in this excerpt of her poetry uses the metaphor of dew to refer to Christ's tears and bloody sweat:

> Remember that on your night of agony,
> Your tears mingled with your blood.
> Dew of love, its infinite worth
> Made virginal flowers spring up.[37]

Genuine contrition that releases the tears of the soul can conquer even the gravest of sins. No matter how great our sins, if we approach penance in the right way, we need not despair. Gregory himself offers as an earlier, Old Testament example of the power and extent of God's mercy the Judean king Manasseh's reconciliation with God. Only twelve when he succeeded his father, Hezekiah, Manasseh is said to have done "evil in the eyes of the Lord," worshipping idols, practicing divination, and shedding the blood of innocents (2 Kgs 21:1-17). The accounts in 2 Kings and 2 Chronicles do not provide that much detail about Manasseh and his deeds or his penance. Gregory uses a couple of apocryphal texts to fill out the narrative. He seems familiar with the Jewish pseudepigraphical *Martyrdom of Isaiah* and its description of Manasseh's torture and murder of Isaiah, which are not explicitly mentioned in the canonical Bible. Gregory also knows the *Prayer of Manasseh* which exists in Armenian translation and may have been in his day part of the biblical canon.[38] The Bible mentions that Manasseh's prayer was a "cry heard by God" (2 Chr 33:13). Manasseh's sins are many and grave; Achan's pilfering of clothing and coins pales in comparison:

[37] St. Thérèse de Lisieux, 1996, *The Poetry of St. Thérèse de Lisieux*, Donald Kinney, OCD, ed., Washington, DC: ICS Publications.

[38] For English text and commentary on the *Prayer of Manasseh*, see Michael D. Coogan, ed., 2010, *New Oxford Annotated Apocrypha*, 4th ed., Oxford: Oxford University Press, 298–99.

He broke the wall of the Mighty One and offered to fortune tellers
The altar of the great sacrament of the sprinkling of blood.
He extended the many paths that run toward scandal,
A shepherd of perdition for the destruction of his flock,
A violent teacher of deviance,
All this while knowing the law of worship,
As his father was the great Hezekiah, the likeness of David.[39]

And yet Manasseh's contrition, unlike Achan's, was not forced but heartfelt and sincere. Therefore, God received his prayer and forgave Manasseh:

God granted him once again
Forgiveness of his sins,
And restored him to the kingdom,
So that You, Beneficient Lord, may multiply and arrange
The ineffable and unceasing praise
Among all nations and tribes, all ages and times,
And that you may keep the door of hope open for entry,
For the glory of Your exaltation,
And for my salvation, I who am condemned.
May Christ, the giver of the gifts of immortality,
Be praised forever.
Amen.[40]

If Manasseh's great crimes, including his brutality against a prophet, may be forgiven because of his sincere sorrow, we need not lose hope over the weight of our sins. Gregory refers to the story of Manasseh as a "faint image" of the gospel of God's mercy and forgiveness wrapped up within the veil of the Old Testament. For he says that while the Old Testament emphasizes the justice rather than mercy of God and is an "effaced letter" that serves to condemn sinners, it also contains depictions of God's extraordinary mercy, a foreshadowing of the mercy proclaimed by Christ in the New Testament.[41]

[39] *BL* 51.4; *MH* 12:330.101–7.
[40] *BL* 51.5; *MH* 12.331.125–36.
[41] *BL* 51.4; *MH* 12.327–28.56–60.

Gregory's plea for sincere and reflective confession must be understood in the context of a general concern about the practice of confession in his time. Confession of sins is mentioned in the New Testament and early Christian texts like the Didachē, a short catechism written in the first century and attributed to the apostles, but its implementation took different forms depending on the time and location.[42] Both individual and collective forms of confession seem to have existed from the beginning of the Armenian Christian tradition. The two practices may have alternated throughout the centuries, with private and more spontaneous confession sometimes dominating and at other times a public and more formulaic mode prevailing. In Gregory's time, reconciliation generally followed a conventional recitation of sins by the penitents. That, at least, is the conclusion that we can draw from a letter, cited by the Mahés, written by the Syrian patriarch John (Yōhannān) bar Shushan to the Armenian catholicos Gregory II Vkayasēr ("the Martyrophile," *r.* 1065–1105) criticizing a method of confession that simply enumerated sins, even ones that the patriarch considered outlandish.[43] The patriarch's concern was that this contrived approach to confession did not encourage the proper contrition necessary for genuine reconciliation. We have already seen Mkhit'ar Gosh's fable of the corrupt priest and his congregation of birds that implied abuse of the sacrament was a problem at least during the twelfth century, but most likely even earlier. Gregory himself is seeking to instill in the faithful a more fervent, personal penance in opposition to the passionless expression of remorse promoted by the recitation of a formal statement of confession.

[42] See Bart Ehrman, trans., 2003, *The Apostolic Fathers,* vol. 1, Cambridge, MA: Harvard University Press, 438–39.

[43] Mahé 2001, 122. For the Armenian text of this letter, H.A. Vardanean 1923, *Yovhannēs Bar-Shushan Hayots' Kat'oghikosin grats t'ught'ĕ*, Vienna: Mkhitarean Press. The Mahés state that by the twelfth century there was a return to private confession, citing the existence of penitential manuals from that period, particularly that of David of Ganjak. But this genre is rare in Armenian literature and Ganjak is on the periphery of the Armenian world, so this revival or return to personal modes of confession may have been rather restricted in its scope.

Gregory's focus on confession thus was occasioned in part by the need to instruct the faithful in proper penance. He emphasized the need for the penitent to turn inward and through the prayer of tears and lamentation allow the words of the confessional to penetrate one's heart and kindle a love of God, a corrective to a superficial and mechanical approach to confession. Yet we should not think that confession is ever adequate if it is simply a withdrawal into oneself done to the exclusion of one's relation with the church and fellow penitents. Gregory sets his main professions of sin here in the first part of his poem, the narthex of the cathedral, in which we are surrounded by our fellow penitents seeking entry into God's house. Sin is never a solitary affair. Gregory is well aware of the impact of the first sin on all the generations of human beings. Since humanity sank into iniquity as a whole, redemption is only possible collectively as one body standing before God and through the mediation of the church and its priests. When Gregory offers his prayers of penance, it is always in solidarity with another sinner, usually a figure drawn from the Bible. In this case it is again Manasseh with whom the poet identifies:

> And now, joining my laments with those of the great sinner,
> He who willingly sinned unto death,
> I will repeat his cry and say with him,
> "I have sinned, Lord, I have sinned;
> To my lawlessness I myself testify." (cf. *Prayer of Manasseh* 12)[44]

Throughout the book Gregory imagines himself with biblical persons and asks that he be granted the same graces that they were. For example, he adduces the man blind from birth of John 9:1 and asks to be healed of his spiritual blindness just as the man in the gospel is cured of his physical blindness.[45] Even more dramatically, he imagines himself imprisoned with the captive souls of hell pleading for Christ to release them from their bondage.[46] These supplications for God's salvation indicate that confession is

[44] *BL* 47.2; *MH* 12:299–300.8–10.
[45] *BL* 18.4; *MH* 12:141.35–40.
[46] *BL* 18.10; *MH* 12:144.94–97.

a communal act done in solidarity with those who share our afflictions.

Millennial Concerns

One might think that Gregory's preoccupation with sin and confession is driven by an urgent resolve to call people to penance in anticipation of the turn of the millennium, when many Christians expected Christ's imminent return. While we cannot preclude that such apocalyptic concerns affected Gregory's thinking, we should first keep in mind that for the Armenians the millennial year would have been counted as 450 because their calendar was set at year 1 at the Council of Duin in 551. Nevertheless, people would have been aware, as they clearly were in Byzantium, that the thousandth anniversary of Christ's birth, and three decades after that (his resurrection), was drawing near and that the end of this world may have been imminent. That expectation may help to explain one of the great enduring mysteries of Byzantine history, why the emperor Basil II never married. Basil's behavior is highly unusual, given that monarchs are usually very anxious about their succession. But it could be explained if Basil believed that the end of his earthly empire was near and that no ruler but Christ would henceforth be needed.[47]

Whatever conclusions Basil may have drawn from calendrical speculation, Gregory did not think that the turn of the millennium would presage the end of the world. In the commentary on the Song, he states that in the eighth millennium the saints will be glorified in Christ.[48] Since the incarnation occurred at the beginning of the sixth millennium, the world still had, in Gregory's reckoning, about a thousand years to go before the *parousia*, or second coming. While concerns about the millennium may have been on many people's minds during Gregory's life, there is no indication that his urgent call for penance and vigilance is due to the calen-

[47] "Basil II" in Alexander P. Kazhdan, 1991, *The Oxford Dictionary of Byzantium*, vol. 1, Oxford: Oxford Unversity Press, 261–62.

[48] *MH* 12:839.53; Ervine 2007, 166 and 122n151.

dar. Given his fondness for the parable of the wise and foolish virgins, he believed that Christians must be ready at all times to meet the Lord regardless of the hour or year. It is much more likely that Gregory was troubled by indifference to the sacrament of confession rather than any specific apocalyptic presentiment, and thus he offered his great book as a series of spiritual exercises that would renew and revitalize the discipline of penance.

These exercises of purification are demanding and fraught with danger if not done with the proper direction. That is why this work is first addressed to the monks, who constitute the frontline in spiritual battles. They are supposed to provide the necessary education so that the faithful can benefit from the healing that the *Book of Lamentation* is meant to offer. With the proper instruction, the faithful will be prepared to receive the grace of absolution. For even though these exercises demand the serious efforts of the individual Christian in the path toward reconciliation and union with God, Gregory never lets us lose sight of the essential role of grace in every step of this journey. Without the grace freely dispensed by God, the way leads nowhere and any attempt to reach God is futile. Gregory impresses this point on us in Prayer 31:

> More than to my works I hold fast to your grace,
> Many times more exalted and glorious,
> More sublime than the weight of my words.
> There is but one forgiveness of sins,
> The conciliator and mighty redeemer of my agitation.[49]

Gregory includes the remission of sins together with baptism and ordination in his poetic discourse on the church and its unity in Prayer 75, indicating that he recognizes it as a distinct sacrament entrusted exclusively to the church through which God's graces flow:

> There is but one forgiveness of sins,
> More through grace than acts of penance,
> So that the truth not be confounded with appearance.[50]

[49] *BL* 31.2; *MH* 12:219–20.39–42.
[50] *BL* 75.7; *MH* 12:469.7.

Having confessed our sins and received the grace of absolution, we now stand at the threshold of the nave prepared to receive the sacrament of baptism that will mark our transition to the next stage, the life of holiness and virtue pursued by the baptized faithful.

Chapter Seven
Baptism, Eucharist, and the Virtuous Life

A Sacramental Vision

According to Pseudo-Dionysius, those who ascend to the second level of Christian initiation "enter upon the contemplation of certain sacred things and being well purified, they commune in these sacred things to the extent possible for them."[1] This second stage in the journey to God is illumination. Through participation in the sacraments, above all the Eucharist, and through their continued advance in learning and contemplation of holy things, the faithful progress toward a greater love of God and come to reflect his glory ever more brilliantly.

For Origen this intermediate station in the ascent to God corresponds to the teachings of the book of Ecclesiastes.[2] Certainly the author of the book, traditionally held to be Solomon, wanted to convey the empiness of material concerns. That is why Gregory refers to it as the "vanities," identifying the book with its opening statement—*Vanity of vanities, all is vanity* (Eccl 1:2).[3] The notion that the natural world is filled with vanity—things that seem to have great value but are in truth empty—courses throughout Ecclesiastes. The author has learned to hate life because all the work done under the sun was evil (2:17). No one is ever satisfied when they acquire what they covet. The man who loves money is not satisfied with his wealth (5:9). Everything that appears good perishes

[1] Luibheid 1987, 244 (532B–C).

[2] Louth 1981, 54–61; Greer 1979, 241.

[3] *BL* 48.5; *MH* 12:308.123.

and is given over to death, a power over which no one has authority (8:8) but which consumes all else.

As pessimistic an assessment of the world as this may be, Ecclesiastes recognizes something of lasting value. Wisdom excels foolishness as light excels darkness (2:13). But what is true wisdom? It is to fear God and keep his commandments (12:14). For all the goodness in the world is from God, who has made everything beautiful in its time (3:11). And so the wise look at the things of this world and see a dim reflection of the divine splendor. Thus is the world redeemed and made whole.

Understood in this way, Ecclesiastes provides us with a sacramental vision of the world. A sacrament in the broadest sense is God's use of a material thing, something that may have little value but from which divine graces flow and through which we encounter God. The bread and wine of the Eucharist are merely material substances but through their consecration they become something more: our offering to God and God's offering of himself back to us. The water of the font may be mere bathwater, as Gregory says the T'ondrakeans believed, but when it is sanctified it becomes more than water. It becomes the instrument by which the faithful are restored to the original state of glory washed of sin and brought into the body of Christ. So Gregory makes clear:

> We believe that in our descent into the luminous font,
> And through the washing of our flesh,
> We assume holiness.[4]

The Armenian word that I translate as "luminous font" literally means a place of illumination, and it is used in religious contexts to refer to the baptistry. This linguistic association of baptism with light makes clear the relation between baptism and illumination.

But, more broadly, whenever we reflect on the presence of God in the world and evaluate things in the manner of Ecclesiastes, we are experiencing the kind of illumination familiar from the Dionysian tradition. This is what it means "to commune with the divine

[4] *BL* 93.3; *MH* 12:568.3.

symbols" for the sacraments are material symbols of the divine.[5] By extension, the entire world, being God's creation, consists of signs and symbols pointing to God and reflecting in their own finite ways the divine glory. In this chapter I will present more fully Gregory's teachings on the sacraments, particularly baptism and the Eucharist, and how we are expected to live in order to reflect more clearly God's glory in our own lives. Since for Gregory the sacraments are mediated through the church, and we now have left the narthex to be received into the congregation that comes together in the body of Christ, I will also discuss Gregory's ecclesiology, his understanding of what the church is.

Faith, Hope, Love, Baptism

In his anti-Chalcedonian treatise, Anania of Narek argued that Chalcedonians had to be rebaptized in order to be received into the Armenian church.[6] This matter was clearly a sore point between the Byzantines and Armenians now that the period of mutual tolerance had come to an end. Anania's argument was based on a presumption that the Chalcedonians believed that Christ died only in his human and not divine nature. For, according to Romans 6:3, all who are baptized into Christ are baptized into his death. Yet Chalcedonian baptism, Anania claims, is only baptism into the death of a man and therefore cannot be a means of salvation. Consequently, such baptism is invalid. The question of rebaptism was by no means peculiar to the christological controversies of this time. Much earlier, the church in North Africa was plagued by similar debates concerning the validity of baptisms performed by priests who had collaborated with the Roman authorities rather than undergo martyrdom. There, the matter was not over the validity of the sacraments of heretics but rather the conduct of the priests administering baptism. No less a figure than Augustine entered the debate on the side of those who did not require rebaptism

[5] Cf. Luibheid 1987, 244 (532B–C).
[6] Cf. *MH* 12:483.26–28.

and argued for the validity of the baptism performed by the compromised priests.

Characteristically, Gregory does not explicitly take a stand on the rebaptism question, but several lines of Prayer 93 indicate that he opposed the position of his teacher and recognized the validity of baptism even in Chalcedonian churches:

> For in [the Church] there is but one washing
> Into the death of Christ, lest his Divinity,
> Offered freely to those who do not know him,
> Suffer a second death for those who already do.[7]

Gregory alludes here to Hebrews 6:4-6:

> For it is impossible for those who were once illuminated, and have tasted the heavenly gift, and have become partakers of the Holy Spirit, and have tasted the good word of God and the powers of the age to come, if they fall away, to renew them again to repentance, since they crucify again for themselves the Son of God, and put Him to open shame.

The author of Hebrews is talking about baptized Christians who have fallen away from the faith. The letter addresses Jewish Christians who are contemplating a return to Judaism. In that context, it is a harsh doctrine that seems to preclude any return to Christianity after an act of apostasy. But in the context of tenth-century Armenia, with the attention of the church authorities on the validity of the baptism of distinct communions, Gregory applies these verses to the opposite effect: lenience toward Chalcedonians and acceptance of the validity of their sacraments lest by demanding rebaptism we risk crucifying Christ a second time. Those who received the rites of initiation in Chalcedonian churches, Gregory implies, already know Christ and so are not in need of rebaptism. But these verses are also directed against the Byzantines, who had themselves begun to require rebaptism of non-Chalcedonians. Against the general deterioration in relations between the two

[7] *BL* 75.7; *MH* 12:468–9:5.

communions at the end of the tenth century, Gregory continued to affirm the unity of the churches who, in the words of Ephesians 4:5, share "one Lord, one faith, one baptism."

In the Armenian rite of baptism, the officiating priest asks the sponsor what the candidate for baptism requests. The answer is "faith, hope, love, and baptism . . . to be cleansed of sins . . . and to serve God."[8] Through the initiation of baptism the candidate begins to enter fully into the Christian life and is prepared to receive the full graces of the Spirit and to grow in virtue, especially the three theological virtues of 1 Corinthians 13:13: faith, hope, and love.

For Gregory, these three form a trinity that mirrors the trinitarian God:

> [Faith] is honored in the name of the glorified Trinity
> Together with love and hope.
> For these three exist separately,
> But if you view them as the same,
> United in one mystery
> You will always be magnified in God,
> For if you believe in Him
> You will also love Him,
> And through love you will have hope in
> His invisible gifts.[9]

Without faith, we cannot come near to God or receive his salvation:

> For not even the Lord of glory
> Will work his miraculous powers on us
> Without first asking that our faith be tied
> To the same yoke as his bounty.
> It has the power to give life,
> Sufficient to itself, being near God,
> For "Your faith has made you well" (Matt 9:22)
> The blessed mouth of God testified.[10]

[8] Mesrob Tashjian et al., 1992, *The Rituals of the Armenian Apostolic Church*, New York: The Armenian Prelacy, 39.

[9] *BL* 10.4; *MH* 12:103–104.69–75.

[10] *BL* 10.3; *MH* 12:102–103.47–54.

The power of faith is revealed by the gospel accounts of Jesus' healings. The author of Hebrews asserts that faith is "the assurance of things hoped for, the conviction of things not seen" (Heb 1:11). The apostles and the people whom Christ healed witnessed with their own eyes Christ's miracles. They did not need the same faith that we need to believe because Christ was visibly with them. The disciples saw the risen Christ. But even those who had seen, like Thomas, needed faith to believe. We who do not see Christ with our physical eyes and are not touched by his physical hands may still see and be blessed by Christ through our faith in his presence. Faith is the virtue that spans the distance between us and Christ, and it is faith that brings us near to God. While many of the examples in the gospels of Christ's healing are done through his physical presence and the laying of his hands on the sick, the example of the centurion (in the version of Luke 7:1-10) shows that through faith one can be healed from a distance:

> There is no room for doubt in your word
> Nor any indication of uncertainty
> Between your will and mercy,
> But you will to heal, for you are compassionate,
> And you can heal, for you are the Creator,
> Say only the word and I will be healed,
> Let me join the centurion in his faith.[11]

The curing of the centurion's servant is an important example because it is done at a spatial distance and vicariously through the centurion's faith. For Gregory, the servant's healing shows us that, even though we are separated in physical time and space from Jesus, we, too, may be restored to health with the same faith as the centurion's. The sick servant was only a few tents removed from Christ, while we are even farther removed. But still through faith Christ is near and with us:

> And it is not only when you are a short distance away,
> Being as far away as one tent from another

[11] *BL* 17.3; *MH* 12:137.72–78.

That I believe your power is effective
For resurrection and healing
But even when you are seated on high in heaven,
Or fully in the bowels of the earth.[12]

The import of these verses for the infinite reach of Christ's resurrection and healing is lost in translation because the Armenian contains an ambiguity that is difficult, if not impossible, to represent in English. The word that bears a double meaning in Armenian is translated here as "tent." Read literally, it refers to the dwellings in Capernaum and signifies that Christ neither met the centurion nor his servant, but healed the servant through the centurion's envoys, the Jewish elders and his friends (Luke 7:3, 6). Jesus literally remained several tents away from the centurion's home where his sick servant lay. Still, through the centurion's faith, he and his servant encountered Christ and found salvation. But the Armenian word that means "tent"—*khoran*—also refers to a tabernacle or the canopy of an altar. The implication here is that even though Jesus is no longer with us as a man walking on earth, he is still fully present to us on the altar. His sacrifice on the divine altar of the cross is brought down to us and placed on the altar of the Eucharist. There is thus a eucharistic aspect to this account of healing. We are in a position similar to that of the centurion. We encounter Christ not as his disciples did, as a man walking the earth, but through the grace of the Eucharist that is mediated through Christ's envoys, the elders, who are the priests, a word derived from the Greek word *presbyter*, which means "elder."

I read the last line of these verses differently from other translators. Both Samuelian and Mahé translate the last two lines as "over the whole world below." But I understand this last line to be a reference to Christ's descent into the bowels of the earth after his death and before his resurrection.[13] On my reading Gregory's point is that not only when Christ is seated at the right hand of the Father in heaven but even in death, when he descended into hell,

[12] *BL* 17.3; *MH* 12:137.79–84.

[13] The Armenian is *i storins erkri*. See the entry for *stor* in *NBHL* 747, which defines it strictly in the sense of "under, below," so the verse must mean "below the earth."

his saving graces still operate on earth. Thus, when Gregory says that faith brings us next to God, he means that however removed we may be from the physical presence of Christ on earth, through our faith and through our participation in the Eucharist, itself an act that proceeds from faith, we remain near Christ and are healed through his spiritual touch.

The Trinitarian analogy that Gregory applies to the theological virtues entails that all three share the same nature even though they may be distinct in their relations to each other, with love proceeding from faith, and hope coming from love. There is a unity of virtue, so that whenever faith increases, love also deepens and hope is strengthened. As the three virtues blossom in the soul, the soul begins to recover its divine image as it more clearly reflects the Trinitarian image through the three virtues. It is not the case that the Trinitarian image is ever completely lost even at the lowest depths of the soul's sinfulness. Though it is a warped and deformed trinity, the image is still apparent in the threefold nature of its depravity. The poet conveys the tarnished Trinitarian image through the verses that describe his fallen state in triplets: "wandering, exiled, spurned" and "filled with doubt, miserable, dejected":

> Ashamed, trampled upon by the Accuser,
> Delivered over to incurable ills,
> I have reached the bottom of death,
> Deformed, your call has found me vile,
> Fallen suddenly into destruction;
> Wandering, exiled, spurned;
> Filled with doubt, miserable, dejected;
> Overthrown, crushed, broken;
> Afflicted, saddened in my soul, reproved.[14]

Even in the most hopeless and desperate of conditions, the underlying divine image appears in a dim and shadowy form. And that is enough to give the poet hope for salvation. As his soul is cleansed of its impurities, he begins to manifest the three virtues and more clearly display the splendor of the divine image within him.

[14] *BL* 20.7; *MH* 12:156–7.96–104.

The path toward God begins with faith, even faith that is as small and insignificant as a mustard seed:

For if there is just a little seed,
Faith as small as a mustard grain,
It will have the power to move the greatest mountains
Into the heart of the sea.
Therefore, let us accept this gift
As the first path toward the author of life.[15]

Strengthened by faith, one will also have hope in God's gifts. For if we believe in the resurrection and Christ's triumph over death, we will also believe that he can restore us to life from the death of sin:

Even the sinner drained by sorrow,
All expectation of goodness removed,
All certainty of grace lost,
Can still hope once more to attain
Anew the glorious ornaments of the first gifts.
For it is from God that this hope is prepared and acts in us.
This hope proclaims the good news of the almighty power of its giver;
In this hope God smells the pleasant incense,
Sweeter than any perfume,
More than the mixture once broiled in the service of the tabernacle,
It is a figure of the humble soul laid low by its dissolution,
Reaching to union in its likeness.[16]

The broiled mixture of the tabernacle is a reference to Exodus 30:7-8 and the altar of incense on which Aaron is commanded to burn "a perpetual incense before the Lord throughout your generations." Like this fragrant incense, a figure of our soul aspiring to reach God, so too is the hope of the humble soul that wafts into heaven and is pleasing to God.

If we live a life of faith and repent for our sins, then we, too, may have hope for the future. Just as Gregory invoked the story of Manasseh as an Old Testament model of penance that prefigures

[15] *BL* 10.4; *MH* 12:103.62–65.
[16] *BL* 11.2; *MH* 12:106–7.31–42.

God's forbearance and mercy under the new covenant, so too the example of Enoch shows us that through a life of faith and repentance death can be overcome:

> Even before the giving of the Law
> He who guarded the ancestral traditions,
> So that he was closer to our first father in faith,
> Took the ancestral debt to be his own,
> Made amends for it by dulling his passions,
> And instead of being forgiven by being interred,
> But because he was tormented in the flesh,
> He was taken up,
> A precursor of the life of rational beings,
> Triumphing mightily over the grip of death.[17]

This Enoch is not the son of Cain mentioned in Genesis 4:17 but the father of Methusaleh who appears in Genesis 5:18-24. The assertion in Genesis 5:24—"Enoch walked with God; then he was no more for God took him"—is cryptic and does not provide much detail for understanding the significance Enoch has for Gregory. The phrase "he was taken up" is based on Sirach 44:16: "Enoch pleased the Lord and was taken up, an example of repentance to all generations." The more detailed background that Gregory alludes to comes from Armenian apocryphal literature. Michael Stone cites an Armenian miscellany in which Enoch is said to abstain from eating and did not look at the heavens, making him the first penitent.[18] As such he is a figure of hope for those who follow his prac-

[17] *BL* 11.3; *MH* 12:108–9.70–78.

[18] Michael E. Stone, 1982, *Armenian Apocrypha Relating to the Patriarchs and Prophets*, Jerusalem: Israel Academy of Sciences and Humanities. Also in *Good Tidings of Seth* 10–16, translated in Lipscomb 1990, 191–92, it is said that Enoch did not marry, planted an orchard but did not eat of its fruit, and wore an iron helmet so as not to look at the fruit. In the *Descendants of Adam*, he covers his face with a linen cloth so as not to look at heaven. See Michael Stone, 2010, "Some Texts on Enoch in the Armenian Tradition" in Jeffrey Stackert, Barbara N. Porter, David P. Wright, and I. Tzvi Abusch, 2010, *Gazing on the Deep: Ancient Near Eastern and other studies in honor of Tsvi Abusch*, Bethesda, MD: CDL Press, 525–26.

tices of penitence. For through his acts of piety and asceticism, Enoch was freed from the curse of Adam and the inherited bondage of death. And if this act of God's mercy took place under the old covenant, Gregory asks rhetorically, how much greater should be our "hope in the new and pure illumination/without veil or shadow/through Christ our Lord's covenant"?[19]

Indeed, when Gregory turns to the New Testament accounts of healing and resurrection, he emphasizes how Christ's grace is given to all who simply believe in his word without their having to undergo Enoch's arduous asceticism. The examples he brings forward show that Christ's mercy and compassion are boundless and offered to all. We have already discussed the example of the centurion, but the centurion's faith took some effort on his part as he had to send his emissaries to meet Christ. The other examples show Christ's miraculous mercy bestowed on those who are reduced to complete passivity and lack any capacity to move toward Christ. In these cases of total infirmity, it is Jesus who comes to the person in dire need. Jesus' urgent advance toward the afflicted is best revealed in the story of the good Samaritan (Luke 10:25-37), perhaps the most familiar of the gospel parables.

Gregory devotes Prayer 14 to this parable. Modern interpretation of this story has focused on the moral applications of its lesson. The good neighbor is the one who helps people in need even if doing so may be dangerous. And there are good people in all nations, including the Samaritans, against whom Jesus' audience harbored strong prejudices. But Gregory's approach to the parable is different. His portrayal is based on the ancient tradition of Christian interpretation that reads the story as an allegory. While this allegorical approach does not exclude the moral reading, it also understands the characters and figures of the story as symbols. As usual, although Gregory follows this allegorical tradition, he also displays his originality. Instead of simply presenting a breakdown of the symbolism, he asks us to imagine ourselves in the place of the traveler who has been severely beaten and left for dead:

[19] *BL* 11.4; *MH* 12:109.88–89.

There is no indication that he cried out to you
When he was pierced by the robbers' sword,
For he was petrified;
He could not even let out a groan,
For he was unable to speak;

Nor with trembling fingers
Could he point out to you who see all
The vicious assault he suffered,
For he had been badly bruised.[20]

But just as our compassion for the victim builds, we are told that he is an unrepentant sinner:

He could not fix his eyes,
Filled with plaintive tears of sadness
On you, Beneficent One,
For he was a sinner;

Nor did he try to move your compassionate heart
By showing you his crushed body,
His blood-stained clothes,
For he was without hope.[21]

Does that change our attitude toward him? Do we try to justify the violence done to him because he was a sinner? We might think: he was traveling on a dangerous road; he should have known the risks; he should have known better. We may think this way when we hear about someone in trouble and needing help, but the good Samaritan does not. He does not judge the victim but simply acts to help the beaten man and restore him to health. The difference between us and the good Samaritan is like the difference between sinners, judging others and perhaps blaming them for their misfortunes, and Christ, who simply aids those who are downtrodden, knowing that they may never repent of their sins. Indeed, Gregory makes it very clear that the good Samaritan symbolizes Christ:

[20] *BL* 14.2; *MH* 12:120.7-13.

[21] *BL* 14.2; *MH* 12:120-1.14-20.

But You, Benefactor of myriad gifts,
Without fault, Giver of all life,
Not only did you not keep a memory
Of his wicked, sinful deeds,
But you did not even reproach him;
You did not trample him with your feet
When he fell,
But you ran to him with affection,
Showing him the utmost care.[22]

The connection between the Samaritan and Christ is not new. It predates Gregory by more than 700 years. It is first found in the writings of Origen. Gregory probably knew about Origen's allegorical reading from the eighth-century gospel commentary of Stephen of Siwnik'. Stephen was well-versed in Greek patristic texts, especially the works of Origen, and he rarely shies away from displaying his erudition. Here is what, following Origen, he wrote in his commentary on the Gospels:

> The man who was going down from Jerusalem to Jericho signifies Adam and all those who sin in imitation of Adam's transgressions. Jerusalem signifies the paradise from which they were expelled and Jericho this world which he entered after leaving paradise. The robbers signify Satan and his legions. . . . The priest and the Levite signify, it seems to me, the prophets and teachers who came before Christ. The Samaritan is Christ, for He was called both a Samaritan and a demoniac [John 8:48].[23]

Not only was Christ accused of being a Samaritan, but also the question, "Who is my neighbor?" which occasioned the telling of the parable, brings to mind the Song of Songs in the Old Testament. The bride and groom refer to each other periodically as neighbor. In Song 5:16—"this is my beloved, my neighbor, O daughters of Jerusalem!"—the bride lovingly describes her groom to her attendants. Readers of English translations will miss this, because most English translations render the word for neighbor as

[22] *BL* 14.3; *MH* 12:131-36.
[23] *MH* 6:221.4.

friend (see, for example, the NRSV). But the word in the Song that the bride uses to describe her groom is exactly the same word in Greek (and Armenian) in the lawyer's question to Jesus, "Who is my *neighbor*?" Thus, there is already in the Old Testament a symbolic prefiguring of Christ as the true neighbor.

The allegorical reading that the ancient interpreters preferred does not obviate the moral reading. The vocation of Christians is to live like Christ and, ultimately, unite with him and become like God. Christ ends his parable by commanding his listeners to show the same mercy that the Samaritan did (Luke 10:37). The parable is therefore not only an allegory about Christ and the unfolding of salvation in history, but also about how Christians are to live. They are called to be like the good Samaritan, not the priest or Levite, because the good Samaritan acted as Christ. We should not think of these two interpretations as mutually exclusive. They are in fact perfectly complementary, since Christ, as perfect man, exemplifies what humans are meant to be.

Later in the same poem Gregory continues to reflect on the Samaritan. He states that the word "Samaritan" means guard, and he alludes to the biblical account of the Samaritans' origins:

> Like the pagans of Assyria whose name means guard
> Because they received the Law from the Jews,
> And did not forget it as they did,
> But guarded it in its entirety.
> You have come to unite Yourself with us.[24]

Here, Gregory is referring to the passage in 2 Kings 17:24-28, in which the inhabitants of Samaria are said to be the descendants of Babylonians settled there by the Assyrian king. Because they were not pious, the Lord sent lions that devoured some of them. As a result, the king dispatched a priest from among the exiled Jews who taught them the Law. According to the Samaritans, at least, they guarded the Law while the Hebrews deviated from their own traditions. This reference to the Assyrian origin of the Samaritans and Gregory's affirmation that they are the true guardians of the tradi-

[24] *BL* 14.3; *MH* 12:122.49–52.

tions of Israel has a special significance since, as we know, the Artsruni dynasty claimed descent from the Assyrian king Sennacherib. Gregory was no doubt aware that by implying a relation between the Artsruni and the Samaritans (and thus, at least symbolically, with Christ) he would enhance the standing of his Artsruni rulers over the Bagratuni. This is a rare and subtle instance of Gregory's nod to Artsruni political aspirations in his poem, which alludes sparingly to specific local landmarks and circumstances, perhaps in order to accentuate the universal appeal of the prayers.

Encouraged by the accounts of God's bountiful grace extended to both Enoch and the beaten traveler, and filled with the hope of God's love, Gregory exults:

> But taking refuge in this shadowless confidence,
> I who was laid low am raised;
> Once miserable,
> I have conquered;
> Having been deceived,
> now I am converted to life;
> From the most miserable evil deeds,
> I have come to hope;
> I was handed over to death,
> But now I am restored to life;
> Once combative and quarrelsome,
> Now I am forgiving.[25]

Love completes the trinity of virtues that the baptized faithful are called to perfect in order to restore in themselves the image of God. Of the three virtues, it is love that scripture most clearly identifies with God. Paul says it is the greatest of the theological virtues (1 Cor 13:13). So the life of faith and hope culminates in love of God and love of neighbor. Yet this love is not selective but offered to all. Its highest form is a seemingly incoherent form of love: the love of one's enemies. For Gregory, love is perfected when it goes beyond the natural love of friends and neighbors

[25] *BL* 11.5; *MH* 12:110.103–9.

and is offered to those who revile and persecute us. To possess this supernatural love, we need the greatest of grace. But it is only by achieving this most extraordinary form of love that we can dare approach God's love.

> Remember your magnanimity, Lord,
> In regarding my unworthiness,
> And with my prayer that good come to my enemies,
> May you too work your ineffable miracles on them,
> In accordance with your magnanimity;
> Do not destroy those who oppress me,
> But convert them, uproot our vile ways,
> And plant goodness in me and them.[26]

God's love extends to all, even to the souls in hell, as we have seen in the hymn of the crucified lion. Gregory remembers these tormented souls also in the *Book of Lamentation*:

> You turned the shadow of death into dawn,
> as the prophet says,
> And willingly descended into Tartarus,
> To the prison of the ones confined below,
> Whose door was closed even to prayers,
> You cut the destructive bond of death
> That held captive the plundered souls exiled there,
> You scattered all thoughts of sin.[27]

The author of Ecclesiastes thought that death would overpower all else (Eccl 8:8) while the author of the Song recognizes love as equal in strength to death (Song 8:6). But Christ's love vanquishes even death. Now we can speak more boldly than Solomon as we apprehend more clearly that this greatest of loves—the love of the wicked and accursed—is even stronger than death and transcends all other forms of love. To be fully in the image of God means that we too must share in Christ's love for sinners and for enemies, for those who crucify him and us.

[26] *BL* 83.2; *MH* 12:516.27–31.
[27] *BL* 16.1; *MH* 12:131–32.19–25.

For Gregory, the root of such love is found in humility, the virtue that Anania especially praised in his writings. Humility requires that we not judge others nor condemn them for their sins. It demands us to recognize that God offers his love to all regardless of their sin:

> You created all, and all are yours,
> You have mercy on all, you alone are compassionate,
> For although they sin, they are yours,
> They are in your accounting.[28]

It is not our place to judge others or to claim to know who is righteous and who is an unrepentant sinner in God's eyes. This forbearance toward others manifests the same refusal to judge found in the sayings of the desert ascetics. Inspired by their model, Gregory insists that we reserve all judgment to God and approach others in a spirit of humility:

> I am never fit to judge correctly
> About who among the earth-born
> Is predestined to be your heir;
> You alone reproach with impartiality,
> By the authority of your righteousness,
> The impious who seem pure
> And the prostitutes who repent.[29]

This humility born of contrition allows us to love others even though they sin. The love Christ embodied is the love that scandalously ate with and ministered to the poor and oppressed, the criminals and prostitutes. That love is the one Gregory desires to imitate, but which he realizes he can only achieve through God's grace. He reads the admonition of Proverbs 25:6—"Do not put yourself forward in the presence of the king, or stand in the places of the great"—and its echo of Christ's words in Luke 14:8-10—"When you are invited to a wedding feast, do not sit down in the

[28] *BL* 31.4; *MH* 12:221.81-83.
[29] *BL* 31.4: *MH* 12:222–23.101–4.

best place . . . but go and sit down in the lowest place"—as a call not to exalt oneself among the proud and vain but to sit in fellowship with the humble and disgraced and share in their humility:

> Now especially desirable to me here is
> The ancient admonition, newly received, of the spiritual sage
> That the Lord himself repeated
> Not to go and sit before the throne of the proud,
> When the impious assemble with their vain thoughts,
> Which David and Jeremiah,
> Standing firm in the law of the covenant, renounced,
> But with those who repent in their heart and are ashamed at their sin,
> Who are terrified and in fear of the great day of judgment,
> And willingly equal in their humility the least of those on earth;
> For their sake God on high exults and rejoices.[30]

Taken to its furthest extent, humility even permits us to love our enemies. Recalling Jesus' equation in Matthew 5:21-22 of anger and abusive expressions with murder, Gregory observes first that God has granted him the grace to master his hateful feelings and words against his enemies. The profundity of this prayer for one's enemy is underscored by the explicit presence of the entire person of the supplicant. Gregory pledges to commit himself to reconciliation with his enemies with all his mind, heart, and body, which is symbolized by the knees on which he prays:

> The cruel desires of my wicked voice having been shut up by you,
> I now in all my thoughts grant pardon to my debtors,
> With all my heart, I seek to be reconciled
> With those who have violently betrayed me
> Together with those who have done me good;
> For their sake, I pray on my knees repeatedly.[31]

With even greater magnanimity Gregory asks to be granted the grace to bless not those who curse him, but rather those whom he

[30] *BL* 50.2; *MH* 12:320–21.30–40.
[31] *BL* 55.3; *MH* 12:349.28–32.

had offended. If he is unable to pray for those whom he has hurt, all of his other prayers are in vain:

> Now what prayers in this book may be pleasing to you,
> What smoke of incense acceptable to you shall I offer,
> O Christ, praised Heavenly King,
> If I do not pray to you to bless those who are cursed by me,
> To release those whom I have bound,
> To free those I have condemned,
> Benefit those I have anathematized,
> Crown those whom I have offended,
> Console those whom I have made sad,
> Tend to those I have bruised,
> Care for those I have alienated,
> Give refuge to those I have betrayed,
> And heal the souls of those whom I have wounded in body?[32]

Among those whom Gregory has condemned and anathemized, of course, are the T'ondrakeans and Nestorians and those of other faiths. But here he asks that God allow him to console and care for these people as well. We should also understand Gregory to be speaking not only for himself but in his role as a priest asking forgiveness for his congregation, pleading for all the members of his Church, including the hierarchs who have through lack of charity condemned their fellow faithful, among whom were Gregory's own father and abbot.

The Centrality of the Eucharist

As the Mahés have observed, these prayers for the extraordinary grace to bless those who are hateful to oneself come immediately after the prayers of communion and the Eucharist. This juxtaposition is meant to show that progress in the virtues is accomplished not through one's own efforts alone but only through participation in the sacraments of the church, and especially

[32] *BL* 55.2; *MH* 12.349.15–25.

through the Eucharist.[33] By taking within oneself Christ's body and blood, one becomes conformed and restored to his image, the image of perfect love that knows no bounds. Indeed, the theme of the necessity of the Eucharist in cultivating the life of Christian virtue is apparent throughout these central prayers. The way of illumination highlighted in these middle prayers is thus connected to the nave of the church which the congregation enters through baptism and where they now assemble to receive holy communion:

> How long would it take the members of our bodies,
> Inclined toward sin, to be saved?
> It could happen only when you, God of all,
> According to your will and desire,
> Accepted the sacrifice and bore death,
> And shared yourself for our forgiveness.
>
> For it is not that you, source of purity,
> Are obliged to die each day,
> But according to your will,
> Through the cooperation of your Spirit,
> And to please the Father,
> For our reconciliation,
> You offer yourself continuously.[34]

Although the Eucharist is a focus of this part of the book of prayers, the centrality of the sacrament underlies the entire work, though usually it is done subtly and in ways that are difficult, if not impossible, to convey in translation. Consider, for example, these verses from Prayer 11:

> [The Word] holds nearby a portion of salvation, a glimmer of life,
> Like a spark of light guarded in his mind and soul,
> Like the remarkable and amazingly intense fire
> That miraculously was ignited at the command from on high,
> After lying dormant at the bottom of the well.[35]

[33] Mahé 2001, 175.
[34] *BL* 53.3; *MH* 12:338.50–58.
[35] *BL* 11.2; *MH* 12:26–30.

The fire is a reference to the miraculous light of 2 Maccabees 1:18-23 that shone forth from a thick liquid. That residue was the remnant of the temple altar fire hidden at the bottom of a well after the return of Nehemiah from captivity to Jerusalem to restore the city walls and the temple. This is one of the miracles commemorated in the Jewish Feast of Lights (Hanukkah). For Gregory, though, the dormant substance is a symbol of the bread and wine that when consecrated become Christ's body and blood. The connection with the Eucharist here is clear from the word I translate as "portion" (Armenian: *nshkhar*), but which can also refer to the host or the bread that is consecrated. As unimpressive as the matter of the host may appear, like the viscous substance found at the base of the well, through the gift of the Spirit it is transformed into the most brilliant and enduring light that restores those who receive it to holiness.

Not only is the Eucharist present throughout the work, but Gregory implies that his book itself can be compared to the sacrament. Returning to his eucharistic prayer, we read:

> I will pray to you with your prayer,
> As is appropriate to the matter of these words,
> The letters of lamentation in this book,
> Which I will fill with sorrow and deep sighs.
> But I will mix in to it what I have received from you,
> that it may be pleasing to you who have given it.[36]

Here, the key word is *matter*, which translates the Armenian word *niwt'*. The word *matter* carries some of the same ambiguity of the Armenian word. The English can refer to a material substance but also the words or contents of a literary work, as when we speak of reading matter. Gregory is playing on a similar ambiguity in Armenian, since *niwt'* can mean matter but also can refer to the letters or elements that the poet is weaving together, since the verb form of the noun, *niwt'em*, means "to weave, contrive." The poet's words are compared to matter, like the elements of the Eucharist that by being mixed with what is received from God are transformed into Christ's flesh and blood. The word for mix here is also significant

[36] *BL* 53.2; *MH* 12:337.29–33.

since it is the same word that he uses to describe the incarnation, the mixture without confusion of the Word with the flesh. Thus, the book is itself a poetic sacrament that Gregory offers to God to be consecrated and distributed among the faithful for their spiritual sustenance. Understood in this way, the book takes on an inspired quality akin to scripture.

The prevalence of the subject of the Eucharist in Gregory's poem is meant to impress upon the faithful the vital importance of communion in Christian life. He is presenting a counterpoint to the T'ondrakean rejection of communion as well as to those charismatic clerics like Jacob of Hark' who discouraged frequent communion. For Gregory, the Eucharist is indispensable as the means to encounter God in our world and to fortify and magnify the virtues that bring us closer to God and restore his image in us. There are limits to how often one can receive communion. But Gregory does not object to daily participation in the Eucharist:

> [The Church] does not allow one
> to come forward twice on the same day
> for the ineffable sacrament of the Lord
> lest the offering be carelessly dishonored.[37]

Although communion twice in one day is barred, daily communion is by implication neither forbidden nor discouraged.

Since the sacraments are effected through the church and its priests, the way to God must be taken through the church. As we have seen, for Gregory fidelity to the apostolic teachings is a sign of the presence of the true church guided and inspired by the Holy Spirit. We can be sure of the validity of the sacraments because they proceed from the universal church that has its origins in the descent of the Spirit upon the apostles at Pentecost:

> [The apostles] are our forebears, our parents who begot us through the holy font, the pedagogues of our learning, teachers to us who are being discipled, our instructors in good confession, the founders of the holy Church, the conveyors of true worship, the prodders in

[37] *BL* 75.9; *MH* 12:472.2.

> real piety, the ordainers of our priesthood—which they received from Christ and passed on to us, the faithful covenanters, the foremost witnesses to our order established by God.[38]

The Church Universal

We have already seen that Gregory, in agreement with the general ecclesiology of the school of Narek, identifies the apostolic church not only with those who profess the miaphysite Christology and do not accept Chalcedon, but also with the Chalcedonian church. Unlike some Armenian miaphysite theologians who equate Chalcedonianism with Nestorius's heretical teachings, Gregory realizes that Chalcedonian Christology is within the sphere of orthodoxy. He praises the Chalcedonian emperors Basil and Constantine and recognizes them as defenders of the faith. The oil of confirmation unites all Christians into one body throughout the world without regard for ethnicity. In a surreal portrayal of the diversity of peoples that constitute the church, there are even strange beings like the dog-headed giant who seems to exist on the fringes of the human species:

> This wonderful oil brings the light of blessing
> To Jew and savage alike,
> The Indian and barbarian,
> Scythian and Greek,
> The violent brute, the fearsome dog-headed giant,
> To the free master and his serf born into slavery,
> Making of them all Christians.[39]

The creatures with a dog's head, the cynocephali, appear in various legendary tales, including the *Romance of Alexander*, a work that was translated into Armenian in the early Middle Ages.[40] They were supposed to be an exotic race living on the edges of civilization.

[38] *Encomium on the Holy Apostles*, *MH* 12:976–89; Terian 2016, 342–43.

[39] *BL* 93.12; *MH* 12:581–82.2.

[40] Pseudo-Callisthenes, 1969, *The Romance of Alexander the Great*, Albert M. Wolohojian, ed., New York: Columbia University Press, 146.

Augustine discusses in the *City of God* whether they are humans.[41] He does not pronounce a verdict on their status, but insists that regardless of whatever unusual appearance rational animals may have, they are human, and thus children of Adam. Gregory is more forthcoming on the question of the cynocephali. Not only are they children of Adam but through the sacraments they also may become children of God, members of the body of Christ.

Although Gregory acknowledges the unity of the universal church, embracing both the Chalcedonian and miaphysite communities, he does not venture into questions of jurisdiction and primacy. His reticence is a mark of prudence, given the troubles his father encountered in arguing against the catholicos for the equal privileges of all bishops. In Prayer 3 of the *Book of Lamentation*, in his listing of all the ranks of people for whom he writes his poem, he distinguishes the bishops from the primates who occupy a see.[42] Samuelian translates this phrase as "patriarch" but the Armenian is not as definite and could more generally be applied to diocesan bishops instead of only the patriarchs. The ambiguity is perhaps deliberate in order not to offend either party in the dispute on the authority of the patriarch over the bishops.[43] Gregory describes Peter as the "rock of faith," "chief of disciples," and "first in number and primacy," but he does not connect this status of primacy to any see.[44] If the T'ondrakeans inherited the antipathy toward Peter of their precursors, the Paulicians, then Gregory would have ample cause specific to his time and place to exalt Peter as a corrective to the heretics' disparagement of the apostle.[45]

[41] Augustine, 1984, *City of God*, Henry Bettenson, tr., London: Penguin, 16.8, 662.

[42] In Armenian, *at'oṛakalowt'eants' nakhagayits'*, "those who preside in occupying a throne or see."

[43] *BL* 3.2; *MH* 12:66.76; and Samuelian 2000, 49. See also the comprehensive treatment of Gregory's ecclesiology in Mahé, 2006, "L'Ecclésiologie de Saint Gregoire de Narek" in Mahé and Zekiyan 2006, 205–27.

[44] *BL* 70.2; *MH* 12:431.29, *BL* 71.4; *MH* 12:441.136; *Encomium on the Holy Apostles*, *MH* 12:981.45; Terian 2016, tr., 332.

[45] See Garsoïan 1967, 42.

In any event, he does not show any interest in disputes about the ranking and ordering of the patriarchal sees.

The congregation assembled now in the nave of the church stands before the altar following the way of the sacraments and the theological virtues in order to come closer to the altar, where God dwells as on his throne in heaven. It is a motley and wondrous spectacle, this collection of God's children: some appear to have canine heads and others are adorned in the peculiar dress and utter the strange speech of the nomadic Scythians. But all have received the grace of the Spirit and all have come to seek God. God is the end of all human longing, and we yearn to encounter him immediately and eternally, not only through the mediation of the church and its sacraments. Some of the faithful have devoted all of their efforts to this journey to union with God. They are the monks, who lead the way. But all Christians are called to consummate their love of God. This consummation and perfection of the journey to God is *theosis*, our becoming one with God, and it is for Gregory as for all the Eastern Christians the only goal of all the exercises and exertions that constitute the Christian life. It is the topic that we turn to in the next chapter as we enter the sanctuary of the church and ascend to the altar.

Chapter Eight

Theosis and the Doctrine of God

To many Christians in the West, and for some Eastern Chrisians as well, the concept of *theosis* appears alien and perhaps even heretical. It seems to imply that humans and God merge into one being in some version of pantheism. Perhaps even worse it appears to honor the blasphemous conceit that we are gods. But the idea of *theosis*, although sometimes suppressed or disguised in other Christian traditions, is part of the common patrimony of the Christian faith. The idea that human beings are made in the image and likeness of God should be familiar to all Christians. If the fall of Adam is understood as tarnishing that image, then everything that Christians do should aim at recovering that primordial and pristine divine likeness. Yet it is only through Christ's incarnation, in which he descends to humanity in order to raise it back to God, that this likeness can ever be restored. If one sees *theosis* as that process in which Christians receive the grace of God to be reconciled with him, then the idea of becoming like God no longer seems so strange or heterodox. Indeed, the gospels themselves make clear that Christians are to achieve such divine perfection: "Be perfect, therefore, as your heavenly Father is perfect" (Matt 5:48).

Gregory understands deification to be the ultimate goal of his life as a monk but he also makes clear that it is the end of all human beings, the fulfillment of our promise as God's beloved creation. The commentary on the Song gives Gregory ample opportunity to develop his conception of *theosis* since the Song is a poem of God's love of human beings, allegorized as the love between a bride and groom. The bride, representing the human soul or collectively the Church, the body of the faithful seeking God, yearns to be with her groom. Read allegorically, the entire book is a symbolic display of the love between Christ and humans presented in terms of earthy and sensuous images and metaphors that arouse our affection for God. Commenting on verse 6:4—"The groom says to the bride, 'You are beautiful, my neighbor, like sweet fragrance, you are beautiful like Jerusalem, arrayed in wonder' "—Gregory remarks that Christ the groom notices the beauty of his bride, who has recovered her former brilliance after being baptized. But he also notes that by looking at the groom and drawing near to him, she has acquired his beauty in the same way that a wick brought near a flame becomes the very light that it touches.[1] And yet immediately after acclaiming her beauty, the groom commands the bride to avert her gaze—"turn your eyes from me for they have roused me" (Song 6:5). This is a puzzling verse, but Gregory interprets it to mean that the groom has been roused with wonder at the bride's sharp vision but also that he fears that in gazing at him the bride would be blinded by his divine splendor. Gregory compares the bride's situation to Moses, who had to hide his face from the burning bush (Exod 3:6), and to Elijah, who wrapped his face with a mantle when the Lord's voice came to him (1 Kgs 19:13). Of course, Moses and Elijah also appear to the transfigured Christ and converse with him while his disciples fall on their faces at the sound of the voice of God from the cloud (Matt 17:6). This interpretation of the groom's words indicates that in our current state we are not prepared for anything more than fleeting glimpses of the divine but that only as we are perfected will we be able to abide the divine light in its fullness.

An especially striking depiction of *theosis* also appears in the commentary's description of the bride's body and words becoming like the groom's. This depiction occurs in the commentary on 6:7 where the groom says (in Gregory's Armenian version of the verse): "Your lips are like a red thread, and your words are beautiful, like a pomegranate's rind are your cheeks from silence." Gregory's reading is based on Nyssen's interpretation:

[1] *MH* 12:835.18–19; Ervine 2007, 162.

> Her eyes come near the divine eyes, her locks to his luminous locks, her head to Christ the head, her lips to the lips that produced life, for her lips became red from the blood of Christ, and they speak the very words that He taught her to speak: to pray for her enemies and to bless those who persecute her, and all such like things.[2]

The reddened lips of the bride symbolize the Eucharist through which the sacramental graces flow. Just as we saw in the last chapter that the Eucharist has an essential role in the growth in virtue, here too Gregory indicates that the progression toward likeness to God's image is accomplished through the reception of Christ's blood in communion.

We also find numerous references to *theosis* in the *Book of Lamentation*. In Prayer 19, Gregory paraphrases the famous statement of Athanasius on deification:

> You for our sake alone became flesh with us,
> So that you may make us for your sake like yourself.
> Light for all, in all things merciful, almighty, heavenly.[3]

And in Prayer 32, Gregory implores Christ to come and dwell inside him:

> O most-bounteous hand of Jesus Christ,
> May you turn also toward me and
> Extend the grace of your holy right hand;
> Dwell within me, become one with me, and never leave
> My anguished heart, my chamber of love.[4]

The erotic language here echoes the romantic imagery of the Song of Songs, evoking the bridal chamber of Song 8:2: "I would lead you and bring you to the house of my mother, and into the chamber of the one who bore me." On this verse, Gregory comments:

[2] *MH* 12:837–38.46–47; Ervine 2007, 165 .

[3] *BL* 19.1; *MH* 12:146.10–12.

[4] *BL* 32.6; *MH* 12:230.117–20.

> Now having found him outside and having been made worthy of a kiss, and then having taken the groom into the chamber and into the house of the soul and into the heart, and having become the abode of the Trinity, she promises to have him drink the wine of happiness and the fruit of pomegranates.[5]

Gregory alludes in this passage to the food offered to God as a sacrifice, but he makes clear that it is the heart's awareness of his goodness that is truly nourishing and pleasing to God.

The human soul, like the bride of the Song, longs most of all for this spiritual wedding with God. But what does Gregory say about this God with whom we seek union and in whose image we are made? We already know that God is Trinitarian and that one of the Trinity became incarnate for our salvation and restoration. But are there any other details about Gregory's doctrine of God that are distinctive or especially notable? In ths chapter I will focus on what Gregory has to say about Trinity and Christ, and how through Christ humans are reconciled with God.

The Trinitarian God

The long profession of faith in Prayer 34, which the Mahés read as the creed that the candidates recite in the vestibule between the narthex and the nave before their baptism, proclaims faith in the three persons of the Trinity. The unity of the three persons is a mystery that transcends all attempts to describe or understand it:

> We confess and proclaim, worship and bow down to
> The unity of the All Holy Trinity, equal in glory,
> Ineffable divinity, ever good, one in being,
> Equal in honor, inaccessible to the mind's soaring wings,
> Higher than any image, beyond any likeness.[6]

[5] *MH* 12:864.22; Ervine 2007, 191.
[6] *BL* 34.3; *MH* 12:243.3.2.

Denying both the Arian heresy that makes the Son a created being as well as the heresy of Macedonius (d. ca. 360) that considers the Holy Spirit a creature, the church recognizes the Father as creator of everything besides the other persons of the Trinity:

> Compassionate Father, Ruler of all and God of the universe
> Of all that is in heaven and on earth
> Except for the Only-begotten Word,
> Through whom He rules all things;
> The Creator and Giver of breath to all beings
> Except for the consubstantial Spirit,
> Through whom He gave form to the world.[7]

There is no ranking or order of the three persons, all of whom exist in an essential relation with the other persons. The doctrine of subordinationism, which renders the Son and Spirit subservient in their nature and essence to the Father, is thus repudiated. Nor does the unity of the persons result in a confusion that produces a fourth being distinct from the three persons or the existence of three distinct gods each with their own wills:

> For placing the Father first in the Trinity
> Does not mean that one is greater than the other,
> Nor by naming one after the other
> Does it mean that one is lower than the other.
> Nor by saying that they form a unity
> Do we imply any confusion among the persons;
> Nor by distinguishing the three persons
> Do we imply a separation of their wills.[8]

The identity of each of the persons is essentially bound to the other persons. The Father without the power of the Son would be bereft of glory, and without the Spirit would lack breath or life. Likewise, the Son without the Father would be an abandoned orphan capable of being annihilated by some mortal being. The Spirit too would be a chaotic wind if it were detached from the origin from which it

[7] *BL* 34.4; *MH* 12:244.4.1.
[8] *BL* 34.8; *MH* 12:247.8.1.

proceeds. Gregory does not specify here from which person the Spirit proceeds though he does use the singular to refer to the Spirit's principle or cause. This omission is not surprising given that questions about the procession of the Spirit surrounding the insertion of the *filioque* into the Nicene Creed that would aggravate relations between the Eastern and Western churches were not a major concern for the Armenian church, which has not taken a dogmatic stance on the matter.

The Motherhood of God

The trinitarian theology expressed in Gregory's profession of faith is standard and certainly orthodox from the perspective of the Nicene-Constantinopolitan creed professed by all the orthodox ecclesial communions. More remarkable are Gregory's claims about the motherhood of God. Gregory is not unique in speaking of God as mother. The patristic and medieval Christian tradition contains many such descriptions of God. God is even portrayed as a mother in the Bible, most notably in Isaiah, where God is compared to a comforting mother (Isa 66:13) and described as a woman in labor (Isa 42:14). In the gospels, Jesus compares himself to a hen gathering her chicks (Matt 23:37; Luke 13:34). So Gregory's use of feminine and maternal images to describe God is not a radical departure from tradition, though it may seem so to many who are unaware of its presence in scripture. While recognizing the first person of the Trinity as Father, Gregory also speaks of the Father as a mother or at least he attributes traditionally maternal and feminine qualities to him. In Prayer 17, a meditation on God's grace, the poet writes:

> For when dawn arrives and the light of day breaks,
> Who can still dread the dark?
> Or can fear death when life is at hand . . .
>
> Who can hunger when there is a wealth of bread,
> Thirst when flowing streams are near,
> Feel betrayed when there is motherly compassion,
> Hatred when under care of the right hand of God?[9]

[9] *BL* 17.2; *MH* 12:135–36.44–57.

And in Prayer 5, a prayer of confession addressed to the Son, Gregory brings together both the masculine function of God as begetter and God's feminine role as nourisher:

> You begot me as a father,
> Nourished me as a wet-nurse.[10]

We may add to these verses of the *Book of Lamentation* some other examples of God's motherhood from the commentary on the Song. Notably, verse 1:2 in Gregory's version based on the Septuagint—"for your breasts are better than wine"—is a declaration made by the bride about her groom. Symbolically, therefore, Christ is the nursing mother whose breasts, here representing the two testaments of scripture, nourish the church. In her discussion of the theological themes in the commentary, Roberta Ervine points to Gregory's remarks on Song 8:5, a verse spoken by the groom and which reads in Gregory's commentary: "I shall awaken you under the apple tree; there my mother was in labor with you, there she who bore you was in labor." Here, Gregory's lemma mistakenly replaces the word *your*, which occurs in both the Septuagint and the Armenian version, with *my*, thereby facilitating his reading of the mother as Christ's. Gregory comments that labor pains pertain specifically to mothers, and so the groom, as Christ, is speaking of the Father as his mother. He notes that God was in labor "in his messages through the Law and prophets" and, in a reference to John 3:5, that he gave birth to his children "through water and the Spirit as brothers of Christ." He concludes that "our Mother is One—the Father begetter, the omnipotent God."[11]

The motif of God as a mother in labor in Gregory's work evokes also the circumstances of his own mother's death. At the beginning

[10] *BL* 5.2; *MH* 12:76.19.

[11] *MH* 12:866–67.41–42; Ervine 2007, 193. Ervine observes that the theme of the motherhood of God in the Armenian tradition is not isolated to Gregory but is also developed further by John Vanakan Vardapet (1181–1251), a learned and important theologian who chided his students for taking offense at the use of feminine imagery to describe God. See Ervine 2007, 63.

of prayer 18, Gregory seems to assume some guilt for his mother's death:

> I was born in sin, the child of deathly labor,
> One who must pay back in one day
> A penalty of countless myriads of talents;
> I beg for your forgiveness.[12]

And in the opening of the poem he presents his work as "remedies for the multifaceted life-threatening labor pains."[13] I do not mean to reduce Gregory's contrition and search for a maternal God to a mere projection of his personal psychological trauma and feelings of guilt. If God is the end of all human desires, and one of the deepest longings of the human soul is for the care and love of a mother, then it makes sense that God would be revealed to us as both father and mother. And if Gregory's personal experience made him especially solicitous of maternal protection, it may have been that very sensitivity that heightened his attentiveness to biblical references to God as mother and his acceptance of the appropriateness of imagining God in terms usually associated with women. In the next chapter, we will see that the same longing for maternal love and concern about the pain of childbirth inform his devotion to the Virgin Mary. But because theological questions surrounding the second person of the Trinity, the eternal word of God, were in Gregory's time (as they remain today) of key importance to the doctrine of the Armenian church and its relation to other churches, let us turn to matters of Christology.

Gregory's Christology

As we have seen, the school of Narek, with the exception of Anania's anti-Chalcedonian treatise, normally approached Chalcedonian Christology in a conciliatory and charitable manner, recognizing that it differed from the Christology of Nestorius and that it fell within

[12] *BL* 18.1; *MH* 12:139.1–5.

[13] *BL* Intro; *MH* 12:49.13.

the parameters of orthodoxy. Nevertheless, they affirmed the primacy of the miaphysite position of their own church because of the conviction that it better expressed the perfect interpenetration of the divine and the human in the person of Christ without any space or interval separating them. Any such gap would keep the word of God from fully entering the fallen human condition and bringing about its redemption. It would prevent a consummation of *theosis*, since humanity would still remain at a distance from God, who would not touch the entirety of humanity and its afflictions.

Gregory professes his devotion to this one-nature Christology. While remaining one in essence with the other persons of the Trinity, the Son descended and assumed the humanity that he shared with us:

> The only Son of the only Father,
> The first-born, only child of the Virgin,
> The Mother of God, Bearer of the Lord,
> The Creator who became in his creation
> The genuine first-formed man.
> Not after the likeness of the earth-formed beings,
> But as a new and blameless man,
> Among the kings the most sublime,
> Never before seen in the centuries,
> Never before existing in the ages.[14]

There are some interesting linguistic peculiarities in these verses. Gregory uses the term "Bearer of the Lord," perhaps the only occurrence of this term, a single word in Armenian (*tiratsin*).[15] Its Greek equivalent (*kuriotokos*) is equally rare, occurring only in one of Athanasius's homilies.[16] Gregory also uses "only-begotten" (*miatsin*), but instead of employing it in its more common sense of Christ as the only-begotten of the Father, he says that Christ is the only-born—I translate it here as "only child"—of the Virgin, presumably to confirm the perpetual virginity of Mary before also re-

[14] *BL* 34.5; *MH* 12:245.5.1a.

[15] This verse of the *BL* is the only passage cited in the *NBHL* entry for *tiratsin*. See *NBHL* 876.

[16] Athanasius, *Sermon on the Nativity of Christ*, PG 28.965.33.

ferring to Christ as Mary's "first born." The repetition of the Armenian suffix *-tsin*—derived from the verb *tsnanem* ("to give birth to" or "beget") and yielding terms such as *first-born*, *Lord-born*, and *primal-born*—places the emphasis on Christ's nativity. The last designation—which I translate above as "first-formed"—corresponds to the Greek *archegonos*, a rare word but one most often found in the writings of Nazianzen, who uses it to refer to Adam. Thus, Gregory connects Christ's assumed flesh to that of Adam's pre-fall flesh, with Christ taking over Adam's role as the genuine first man.[17]

Gregory proceeds to offer several analogies for the incarnation:

> The first born, according to the psalmist,
> Higher than the kings of the earth (Ps 88:28),
> Assuming our form in the flesh,
> In an incorruptible mixture,
> As in the example of the soul and body,
> And gold with fire,
> Or light with air,
> Neither changed nor separated.[18]

The christological language here is familiar. The union of the divine and human is a mixture without confusion, the same language that Gregory uses in Prayer 93 (as discussed in chapter two). Here, though, instead of the example of the intertwining wick, we have the mixture of the soul and body to form the unity of the person, although the soul and the body do not dissolve nor lose their own distinctive identity and powers. This particular metaphor of soul and body could be construed as a heretical denial of Christ's full humanity, for if the Word, on analogy with the soul, simply assumed a human body without a soul, Christ would not be a complete human. That conception of the incarnation was advocated by Apollinaris and condemned as Docetism at the first council of Constantinople in 381. Gregory makes clear, though, that he affirms the full and perfect

[17] Based on a *TLG* search on *archegonos* and its cognates.

[18] *BL* 34.5; *MH* 12:245.5.1b.

humanity of Christ, "lacking in nothing as to his humanity."[19] So he intends the soul-body analogy simply as a metaphor for the union, a natural example of how two substances can exist together in an intimate bond without either one losing its integrity. Likewise, the refining fire does not cease to be fire but produces a pure metal when the dregs of the original gold are skimmed off from a molten mixture. This image of the purification of gold through fire is significant because it suggests that through the incarnation, the divine Word, like fire, effects the purification of impure humanity, the debased gold. If we extend the metaphor to the question of the incorruptibility of the assumed flesh, then it would seem that the assumed flesh, like the gold, is impure and corruptible and it is through its assumption in the incarnation that it becomes incorruptible. The metaphor therefore coheres with the anti-Julianist position affirmed as orthodox at the Council of Manazkert, the council that would define the emerging orthodoxy of the Armenian church in relation both to the Chalcedonian definition of Christ and to the debate between Julian and Severus. Likewise, the metaphor of the light and air illustrates the light of God that illuminates the obscure body just as the light of the sun turns the dark, misty air of night into the clear splendor of dawn.

Though the incarnation turned the naturally corruptible and passable flesh of humanity into the pristine body of Christ, Christ deigned willingly to suffer with us:

> He came himself voluntarily to the cross of death,
> Like the immaculate lamb led to slaughter;
> He prepared through his mighty free will
> The salvation of his creatures;
> He truly suffered in the way all living beings do;
> He was placed in the tomb
> While never separated from his divinity.[20]

Gregory's creed on the incarnation sets his Christology firmly in line with the doctrines affirmed at Manazkert. If there is any further doubt that Gregory rejects the currents of Julianism still in his

[19] *BL* 34.5; *MH* 12:245.5.1a.
[20] *BL* 34.6; *MH* 12:245.6.1.

time influencing theology in Armenia, we need only turn to his commentary on the Song to dispel it. Armenian Julianists like John Mayragomets'i did not deny that Jesus suffered. Because the body he assumed was impassible by nature, his suffering was both voluntary and the result of a miracle through which the body's natural impassibility was overridden. But for Mayragomets'i there were certain kinds of suffering unbecoming of God. Among these were fear and mourning. These passions seem to entail some deficiency of virtue or power, particularly a lack of faith or hope in God. And yet Jesus is depicted mourning at the death of Lazarus and in a state of profound fear and despair in the garden of Gethsemane on the eve of his crucifixion:

> They went to a place called Gethsemane; and [Jesus] said to his disciples, "Sit here while I pray." He took with him Peter and James and John, and began to be distressed and agitated. And he said to them "I am deeply grieved, even to death; remain here, and keep awake." (Mark 14:32-34)

An even more striking depiction of the depths of Jesus' distress is the pericope of the bloody sweat. After asking that his Father remove the cup before him but then assenting to the Father's will, an angel came to minister to him and he began to sweat drops of blood (Luke 22:41-44). Mayragomets'i would not deny that Jesus perspired like an athlete in intense competition with his opponent. But for Mayragomets'i the peculiar and pathological sweat of blood could only indicate an extreme distress and anguish inconsistent with Christ's divinity. He could not accept that the Lord would need the comforting of an angel and that he was so severely distressed that he perspired blood.[21] Mayragomets'i's surviving writings and those of his opponents indicate that he believed the pericope of the bloody sweat to be an addition to the gospel text made by Nestorians who were, Mayragomets'i implies, intent on emphasizing Jesus' frail humanity to the detriment of his divinity.

[21] The authenticity of the pericope is a problem in the textual criticism of the Greek New Testament as well. See Ehrman 2005, 139–44.

The absence of the pericope from most of the pre-eleventh century Armenian Luke manuscripts is one more indication of the impact Mayragomets'i's Christology had on Armenian theology centuries after his condemnation at Manazkert.[22] So it is all the more remarkable that Gregory's exemplar contains the pericope and that he directly cites it in his commentary on the Song. Commenting on the groom's declaration to the bride in Song 5:2—"my head is wet with dew, my locks with the drops of the night"—Gregory writes:

> Here [the groom] reminds the bride of the sweat that he bore in the evening from fear of death, and about which the Gospel says *his sweat flowed from him in great drops* (Luke 22.44). He says that through my sweat you have put on this purity of the dove and perfection, and have become my sister and bride. It was through my sweat by which in that night I removed the sweat of the curse.[23]

Noteworthy here is that Gregory says that the sweat resulted from Christ's *fear of death*, the very passion that the Armenian Julianists contended was inappropriate for Christ. There is a difference in the wording of the verse here and in the form found in the Armenian Bible and the Septuagint. The Zohrapean edition of the Armenian Bible reads: "and sweat like drops of blood flowed from him and fell drop by drop to the ground."[24] Gregory does not mention blood, most likely because his focus is on the dew in the groom's hair as a figure of Christ's sweat in the new garden, which annuls the sweat of the curse imposed on Adam in the garden of old (Gen 3:19). Furthermore, the Armenian anti-Julianists considered the reference to drops of blood to be a simile rather than a literal depiction of the sweat. The important point for us remains that Gregory disavows the Julianist denial that Christ experienced the fear of death.

Likewise, in opposition to John Mayragomets'i's rejection of Christ's sorrow and grief, Gregory presents a genuinely sorrowful Christ:

[22] Cowe 1994, 44.

[23] *MH* 12:817.49–50; Ervine 2007, 143.

[24] Zohrapean 1805, Luke 22:44.

For truly did the compassionate Lord weep
Just as we humans do
At the burial of his friend,
So, too, for Jerusalem gone astray [Luke 19:41]
And for Judas gone mad. [cf. Matt 26:24][25]

In presenting Jesus as one who shares in all our sorrows and afflictions but who remains sinless, Gregory is faithful to the general anti-Julianist thought of the school of Narek. Khosrov had already affirmed the passions of Christ in his commentary on the liturgy:

> Christ lived out his life but committed no sin, bearing all the passions of the flesh: He was born, nourished, hungered, thirsted, grew tired, ate, drank, felt, became anxious, sorrowed, wept, and took upon Himself all else entailed by the flesh. And remaining free from sin, He became victorious over fleshly shortcomings.[26]

Echoing his father's words, Gregory goes even further by adding that Christ experienced death as God:

> [He] suffered and took on himself all that humans suffer save for sin: he was spat upon, slapped and whipped, mocked with robes and a crown of thorns, His divine head beaten with a reed, nailed naked to the cross with criminals, and fed with bile and vinegar. God died and was pierced with the spear of the soldier, and was wrapped and buried, and all else.[27]

This affirmation of Christ's sufferings in opposition to Julianism fits well with the general plan of the school of Narek to bring the church closer to the people. A Julianist Christology that mitigates Christ's suffering presents serious obstacles for an effective pastoral theology. Consider how Julianists would counsel a person in grief. Since mourning is for them a symptom of human sinfulness, they would have to advise the bereaved to resist the normal process of grieving. They could not point to Christ and declare that he

[25] *BL* 25.3; *MH* 12:180.54–56.
[26] *MH* 10:201.223; Cowe 1991, 161.
[27] *MH* 12:871.86–87; Ervine 2007, 197–98.

shares the grief of the bereaved, since they do not believe that Christ mourns in the way we do. For Gregory, though, Christ's mourning, sorrow, and fear are identical to our own feelings. Not only can the afflicted take comfort in Christ's participation in our suffering but also through his passions Christ has sanctified the entire range of emotions that humans experience. Gregory's Christ, in contrast to Julian's, is a Christ who is extremely close to us and whose experience is our experience as well.

Gregory displays Christ's compassion perhaps most vividly in Prayer 18 of the *Book of Lamentation*, which is devoted to the gospel accounts of healing and resurrection. Here, Gregory portrays Jesus sharing in our suffering as a fellow human while also recognizing that he provides more than just solidarity with those who are in pain. Christ is both human and divine and, as God, is capable of healing the sick and restoring the dead to life. Gregory associates himself with the afflicted of these stories and asks for Christ's comfort and healing. One of the many remarkable features of this prayer is that Gregory identifies most of all with women, presenting himself as similar to the sinful woman of Luke 7:38-50 (Prayer 18.5) and the woman having a flow of blood for twelve years (Prayer 18.4). However, he also identifies with Lazarus raised from the grave after four days (18.7). Since the next section of the prayer, which portrays the episode of the widow of Nain (Luke 7:11-17), also depicts Jesus resurrecting a man from the dead, one might suppose, as some translations do, that Gregory associates himself with the raised young man. But in reading the verses more carefully we find that Gregory connects his own laments with those of the mourning widow whose son has died. He asks that Jesus say to him the same words that he spoke to the widow: "Do not weep" (Luke 7:13):

> Like the pitiful voice of despair,
> The wails of lamentation
> Of the widow of Nain,
> The mother of an only son,
> Her fingers trembling,
> Her breast heaving,
> Tears flowing on her face from grief's pain,

I too implore You with my last sigh,
And say, "Give me in my despair
The encouraging comfort
of your compassionate word."
Say to me also, most blessed Lord,
Creator of the world, worthy of praise,
"Do not weep" like a captive with much to lament.
But as you restored the young man to life
In consolation of his afflicted mother,
May I too receive from you
my most indebted soul renewed.[28]

The analogy drawn here is somewhat perplexing. As the widow has lost her son, so too has Gregory lost his soul. He has not suffered literal death but rather spiritual death. The relation between the widow's son and the poet's soul seems problematic. But one clue about what Gregory is doing here is provided by the Armenian word in the last line that is translated here as "my soul" (*hogis*). In colloquial Armenian, it is common to call one's child or any other close person "my soul" as a token of one's affection. This usage is already attested in Middle Armenian as early as the fourteenth century and may derive from the analogous Persian custom, also found among Armenians, in which *jan*, a Persian word for soul, is used as a term of affection.[29] Assuming this usage was also current in Gregory's time, it would explain the connection between the widow's son and Gregory's soul. Just as the widow has lost her metaphorical soul, so too Gregory has lost his literal soul to sin and moral debt. And just as Christ restores the widow's "soul" by resurrecting her son, so too Gregory asks that his own soul be renewed and restored to him.

Gregory evokes Christ's compassion for the widow also by drawing parallels between the woman of Nain and the Virgin Mary. The widow's affliction foreshadows Mary's grief, both of whose sons die and are resurrected. When he arrived in Nain and witnessed the burial of the only son of the widowed mother, Jesus' attention was

[28] *BL* 18.8; *MH* 12:143.76–85.

[29] For the medieval Armenian usage, see Ghazaryan and Avetisyan 2009, 432.

drawn to his own mother and the torment she would endure at his crucifixion. That is why without even being asked to, Jesus is moved by compassion to restore the widow's son to life. With these words—"as you restored the young man to life/In consolation of his afflicted mother"—Gregory emphasizes the gospel's statement that Jesus performed the miracle above all out of compassion for the mother who was left with no close male relative. This too ties the widow to the Virgin, for in describing the widow as the mother of an *only son*, Gregory recalls the designation of Christ as the *only child* of Mary in Prayer 34 of the poem, discussed above.

In addition to the clear pastoral advantages of this very human, suffering, and compassionate Christ, the notion of a Christ who is immersed in all the problems of humanity and who descends to the very depths of human despair and suffering is also important for systematic theology. Only such a fully human Christ can truly redeem humanity in its totality and restore us to the divine image. *Theosis* requires a Christ who is both fully human and fully divine. The worry is that a Julianist Christ is not human enough to redeem humanity thoroughly and to reconcile us completely with God. All of Gregory's theology focuses on that ultimate goal of returning humanity as a whole to the Lord; consequently, he disavows all the principles of Julianism that stand in the way of this goal.

The Sacrament of Chrismation

By now it should be clear from our study of his work that for Gregory, the path toward *theosis* is essentially sacramental. The grace to be like God and with God comes from the Eucharist. Commenting on Song 7:9 according to the Septuagint—"I go with my nephew in uprightness, being made sufficient in my lips and teeth"—Gregory remarks that the soul becomes perfect by observing Christ's teachings, which he himself exemplified for us through his actions. Christ's lessons were not just his words but also his deeds. Jesus first acted and then taught, as expressed in the opening of the Acts of the Apostles: "Jesus began to do and then to teach" (Acts 1:1). For our edification, he modeled the virtues:

He became man so he would do all that he taught in word, and through his works he would teach us mildness and humility. . . . He displayed absence of malice in praying for his crucifiers—*Father, forgive them, for they know not what they do* (Luke 23:34). . . . Likewise he demonstrated the completion of his work through a donkey and his humility by sitting on it [Matt 21:5-7; John 12:14-15]. . . . At the wedding he shared in the joy of those who rejoiced and offered them a gift, and in mourning, too, he demonstrated the extent of his sadness by weeping, and taught us to mourn with our brethren in sadness."[30]

Yet we are unable to emulate Christ's perfect life through our own devices. We need the grace of God every step of the way. The grace of becoming like Christ is granted first through the Eucharist:

> Now from where was given such power to the bride to accompany Christ in uprightness? By the awesome sacrament of communion in the body and blood of Christ, which he gave to us for strength. He made us bold to drink with our lips and break with our teeth that on which you angels, the *daughters and queens*, did not dare to gaze, and made us sufficient to break with our teeth the one of whom no bone was broken on the Cross, as the prophet had said before (Ps 33.21).[31]

The Eucharist grants us the strength and power to become like Christ, a privilege not even bestowed upon the angels, who in the Song are represented by the daughters of Jerusalem attending the bride. Taking into one's inner being the body of Christ allows us to exhibit and perform in our outer behavior the virtues epitomized in Christ's life. But it is in the sacrament of chrismation, or anointing with the holy oil (*muron*), that the divine image is perfected. Gregory alludes to Anania's anthropology of the inner and outer person in claiming that through anointing the two aspects of our being are reconciled and together sanctified:

[30] *MH* 12:857–58.87–92; Ervine 2007, 184. Cf. *MH* 10:202–3.246–53; Cowe 1991, 164–65.

[31] *MH* 12:12.859.98–99; Ervine 2007, 185.

This oil of salvation,
Perfected through light,
Is poured on us
To anoint the outer temple,
But invisibly, unseen,
Penetrates the inner person
And restores it to life.[32]

Having anointed my head
With your immaculate heavenly oil,
I come before you in gladness,
Rejoicing and not in sorrow.[33]

The sacrament of anointing unites us with God and restores us to Adam's original state. Here, the poet considers the sacred oil as the fruit of the tree of the crucifixion that reverses the effects of the fruit of the tree in Eden, just as earlier we saw that Christ's sweat in Gethsemane undoes the curse of sweat imposed on Adam:

You gave the oil . . .
So that we who find ourselves
Exiled in the shadows of death
Through the guilt incurred
From the tree of primal perdition
May be illuminated by the flame of faith
And be restored to our original glory
Through the fruit of the tree akin to it.[34]

A Mysticism of Light

The association of anointing with perfection is one more instance of the influence of Pseudo-Dionysius on Gregory's understanding of the sacraments and their role in the ascent toward God. We have already noted the relation of baptism to purification and the role of

[32] *BL* 93.3; *MH* 12:568.3.4.
[33] *BL* 93.11; *MH* 12:581.11.6.
[34] *BL* 93.2; *MH* 12:567.2.3.

the Eucharist in illumination. There are, however, some significant differences between their sacramental theologies. Gregory adds the sacrament of confession in the first stage and grants a sacramental character to marriage in his commentary on the Canticle, while the Dionysian corpus mentions neither marriage nor confession. But Dionysian theology clearly informs the basic tripartite structure of the *Book of Lamentation* and the focus in each part on particular sacraments. Although the general idea of three levels of Christian initiation predates Pseudo-Dionysius's mysticism, the specifically sacramental character of Gregory's arrangement of his poem points to a direct Dionysian influence.[35] We have already remarked on the Dionysian aspects of Khosrov's ecclesiology. Given the imprint of Dionysian thought on the school of Narek, it is natural to ask to what extent the mystical theology of the Areopagite has shaped Gregory's own mysticism. In particular, we may wonder to what extent Gregory's mysticism reflects one of the most distinctive elements of Dionysian mysticism: *apophatic* or negative theology. Although we can make positive statements about what God is—how God is one and goodness and life—this *cataphatic* or affirmative approach to theology fails to do justice to the otherness of God and his separateness from the things of our world. If we describe God as king, we must also be aware that he is not like any of the kings of this world, his creation. Consequently, when we describe God in terms of what he is not, such as when we say that he is *not* mortal or *not* corruptible, we are speaking more truly than when we say what God actually is. All our attempts to define God in our own terms, using the images and metaphors of this world, fall short and must be abandoned in our ascent to God.[36] God is ineffable: we can never use our language and images to express in full what God is. Ultimate knowledge of God is beyond words, even beyond thought. The best we can do in words is to transcend even the apophatic approach and speak of God as beyond the immortal, beyond the ineffable. To express these

[35] On the pre-Dionysian history of the threefold initiation, see Louth 1981, 58–61.

[36] For discussion of Dionysius's cataphatic and apophatic approaches to theology, see Louth 1981, 164–68.

transcendent concepts, Pseudo-Dionysius spoke of the superimmortal and the superineffable. For God is beyond all being, beyond everything that we perceive and can conceive. Pseudo-Dionysius calls this transcendence of all worldly images the darkness of God. Based on ideas already present in Nyssen, which the Cappadocian drew from the biblical account of Moses' ascent of Mount Sinai recounted in Exodus, where *Moses drew near to the thick darkness where God was* (Exod 20:21), Pseudo-Dionysius speaks of God being dark in the sense that when we truly encounter God and are assimilated to him, our knowledge of him is unmediated by any words or images.[37] Breaking free of these images, the mystic, like Moses, "plunges into the truly mysterious darkness of unknowing . . . supremely united to the completely unknown."[38] Knowledge of the divine is a knowledge beyond all perception and all thought, a knowing that is beyond even knowing itself.

To what extent does Gregory share these features of Dionysian mysticism? In speaking of God, Gregory uses both cataphatic and apophatic language. In Prayer 3 of the *Book of Lamentation*, he addresses God in cataphatic language:

> O Lord, my Lord, giver of gifts, bearer of goodness,
> Ruler of all equally, creator of all things out of nothing . . .[39]

He then shifts to strictly apophatic terms for God:

> Unbearable, inapproachable, incomprehensible, unintelligible,
> Ineffable, invisible, imperceptible, intangible,
> Unsearchable, without beginning, timeless.[40]

In the *Book of Lamentation*, Gregory avoids the use of the transcendent terms but, as we noted in chapter four, in his theological trea-

[37] For Nyssen, see Abraham J. Malherbe and John Meyendorff, 1978, *Gregory of Nyssa: The Life of Moses*, Classics of Western Spirituality, New York: Paulist Press.

[38] Luibheld 1987, 137.

[39] *BL* 3.1; *MH* 12:63.1–2.

[40] *BL* 3.1; *MH* 12:63.5–7.

tise *Advice on the Orthodox Faith and the Pure and Virtuous Life*, he does describe God the Father using these peculiarly Dionysian terms after listing the apophatic descriptors:

> limitless, timeless, nowhere, infinite, immutable, unchangeable, super-essential, super-existent, super-light, super-ineffable.[41]

All of these transcendent terms are the Armenian equivalents formed as calques, or translations that reproduce in Armenian the same compound structure of the distinctive Greek terms found in the Dionysian corpus.[42] Gregory's use of these names of God and his procession, beginning with the cataphatic terms followed by the apophatic, and then, at least in his theological treatise, the transcendent terms, reveal a clear Dionysian influence on his approach to speaking about God.

Gregory also repeatedly affirms the ineffability of God:

> The way of the providential creator surpasses
> The limits of the mind of the angels and humans,
> And if I were to try myriad times
> I could not capture it in verse,
> For his limitless beneficence is ineffable.[43]
> Ineffable divinity, always good . . .
> You cannot be expressed by names
> Nor signified by titles,
> Nor likened to a quality,
> Nor bound by a quantity.[44]

But despite this clear Dionysian influence on his mysticism, there is one conspicuous difference: Gregory rarely attributes darkness to God. Instead, Gregory almost always speaks of God as pure light. God is a "shadowless brilliance who dwells and reposes in unapproachable light." He is "by nature light and the ever-splendid

[41] *MH* 12:1024.21.

[42] The adverbial form of the Greek *huperarrētos*, "superineffable," appears in the Pseudo-Dionysian *Divine Names.* See Heil and Ritter 1999, 115.12.

[43] *BL* 44.3; *MH* 12:285.44–47.

[44] *BL* 34.3; *MH* 12:243.3.2.

sun."[45] The only passage in the *Book of Lamentation* in which Gregory admits darkness or obscurity in God is in Prayer 93.19:

> For as God is truly said to be unapproachable light,
> But on account of his boundless, infinite glory,
> He is conceived as though hidden
> Under an impenetrable darkness,
> Sealed off on the outside from our intellect's grasp.[46]

Elsewhere in his wrtings Gregory prefers to concentrate on the light of God rather than the darkness that characterizes many of the mystics' experience of God as they approach union with God. Gregory's preference for light over darkness is all the more remarkable, given that Nyssen, an important theological source for Gregory and on whose writings he relied in composing his commentary on the Song, also propounded a mysticism of darkness, especially in his *Life of Moses*.

In trying to explain this preference for a mysticism of light over darkness, we should keep in mind that Gregory is not only a theorist of mysticism but a practitioner. So in describing in words what mystical encounters are like, he is drawing from his own direct experience. And perhaps for him such visions of the divine were better described in terms of unapproachable light rather than as darkness.

Of course the mysticism of darkness found in Nyssen and Dionyius is not the only form of Christian mysticism. There is also a mysticism of light that is found, for example, in the writings of Origen.[47] And there is no reason to rule out Gregory's familiarity with Origen. Although Origenism was condemned at the Second Council of Constantinople held in 551, the Armenian church neither participated in that council nor formally adopted its conclusions. Armenian theologians were familiar with and read many of Origen's works. As we have noted, in the eighth century Stephen of Siwnik' drew copiously from Origen's books.

[45] *BL* 90.2; *MH* 12:540.33; *BL* 91.2; *MH* 12:547.26 (cf. 1 Tim 6:16); *BL* 93.15; *MH* 586.2.

[46] *BL* 93.19; *MH* 12:591–92.19.5.

[47] Louth 1981, 74.

But another explanation of Gregory's tendency to eschew darkness relates to the so-called Iranian substrate of Armenian culture and folklore, a substrate that influences Gregory's work. Armenia had been for centuries within the political and cultural orbit of the Persian Empire, and its language and cultural institutions bore a strong Iranian imprint long after Armenia's Christianization. Examples of this Iranian substrate in the *Book of Lamentation* include the night demons of Prayer 12.3-4, the agents of Ahriman, the evil deity of darkness in Zoroastrianism, and the wolf-monster (*gaylgazan*) of Prayer 66.[48] Given that Zoroastrianism attibutes to the good deity, Ahura Mazda, only light and no darkness, which is the sole province of the benighted Ahriman, Gregory's mysticism of light may be a vestige of this pre-Christian Iranian theology. But such claims remain at the level of speculation. All we can say with certainty is that Gregory favors a mysticism of light even as other aspects of Dionysian mystical theology have profoundly influenced his theology.

Universalism

We noted in the last chapter that the nave of the church in which the baptized and confirmed Christians gathered was a diverse group drawn from many ethnic groups. Now that we are in the sanctuary preparing for the restoration in us of the divine image and reconcilation with God, we may ask who else is with us. Is the assembly of perfected Christians as expansive as those in the nave? Or since the way is narrow (Matt 7:13-14), are the elect an exclusive group? In recent Catholic theology there has been a revival of the ancient view

[48] The detection of an Iranian substrate in Gregory's work has been explored by Mahé 2000, 126f. and 161, as well as Mahé 1983, "Echos mythologiques et poésie orale dans l'œuvre de Grigor Narekac'i," *REArm* 17, 249–78. See also the fascinating discussion of the influence of Iranian folklore on Armenia in James R. Russell, 1988, *Zoroastrianism in Armenia*, Cambridge, MA: Harvard University Department of Near Eastern Languages and Civilizations, esp. 460–61 for the wolf-monster. But also see Terian 2016, xxiv–xxv, who gives us reason to be cautious in reading such pre-Christian allusions in Gregory's text.

found in Origen and Nyssen, among others, that all are saved. This view is called universalism (Greek: *apokatastasis*), and Catholic theologians such as Karl Rahner (1904–84) as well as several Protestant and Orthodox thinkers have in recent times advanced the thought that God's plan of salvation may be extended to all. A more cautious but hopeful form of universalism is found in the writings of the Catholic theologian Hans Urs von Balthasar (1905–88).[49] In the light of this recent development in Catholic thought, and given Gregory's emphasis on mercy and the universality of the church, it may be worthwhile to consider what Gregory has to say about this question of who is saved.

The evidence is equivocal. In Prayer 40, Gregory presents a terrifying vision of the future life:

> From a distance I see with my mind's eye
> A vision of blazing terror of what is to come;
> I glimpse from here long before
> The day of light, the hope of the saints,
> And the day of darkness, the punishment of the guilty,
> From which none can flee to a place of refuge.[50]

And in Prayer 64, he cites Isaiah 66:24—"for their worm shall not die, and their fire shall not be extinguished"—and adds to these verses that "the fire is inextinguishable/the punishment unending/the place eternal/its image dreadful."[51] Certainly these are very clear statements that some will face eternal torment.

And yet later in the book we read this supplication:

> Through these sighs of sorrow and laments
> Arranged in numerous forms,
> Have mercy on all souls,

[49] For von Balthasar as a hopeful universalist, see Edward T. Oakes, SJ, "Christ's Decent into Hell: The Hopeful Universalism of Hans van Balthasar," in Gregory MacDonald, ed., 2011, *All Shall be Well: Explorations in Universal Salvation and Christian Theology from Origen to Moltmann*, Cambridge: James Clarke, 382–99.

[50] *BL* 40.2; *MH* 12:273.7–12.

[51] *BL* 64.2; *MH* 12:397.27–29.

O blessed, forbearing King,
And especially on those souls
Cut off from any hope
Of a life of salvation,
Those who have gone to their rest unprepared,
Their lamps extinguished from lack of oil.
Remember them, my Lord of compassion.[52]

Gregory alludes here to the foolish virgins who did not prepare for the coming of the Lord (Matt 25:1-13). Assuming that these unprepared virgins represent the souls condemned to hell, Gregory dares even to ask for God's mercy on them, suggesting that he has some hope of universal salvation consistent with his faith in the infinite mercy of God. We have already discussed in chapter five his Ode for the Holy Cross, a hymn sung by the souls in hell at the time of the crucifixion in expectation of Christ's harrowing. That ode represents a particular time in the past and there is no indication that Christ's atonement will be applied to those souls in hell after the resurrection when he escaped hell with the prophets and patriarchs. But there is also a timeless quality to Christ's salvific action and Gregory wants at least to consider that the souls in hell, with whom he seeks solidarity, may themselves still have hope of redemption.

There is one notable exception in Gregory's adumbrations of universalism. Satan is beyond any hope of redemption:

[Satan] was not granted this multitude of graces;
Instead [Christ] poured them all upon me abundantly.
He was not tortured for Satan's sake,
But for me he is sacrificed every day.
[Satan] does not commune with the Life
But I partake of it always for salvation.[53]

Gregory's eucharistic language here implies that by being excluded from Christ's offering of His body, Satan cannot attain salvation. Yet all humans, no matter how sinful, may be redeemed through

[52] *BL* 86.1; *MH* 12:528.1–9.
[53] *BL* 67.1; *MH* 12:416.10–15.

Christ's sacrifice. The theme of universalism in Gregory's work requires further study. If he does indeed entertain the concept of universal salvation, then we would have another important patristic witness in favor of universalism, and in particular one much later than either Origen and Nyssen.

Above the main altar of the Cathedral of the Holy Cross, as in every Armenian church, stands the central icon of the Virgin Mother holding the Christ child. It is through the Mother of God that the Word became incarnate and the hope of salvation was extended to the world. She, being closest to the Lord, was the first to experience the perfection and union with God that we have been exploring in this chapter. So, too, it was through the Virgin that Gregory was introduced to the world beyond Armenia. Given her importance in Gregory's theology, we will devote the next chapter to the place of Mary in Gregory's writings and thought.

Chapter Nine

Gregory's Devotion to Mary

It is through Mary that Gregory of Narek came to the attention of the universal church. The first pope to mention him was St. John Paul II in his 1987 encyclical *Redemptoris Mater* (*Mother of the Redeemer*). There, the pope wrote:

> In his panegyric on the Theotokos, St. Gregory of Narek, one of the most renowned figures of Armenia, deepened with a powerful poetic gift the various aspects of the mystery of the Incarnation, and each of them is for him an opportunity to sing and praise the extraordinary grandeur and wonderful beauty of the Virgin Mary, the Mother of the Incarnate Word.[1]

Subsequently, the new *Catechism of the Catholic Church*, issued in 1992, named as distinct forms of Marian devotion—along with the rosary in Latin Christianity and the Byzantine *Akathistos* hymn—the prayers of St. Ephrem in the Syriac tradition and those of St. Gregory in the Armenian.[2] Gregory's prominent position among the great Marian doctors should come as no surprise given that throughout his works he makes clear that the veneration of the Virgin is crucial for his spirituality and his overall theology. Mary has an essential role in the economy of salvation. It was only through her consent that the Word became flesh and dwelt among us.

[1] John Paul II, 1987, Encyclical Letter on the Blessed Virgin Mary (*Redemptoris Mater*), Vatican City, §31.

[2] *Catechism of the Catholic Church*, 1997, 2d edition, Rome: Libreria Editrice Vaticana, 706 (§2678).

Because of her we become worthy to call God *Abba, Father*. For it is only through her that we come to share in the humanity of Christ and it is through his incarnation that we are able to achieve fellowship with God:

> Praised are you, O bright reflection of the Creator's virtue, for the great reward of glory which you passed on to us—who are the least—through the marvelous miracle performed in you. For that fatherless Child, O Mother, you embraced as a son; and holding up in your arms that unbounded Being who became a human, you drew him close to your lips and greeted him with a kiss. Being found as coheirs with him, we cry out to God, *Abba, Father*, because of your intermediary role, O holy Mother of God.[3]

Gregory describes the union of Mary and the Word in the incarnation in very graphic terms. Mary is a living ark, likened to Noah's, on whose wood the Holy Spirit nails the Word so tightly that there is no "partitioning gap."[4] Mary's body is a correlate of the cross from which the salvation of humanity proceeds. The difference is that the nailing to Mary's body bestows human life upon the Word, while the cross wrenches that life away.

The Daughter of Eve

In this chapter I discuss and develop Gregory's Mariology based primarily on a reading of the two recensions of the encomium to the Virgin Mary, Prayer 80, addressed to the Virgin, of the *Book of Lamentation*, and some of his Marian hymns.

But we should also consider the connection in Gregory's mind between Mary and the bride of the Song of Songs. As we have seen in chapter four, in Gregory's commentary on the Song, the Marian symbolism of the bride, though present, is muted in favor of the ecclesial interpretation of the bride, whom Gregory considers to be an

[3] *Encomium on the Holy Virgin* (second recension) [*EHV2*], *MH* 12:967.23; Terian 2016, 312.

[4] *Litany [K'aroz] for the Assumption*, *MH* 12:708.45–48; Terian 2016, 148–49.

image of the church. Traditional Christian exegesis has treated the romantic and erotic poetry of the Canticle as an allegory of a "spiritual marriage" between Christ and his church or with the individual soul. Although Christian interpreters did acknowledge the bride as emblematic of Mary, the Marian reading did not come to the fore in any known commentary on the Song prior to the twelfth century. Nevertheless, Gregory is very much mindful of the Marian symbolism of the Song. Elsewhere in his writings, he makes explicit the very close relation between Mary and the church. Speaking of the church, he writes in the *Book of Lamentation*:

> This spiritual mother, celestial, luminous,
> Caressed me as her son
> More than my earthly, human, physical mother.
> The milk of her breasts was the blood of Christ.[5]

Having lost his earthly mother early in his life, Gregory was entrusted by his father to the care of the church, which became his spiritual mother. He then adds that the motherly care of the church resembles and is an image of the love of the Mother of God.

> If one were to write that the Theotokos
> Is the icon of the Church,
> One would not be unjustified.[6]

Alluding to *theosis*, by which Christ's image is restored in the children of the church, the poet notes that just as Mary gave birth to and cared for Christ, so too the church gives birth to and fosters the growth of the saints, these "divine creatures, pure icons of the one God, Christ."[7] Given this close relation between Mary and the church, the ecclesial and Marian readings of the Song are perfectly consonant in the poet's mind.

Indeed, Gregory draws this connection between the bride and Mary in numerous places in his writings. Nowhere does he do this

[5] *BL* 75.12; *MH* 12:476.1.
[6] *BL* 75.12; *MH* 12:476.2.
[7] *BL* 75.12; *MH* 12.476.7.

more eloquently and brilliantly than in an antiphon for the nativity, which begins with the words of the bride in Song 1:5 and continues to borrow from the verses of the Song.[8] The first part of the hymn is like a recapitulation in miniature of the Song with the voices of the bride and groom alternating. Here, I have divided the verses according to who appears to be speaking, beginning with the bride, though it should be noted that this is an artificial device not present in the manuscripts. The last stanza of the hymn commemorates the birth of Christ:

> Black am I, beautiful,
> A daughter of Eve, Jerusalem.
>
> Behold this my delightful bride,
> Bound through love with her groom.
>
> My nephew is like the gazelles,
> The young deer.
> Behold the voice of my beloved,
> Made tender and soft through love.
>
> Come my neighbor, come my companion,
> My bride from the cedars of Lebanon.
> See how she exults:
>
> Cover me with apples and
> Lead me to the house of wine!
>
> Her eyes are like a dove's
> her arm a cord of red, her necklace of gold.
> Behold she is a mountain of incense
> redolent of nard and myrrh.
>
> My beloved was beautiful,
> An infant child yet eternal.
> Behold he is a lofty mount,
> a lily of the valleys, a flower of the plain.
>
> The ranks of the prophets
> sing from on top of that hill,
> Behold he is the mount of the lily,
> his fragrance of rose, cinnamon.

[8] *MH* 12.649–50; Terian 2016, 49–52.

Arise and look to Bethlehem,
O children of Zion,
Go forth to the cave;
Bow down before the King.
Sing with the shepherds,
Worship with the magi.
Behold the gold of the King,
the incense of the Only-Begotten of God the Father,
To Whom we give glory and thanks,
And endless exaltation;
Now and forever may
Christ be blessed together by all.[9]

We can understand the bride as the church expectant of the Lord's advent. Just as the bride delights in the presence of the groom, the church is to rejoice at the imminent birth of Christ. But there are also clear indications that Gregory intends this to be an allegory of Mary and the Christ child. The Marian reading is first suggested by the bride's reference to herself as a "daughter of Eve," a distinctive designation that may point back to Genesis 3:15 and God's curse of the serpent that places enmity between his seed and the seed of Eve. The description thus suggests Mary's role as the New Eve, an ancient designation that can be traced back to the earliest

[9] My translation is from the version in the Antelias edition commemorating the millennium of the completion of the *Book of Lamentation* (St. Gregory of Narek, 2003, *Matean oghberkut'ean ew ayl Erkasirut'iwnk'* [Book of Lamentation and other works (in Armenian)], Antelias, Lebanon: Catholicosate of Cilicia, 646–47), which differs in a couple of places from the version in *MH* 12:649–50, upon which the translation of Terian 2016, 49–52, is based. It also differs in other respects from Terian's in a few places. For example, Terian reads the second line as a vocative, the bride calling to Jerusalem, the daughter of Eve. That reading is plausible, given that in the Song the bride addresses the daughters of Jerusalem, her companions. But since Armenian does not have a distinctive vocative case, she could also be describing herself. This latter reading seems to me to make better sense since in the Song the bride never just addresses one daughter but only the collective daughters. Also, she never refers to her companions as "daughter of Eve," an appellation that seems more fitting for Mary, the new Eve. Likewise, Jerusalem is a figure for the church as the New Jerusalem. Since the bride here symbolizes both Mary and the church, it seems to me more likely that the bride is designating herself here as the daughter of Eve and Jerusalem.

centuries of Christian literature.[10] In calling Mary the daughter of Eve, Gregory is drawing not on Greek patristic literature, but the Syriac tradition, in particular the poetry of Ephrem the Syrian.[11] In his Hymn on the Nativity, Ephrem writes:

> Man imposed corruption on woman when she came forth from him,
> Today she has repaid him—she who bore for him the Savior.
> He gave birth to the Mother, Eve—he, the man who was never born;
> How worthy of faith is the daughter of Eve, who without a man bore a child![12]

Further confirmation for the Marian reading of Gregory's hymn is found in the bride's calling her groom "an infant child yet eternal." We find examples of Gregory portraying Mary with the imagery surrounding the bride of the Song also in his *Encomium on the Holy Virgin*. There, he describes Mary as both a flower and an apple, metaphors drawn from Song 2:1 and 2:3. She is also said to be "a sanctified bride for the Father of Christ."[13] So even though the ecclesial symbolism of the bride dominates the commentary on the Song, the Marian reading was certainly present in Gregory's mind. And since he considers Mary as an icon or image of the church, the symbolism of the bride as the church coheres with that of the bride as a figure of Mary. Mary is the prototype of the church, given that the Holy Spirit descended on her as it did later in the upper room on the apostles at Pentecost, the birthday of the church, and also because her body became the first abode and tabernacle of Christ's body.

[10] The idea of Eve as a type of Mary is found as early as the second century in Justin Martyr, who wrote that while Eve was a virgin who brought forth death, Mary brought forth life through the Christ. See Thomas B. Falls, 1965, *Saint Justin Martyr: The First Apology, the Second Apology, Dialogue with Trypho, Exhortation to the Greeks, Discourse to the Greeks, the Monarchy, or the Rule of God*, Washington, DC: Catholic University of America Press, 305.

[11] A proximity search for the words "daughter" and "Eve" on the *TLG* returned no results that used the title "daughter of Eve" specifically for Mary.

[12] *Hymn on the Nativity* 1.14–16, in Kathleen McVey, trans., 1989, *Ephrem the Syrian: Hymns*, Classics of Western Spirituality, New York, Paulist Press, 65.

[13] *MH* 12.966.16; Terian 2016, 310.

Mary's role as the New Eve goes beyond her giving birth to Christ, the New Adam. For Gregory, redemption comes to humanity through Mary and her obedience to God's word. The early theologians and exegetes read Jesus' life as a recapitulation of the fall of Adam, overturning at each step the first man's original disobedience. Jesus' acceptance of the Father's will in the garden of Gethsemane is the mirror image and reversal of Adam's rejection of God's will in Eden. As humanity fell through an act of disobedience at a tree, so too we are raised by obedience to the Father's will at the wood of the cross. In the same way, Mary's acts recapitulate the life of Eve. Her fiat of obedience to God's will, spoken to the archangel Gabriel—"let it be to me according to your word" (Luke 1:38)—undoes Eve's fiat of disobedience, given to the serpent, another angelic being, albeit in disguise. So just as Christ's actions redeem Adam, we can understand Mary's actions as canceling the curse on Eve. And since Eve, as the first mother, represents all women, Mary's reversal of Eve's sin also signifies the salvation of all women.[14] The belief that Mary assumes a special role in the salvation of all women is not new but is found in patristic texts as early as the third century, for example, in the writings of Origen.[15] Proclus, the archbishop of Constantinople (d. ca. 446) with whom the Armenian bishops consulted on doctrinal matters, gives a forthright affirmation of Mary's leading role in the salvation of women: "All women are blessed because of her. No longer does the female sex stand accused. For it produced the offspring that will surpass even the angels in glory."[16] Gregory adopts this patristic idea of Eve's absolution in Mary and represents it in his hymnography as a symbol of the redemption of women. In the treasure-hymn for the feast of the Assumption, Eve and her daughters, representing all women, dance in celebration at the news of

[14] For discussion of this idea in the patristic tradition, see Tina Beattie, 2007, "Mary in Patristic Theology" in Sarah Jane Boss, ed., *Mary: The Complete Resource*, Oxford: Oxford University Press, 75–105, esp. 90–93.

[15] Beattie 2007, 90.

[16] From the *Homily on the Holy Virgin Theotokos* in Nicholas Constas, 2003, *Proclus of Constantinople and the Cult of the Virgin in Late Antiquity: Homilies 1-5*, Leiden: Brill, 260–61. Also cited by Beattie 2007, 91.

Mary's assumption into heaven and her elevation to the rank of the angels, a dignity that they too will share:

> Through you does our forefather Adam prosper,
> You who are his daughter and virgin,
> Through whom was born the One who takes away sin.
>
> Eve dances with her daughters,
> Joyously adorning herself for the banquet,
> Having become part of the circle of the seraphim through you,
> Mother and Virgin, most blessed among women.[17]

As the first of creation to achieve *theosis* through the incarnation, Mary undoes the curse of Eve. Since she is the new Eve, Mary takes over from Eve the role of being the icon of all women. Through her unique holiness, she is exempt from the curse of Eve, and her exemption from this curse presages the lifting of that curse from all the daughters of Eve:

> In you were fulfilled the words of the chosen prophets
> And of the predicting seers
> Speaking for God,
> That you will become in place of Eve
> The mother of the living Word of God
> By whom the creatures were adorned.
> To be restored from ancient sin to glory,
> Thus were the birthing pangs of the curse on the foremother
> Dissolved and replaced with a blessing,
> And the writ of condemnation for sinning was annulled, torn apart.[18]

The belief that Mary gave birth without suffering is not original to Gregory. The apocryphal works on Mary and the nativity, most

[17] *MH* 12:707.32–37; Terian 2016, 148. Terian perceptively notes that while Mary is assumed into heaven among the cherubim (149n16), Eve and her daughters are elevated to the rank of the seraphim. In Dionysian angelology, these two orders of angels share the highest status among the celestial beings, as they are the closest to God (cf. *Celestial Hierarchy* 201A in Luibheid 1987, 160–61).

[18] *MH* 12.707.25-32; Terian 2016, 148.

notably the *Protoevangelium of James*, suggest a painless birth. Several of the apocryphal infancy narratives were translated into Armenian as early as the sixth century, so Gregory could have had access to them.[19] The depictions in these infancy narratives accentuate the extreme harshness that Mary faced as she prepared to give birth. The nativity account in Luke's gospel makes clear that she was traveling without knowing where she would have her child. But the Armenian Infancy gospel also describes the extremely unfavorable weather, noting that the day of Christ's birth was "a cold, wintry day."[20] The cave of the nativity was normally used to house animals, not an especially sanitary location. Yet Mary was able to give birth easily without the services of a midwife.[21] In a time when giving birth even in ideal surroundings could still be very dangerous, the ease of Jesus' birth stood out as a powerful sign of something supernatural and miraculous. The patristic tradition elaborates on the lack of labor pain; one of Gregory's sources, Nyssen's commentary on the Song, refers to Mary's pregnancy as "unique, [Christ's] birth unstained, its pangs, painless." [22] But Gregory takes that thought further and indicates that somehow through Mary's painless delivery of Jesus the curse of painful labor placed on Eve and her daughters has been removed. In the *Book of Lamentation*, he writes that Mary is the "healer of Eve's labor pains."[23] But even this idea that Mary relieves the suffering of bearing children is not original to Gregory. It is already present in the Armenian tradition as early as the beginning of the eighth century in a hymn on the nativity, addressed to the Virgin, by the anchoress and hymnographer Sahakdukht of Siwnik':

[19] For the Armenian translation and commentary on this work, see Abraham Terian, 2008, *The Armenian Infancy Gospel with Three Early Versions of the Protoevanglium of James*, Oxford: Oxford University Press. For the broader patristic evidence, see also Luigi Gambero, 1999, *Mary and the Fathers of the Church*, Thomas Buffer, tr., San Francisco: Ignatius Press, 35–42.

[20] Terian 2008, 42.

[21] Terian 2008, 43.

[22] Gregory of Nyssa 2012, 409.

[23] *BL* 80.2; *MH* 12:500.34. Samuelian renders *erkants'n* as "sorrows" but the specific and primary meaning of the word is the pain of childbirth. See *NBHL* entry for *erkn*, vol.1, 695.

Door of heaven and descent of God,
Intercessor of peace,
You lifted up the labor pains from the first mother, Eve,
Who was conquered by death.
Blessed are you among women,
Graceful virgin and mother of the Lord.[24]

Yet Gregory fixates on this thought. Mary's exemption from labor pain and the attendant annulment of the curse of Eve take on a particular significance as a recurrent theme running throughout Gregory's Marian works, a persistence that assumes a special poignancy in the light of his own mother's sufferings and death. We have seen that he describes God as the Creating-Mother undergoing the pangs of birth. This contrast of God's labor pains with the Virgin's painless birthing produces an interesting reversal of nature: God who is by nature impassable experiences the pangs of birth, while Mary, formed of mortal flesh, gives birth free of any discomfort. This reversal is itself an image of Christ's passion, in which the impassible Word of God takes on the sin and sufferings of humans in order to relieve us of our afflictions.

Some scholars have noted that Mary's exemption from the ordinary experiences of women serves to distance and alienate her from the normal human condition. In her book *Alone of All Her Sex*, Marina Warner sets out a compelling case for the detrimental effects of such Marian exceptionalism.[25] Through the magnification of her special privileges as the Mother of God, Mary begins to lose her humanity in much the same way as the Julianists, in insisting on the incorruptibility of Christ's body, make Jesus more remote and less suitable for the role of mediator between God and humans. Warner argues that by exaggerating the differences between Mary and other women, the church fathers have in effect encour-

[24] *MH* 6:602–3. The hymn is an acrostic with each stanzas' initial letter spelling out her name. The acrostic device ensured that the hymn would be attributed to its composer, a matter of particular concern for a woman whose works may otherwise be ascribed later to a male author. Yet this concern is not exclusive to women authors, since Gregory employs eponymous acrostics too.

[25] Marina Warner, 1983, *Alone of All Her Sex: The Myth and the Cult of the Virgin Mary*, New York: Vintage.

aged an association of women in general with the disobedient Eve and thus fostered the misogyny that has infected much of Christian thought and practice through the centuries.

Warner's critique of traditional Mariology is worthy of particular attention as the church in modern times struggles with questions not only of the legacy of contempt toward women but also in debates on the role of women especially in the ministry. But with regard to Gregory and his praise of Mary's privileges, we should note that her special status heralds the future blessed state not only of all women but of humanity as a whole. The daughters of Eve see in Mary that which they will become. Mary is the archetype of human salvation. Her holiness and purity are the prelude to the blessings and graces extended to all humanity and the daughters have special occasion to rejoice because the promise of sanctification has been fulfilled first of all not in one of the sons of Adam but in one of their sisters. Surely, Gregory imagines among the dancing women his own earthly mother.

Although Mary is ranked among the cherubim, she does not become a normal angel, a bodiless being, but she is assumed among the celestial beings with her incorruptible body, again a preview of our own bodily resurrection. As Proclus noted, she has surpassed even the angels in their glory. And that superiority to angelic glory is a result of her being not simply a spirit like the angels, but an embodied spirit. This notion of humans, composed of both earth and soul and exceeding the angels, also appears in Gregory's commentary on the Song. The daughters of Jerusalem marvel at the bride, the Shulamite, and ask her to turn that they may look at her (Song 7:1). Gregory interprets this as the angels amazed at the transformation of the human body from afflicted and sinful dust to a glorious garment that now adorns the bride, who has surpassed the celestial beings in power and whom the groom regards with greater admiration.[26] The body that once weighed us down now lifts us up above the angels; what was "sown in weakness is raised in power" (1 Cor 15:43).

[26] *MH* 12:847.122; Ervine 2007, 173.

Mary's Perpetual Virginity and Assumption

Among the mariological doctrines that Gregory affirms is Mary's perpetual virginity. Gregory follows the traditions and liturgy of the church, which bestow the title of "ever virgin" on Mary. He calls Mary the ever-virgin Mother of God, for example, in his Litany for the Assumption.[27] Gregory does not elaborate on this title, but the Armenian tradition of biblical exegesis accounted for Jesus' brothers and sisters by viewing them as Joseph's children by another marriage. For example, Stephen of Siwnik' writes in his commentary on the gospels that Jesus' brothers mentioned in Matthew 12:46 are in fact not Mary's but Joseph's children by a previous marriage.[28] As well, Gregory's association of the Virgin with the widow of Nain, the mother of an only son, in Prayer 18 of the *Book of Lamentation* discussed in the previous chapter, implies that Mary too had but one child.

In addition to the question of her perpetual virginity, another concern that drew the attention of theologians was the manner of Mary's departure from the earth. Death normally entails a shadowy bodiless existence awaiting the final judgment when our bodies, now glorified, will be restored to us. In Mary's case, however, there is no delay between her departure from the mortal life and the restoration of her bodily life. Her incorruptible body is assumed on the very same day as her soul:

> The riches of greatness culminated today in a tangible way in you, who soared to the heights of heaven in a body incapable of corruption and disintegration, in the presence of which the indebtedness to death shamefully dissipated. And you were deemed a worthy resident in the land of the living, a cohabitant with your Lord, O holy Mother of the Lord. Plead for mercy always for those who sojourn in this deep abyss.[29]

Although the belief that Mary was assumed into heaven is ancient, the bodily assumption was not officially a doctrine of the Catholic

[27] *MH* 12:708.56; Terian 2016, 149.

[28] *MH* 6:194.31.

[29] *MH* 12:965–75; Terian 2016, 324.

Church until 1950, when Pope Pius XII issued the apostolic constitution *Munificentissimus Deus*.[30] The belief in the assumption, while not defined as an article of faith in the Eastern and Oriental Orthodox churches, is proclaimed in the Orthodox liturgy and calendar, with August 15 marking the feast of the Dormition, as it is usually designated in the Eastern churches.[31] The patristic tradition in the East, however, appears to have been unsettled on the question of Mary's bodily assumption. The Coptic Church commemorates the dormition and the assumption on two different days, celebrating the former on January 29 and the latter on August 22, perhaps a reflection of a belief in the Alexandrian tradition that Mary's body was assumed not at the same time as her death but later. According to a tradition once current in the East, Christ assumed Mary's soul but took her body to the garden of Eden at the foot of the tree of life to await the general resurrection.[32] That tradition, of course, diminishes Mary's exceptionalism, as her own integral presence in heaven takes place at the same time as the rest of humanity. Although there were different views about Mary's assumption in both the Eastern and Western churches, it is notable that Gregory unequivocally affirms the belief that Mary was assumed body and soul into heaven.

[30] The constitution was issued on November 1, 1950. There, the pope declared *ex cathedra* that "the Immaculate Mother of God, the ever-virgin Mary, having completed the course of her earthly life, was assumed body and soul into heavenly glory." See Pius XII and John R. Sheets, SJ, 1980, *Munificentissimus Deus*, Boston: St. Paul Books and Media.

[31] Though the Armenian Apostolic Church refers to the feast (celebrated in this rite on the Sunday nearest August 15) as *Verap'okhoumn*, literally, "assumption" of the Blessed Virgin Mary. On the assumption in the Armenian tradition, see Thamar Dasnabedian, 1995, *La Panégyrique de la Sainte Mère de Dieu de Grigor Narekac'i*, Antelias, Lebanon: Catholicosate of Cilicia, 128–32.

[32] See Bishop Gregorius, 1991, "Feasts of the Theotokos" in Aziz Suryal Atiya, ed., *The Coptic Encyclopedia*, New York: Macmillan; and Emmanuel Lanne, 2006, "Marie Immaculée et Glorifiée dans la Mystère du Salut chez Saint Grégoire de Narek" in Mahé and Zekiyan 2006, 139–76, esp. 159.

Mary Immaculate

The most contentious of the Marian doctrines, at least in terms of the relations of the Catholic Church and the Eastern churches, is the immaculate conception. Controversies surrounding this understanding of the conception of Mary by her parents, Joachim and Anna, divide the communions to this day. It was only in the middle of the nineteenth century that the Catholic Church officially proclaimed the immaculate conception as official doctrine. The dogmatic constitution *Ineffabilis Deus* of Pope Pius IX, issued in 1854, declared that Mary, through a grace granted uniquely to her, was preserved free of original sin from the moment of her conception.[33] But it would be wrong to view this as a doctrine that emerged out of a theological vacuum. For belief in the immaculate conception was much older and was debated by the medieval scholastics with a consensus developing in its favor in the West well before Pius IX's decree. In part, the doctrine emerged as a way to account for a singular feature of the calendar of feasts: the only saint whose conception is commemorated in the calendar is the Virgin. The feast of the Conception of the Holy Mother of God is ancient, dating back as early as the fifth century. Given that human beings are conceived in original sin, it did not seem proper to commemorate an event tainted by sin and the sexual desire of Mary's parents. Jesus' conception was different since his conception was virginal and thus free of all sin. At first the church attempted to suppress celebration of the feast.[34] The failure of that attempt revealed the extent of the popularity among the faithful of this pious observation. As a result, Catholic theologians made an effort to justify the popular practice. This is a good example of theology being used to justify the traditions embraced by the people. Theology need not be an imposition from above of some novel theory but often is grounded in the deep-rooted piety and sense of the faithful. One proposal to justify the feast was to recognize Mary's con-

[33] Pius IX and John R. Sheets, SJ, 1992, *Defining the Dogma of the Immaculate Conception*, Boston: St. Paul Books and Media.

[34] Sarah Jane Boss, 2007b, "The Doctrine of Mary's Immaculate Conception," in Boss 2007a, 207–35, esp. 208.

ception as free from original sin. The church in both East and West had with some exceptions early in the patristic tradition come to the conclusion that Mary never committed any actual sins. It did not seem to be too radical a move also to acknowledge that Mary was preserved by an act of grace from original sin, understood as the human proclivity, inherited from Adam's primal sin, to disobey God. This recognition would validate the preexisting veneration of Mary's conception and also underscore her special status as the blessed woman chosen to bring Jesus into the world. While for the rest of us the stain of original sin is removed through baptism, Mary was not in need of baptism since she was kept immune from the contamination of sin from the very beginning of her existence.

Nevertheless, there was considerable opposition to the immaculate conception among Western theologians. The great thirteenth-century doctor St. Thomas Aquinas, often regarded as the greatest of Catholic theologians, argued against the doctrine. His fellow Dominicans remained mostly opposed to it as late as the seventeenth century.[35] Above all, it was the Franciscans and their distinguished philosopher John Duns Scotus (1266–1308) who championed the immaculate conception, so that by the time Pius IX issued the decree, a consensus had been achieved at least in the West in favor of the doctrine.

The Eastern churches generally rejected the teaching. This was partly due to their different understanding of sin, one not based on the Augustinian doctrine that original sin itself, rather than merely the consequences of sin, was transmitted by parents at conception through concupiscence—that is, sexual desire. But there was (and remains) in the Eastern church an aversion to the Western inclination to define doctrines formally rather than simply to let them be expressed through the liturgy and prayers of the church. Expressing the common belief that Mary did not commit any actual sins, the Orthodox speak of Mary as all-holy (*panagia*). If they specified a time of sanctification at all, the Eastern theologians focused on the moment of Mary's fiat, or her overshadowing by the Holy Spirit (Luke 1:35), rather than the moment of her own conception.

[35] See Boss 2007b, 207.

Also problematic from the Eastern perspective was that the pope's promulgation of the doctrine was made *ex cathedra*, meaning that he was exercising a prerogative, recognized in the Catholic but not Orthodox churches, as successor of St. Peter to define doctrines on faith infallibly and without needing the decision of a church council. The Orthodox have never accepted this as a prerogative of the bishop of Rome or any single bishop.

In his constitution, Pius IX noted that the ancient writings of the church fathers in both the East and West testify to the doctrine of the immaculate conception. Later commentators have brought forward St. Ephrem among other patristic authors as an example of an early advocate of immaculacy, the doctrine that Mary was conceived free of the taint of original sin.[36] In his *Hymns on Nisibis*, Ephrem writes:

> Only You and your Mother
> Are more beautiful than everything.
> For on you, O Lord, there is no mark;
> Neither is there any stain in your Mother.[37]

Since, as we have seen, Ephrem's veneration of Mary influenced Gregory, who extols the Virgin in equally exalted terms, it is reasonable to ask if Gregory belongs to this same choir of patristic authorities who appear to bear witness to the immaculate conception. Armenia would seem to be a promising place to look for expressions of immaculacy.[38] Some of the Eastern objections to the doctrine do not apply as well in the Armenian context. For example, the objection that the East rejects Augustinian notions of original sin and that as a result the question of whether Mary was conceived without original sin is otiose may be a compelling argument in the general context of Eastern theology, but the Armenian theologians were familiar with something like the Augustinian account

[36] See Gambero 1999, 110.

[37] *Hymns on Nisibis* 27, quoted in Gambero 1999, 109.

[38] For discussion of the immaculate conception in the Armenian context and references to the debate among Armenian theologians on Gregory's views, see Dasnabedian 1995, 123–28.

of sin through the influence of Julianism there. Nevertheless, the question of whether Gregory believed in immaculacy is difficult to answer in part because the question was not clearly defined or a matter of immediate concern in his historical context. He explicitly affirms that Mary is the bearer of God because he knows Nestorians who question that title. But the problem of the immaculate conception was not a major point of theological polemics in his time and place. Nevertheless, by examining Gregory's writings we may be able to get a better sense of how he understands Mary's sinlessness. In Prayer 80 of the *Book of Lamentation* she is said to be marked by "spotless purity, unblemished goodness, immaculate holiness, solicitous intercession."[39] But a mere assertion of Mary's spotless and immaculate holiness is not sufficient to establish that Gregory affirmed immaculacy, because essential to the doctrine is that Mary is immaculate from the moment of her conception and that she is preserved from the stain of sin rather than purified of it. It is the moment of her sanctification and preservation from sin that is in question.

The Benedictine scholar Emmanuel Lanne, basing his conclusions on Dasnabedian's research on the *Encomium on the Holy Virgin*, presents a meticulous and well-argued case against immaculacy in Gregory's Mariology.[40] Lanne notes that the orthodox doctrine of the Armenian church articulated at the Council of Manazkert holds that the Word assumed corruptible flesh by nature and by grace transformed it into incorruptible flesh. By being united with the Word at the incarnation, Mary's flesh shares in the same incorruptibility. If we interpret incorruptibility to mean Mary's preservation from original sin, Mary receives this grace only when she accepts the divine Word within her through the Spirit's action. Lanne cites a number of passages from Gregory's work to support his contention that Mary is purified at the *fiat*. For example, in the second recension of his *Encomium*, Gregory says of Mary that she was "praised as the sinless child of the first woman."[41] While this seems to indicate that Mary was always free

[39] *BL* 80.1; *MH* 12:500.17–18.

[40] Lanne 2006 in Mahé and Zekiyan 2006, 139–76.

[41] *MH* 12:971.63; Terian 2016, 318; Lanne 2006, 154.

of sin, Lanne says that Gregory made this assertion in the context of the annunciation. After reviewing a number of passages from Gregory's Marian works, he concludes that all of the attributions of Mary's immaculate condition are related to her fiat. While Gregory never doubts her absolute purity, her sinlessness is always connected primarily to the incarnation and the fact that Mary carries the incarnate Word within her. It is this intimate unity with her Lord that bestows a unique glory on her. Although many of the statements that Gregory makes about Mary are equivocal and may be interpreted in an immaculist light, Lanne thinks in agreement with Dasnabedian that when these assertions are placed within their textual context, as well as against the theological background of Gregory's thought, they all point to a non-immaculist reading.

I agree with Lanne and Dasnabedian on the theological context of Gregory's thought. He does adhere to a position midway between Julian's view that Christ's body is by nature incorruptible and Severus's position that Christ's body is corruptible until the resurrection. The Armenian position, we recall, is that at the incarnation the corruptible flesh assumed by the Word becomes incorruptible. This middle position does suggest that Mary's flesh was corruptible but that when Christ made her body his abode, it became incorruptible. Hence it was only at the incarnation that Mary was cleansed of incorruption.

But the conclusion that Gregory's position is anti-immaculist follows only if incorruptibility in this case refers to exemption from sin. Corruption, especially within the context of the Julianist controversy, is a notoriously ambiguous concept. In that controversy, corruption primarily signifies impassibility; the debate focused on whether Christ's body suffers by nature or by will. But corruptibility could also refer to a liability to moral corruption from the effects of original sin. There is no doubt that something dramatic happened to Mary at the fiat. But we need not conclude that it is the grace of exemption from sin or its effects. Furthermore, whenever Gregory speaks of the change effected in Mary at the annunciation, it usually involves not a change with respect to sin but a transformation in which her "frail nature," incapable of bearing God in her womb, "became the vessel and bearer of the unbearable word of God mixed with flesh from her."[42] Her frailty is not a moral deficit on her part but a physical limitation of being a finite mortal being incapable of containing the infinite eternal Word. Similarly, when in the Song of Songs the bride's companions express their concern about her future because of her small size and lack of breasts (Song 8:8), Gregory reads this as an allegory of the angels doubting the ability of Mary to be the bearer of God.[43] Defiant and emboldened, the bride responds to the companions' doubts by proclaiming herself a battlement and her breasts like a tower (8:10). Gregory interprets this as a reference to Mary's fortification at the incarnation:

> Through the power of the Almighty, my littleness will become greater and more solid than a wall, and from having no breasts, my breasts will become like a tower. For the One who made the heavens and earth and our nature and yours from nothing will magnify my breasts and make them larger than yours. So that which you are unable to hear and bear and suffer, my weak nature made greater than yours, has heard, borne, and believed.[44]

Just as a dramatic change takes place in Mary at the incarnation, so too, Gregory indicates, something extraordinary happens at her conception. The relevant text is from the second recension of the *Encomium on the Holy Virgin* as translated by Terian with slight modification:

> O blessed among women, a worthy abode for the descending Word, a pot for the planting of the divine body, and a reliquary for the oil of divine anointing, you were preserved[45] in immaculate innocence[46] by the shielding wings of angels prior to the birth of the Word in utmost perfection. You whom the glory of the Triune God was pleased to make his resting place, for the Holy Spirit—the author of impeccable sanctity—came upon you, and *the power of the*

[42] *MH* 12.851.30–31; Ervine 2007, 178.

[43] *MH* 12:870.78; Ervine 2007, 198.

[44] *MH* 12:872.98–99; Ervine 2007, 199.

[45] The Armenian is *pahēir*, "preserved, guarded, kept."

[46] The Armenian is *anaght anbtsut'eamb*, "spotless innocence."

Most High Father overshadowed your mother [Anna] in order to prepare you to be the receptacle of the Son.[47]

This passage, understood in the way Terian translates it, is among the most congenial in Gregory's corpus to the immaculist thesis. For the Holy Spirit here descends not upon Mary at the annunciation, but upon her mother, Anna, at Mary's conception and bestowed upon her "impeccable sanctity." The words of the angel to Mary at the annunciation ("the power of the Most High will overshadow you") are repeated almost exactly here, but in this case addressed to Anna ("the power of the Father overshadowed your mother").[48] The connection that Gregory draws between the conceptions of Mary and of Jesus goes well beyond the language of the Armenian versions of the *Protoevangelium*, which depict an angelic annunciation to Anna but without any indication that her conception involved the same overshadowing of the Most High as her daughter's.[49] Gregory implies that Mary is protected from the stain of sin from the moment of her conception rather than simply being fortified to receive the Lord in her womb. If Terian's reading of this passage is correct, then there are two stages to Mary's preparation to receive the Word. First, the Holy Spirit descended on Mary at her conception and preserved her from all sin. Then, before Jesus' conception, Mary's body was strengthened to prepare her physically to be the bearer of God. However, there are reasons to doubt that this is the correct translation of the passage. Dasnabedian, in her French translation, takes the passage to be addressed to Mary and renders it as "and the power of the Father Most High overshadowed you, O Mother."[50] If Dasnabedian's translation is correct, then this passage does not support an

[47] *MH* 12:966–67.17–18; Terian 2016, 310–11; italics added.

[48] The Armenian of Luke 1:35 is *zawrut'iwn Bardzreloyn hovani lits'i i veray k'o* while the *Encomium* says here *bardzreloyn Hawrn zawrut'iwn mawrd hovanets'aw*.

[49] See Terian 2008, 152, 160, and 169 for various versions of the annunciation to Anna from the Armenian *Protoevangelium*.

[50] "Et la puissance du Père Très-Haut te plaça sous son ombre, ô Mère," taking "mother" here, in contrast to Terian's translation, as a vocative referring to Mary rather than Anna. See Dasnabedian 1995, 258–59.

immaculist reading. My own view inclines toward Dasnabedian's version, though Terian's translation cannot be ruled out on strictly grammatical grounds.

There is however another passage from Gregory's Marian writings, this time the first recension of the encomium on the Virgin, that seems to me to contain a more incontrovertible expression of immaculacy. There, Gregory describes Mary as a "spotless lamb" presented to the Jerusalem temple.[51] According to the Armenian versions of the *Protoevangelium of James*, Mary was presented to the temple when she was three.[52] Although the Virgin's dedication was many years before the incarnation, Gregory already describes her as immaculate at this event and calls her dedication "a foreshadowing"[53] of Christ's own sacrifice as the undefiled lamb of God (1 Pet 1:19). So this particular passage of the encomium is noteworthy as an especially clear assertion of Mary as immaculate while still in her infancy.

On the other hand, there are passages in Gregory's works that appear explicitly to reject immaculacy. There is at least one verse in Marian Prayer 80 of the *Book of Lamentation* that seems to deny that Mary was exempted from sin from her conception. In language that resembles the description of the annunciation in Luke 1:35, Gregory says that the Virgin was "prepared and purified by the resting of the Spirit."[54] The word translated as "purified" is a distinctive verb that literally means "to effect purity."[55] The mention of purification by the Holy Spirit apparently at the annunciation implies that Mary is only at that moment purified of sin. Even this, though, is not decisive evidence against the immaculist thesis. Alluding to the infant Jesus' presentation to the temple in Luke

[51] *MH* 956.30; Terian 2016, 293. The Armenian is *oroj anarat*, "a sinless or immaculate lamb."

[52] Terian 2008, 153, 161.

[53] The Armenian is *stuerazgoysh*, a *hapax* that probably means something like "shadowy foresight."

[54] *BL* 80.1; *MH* 12:499.13.

[55] The Armenian is *mak'ragorcel*. The *NBHL* cites only this occurrence in the *BL*, but provides three citations in other authors of the substantive form, *mak'ragorc*, "something that effects purity."

2:22-24, Gregory says, "He was purified, thus he was lauded."[56] If Gregory says of Christ, who is without doubt sinless, that he was purified at his presentation, then the assertion that Mary was purified at the annunciation need not entail that she was purified of sin rather than prepared for her mission.

A much more extensive study will be needed for a more definite assessment of Gregory's position on the immaculate conception. Any further exploration of his Mariology must begin with an engagement with the impressive body of work produced by Dasnabedian, the foremost authority on Armenian Mariology. My tentative conclusion at this point is that although the evidence remains somewhat equivocal, Gregory inclines toward an immaculist Mariology, and that he may accordingly be added to the list of the Eastern doctors whose writings provide support for the doctrine, not only St. Ephrem in the Syriac tradition but also Greek fathers such as St. John of Damascus. The fact that the works of preeminent teachers in three of the major Eastern Christian traditions, if not explicitly affirming immaculacy, are at least strongly suggestive of it, is a significant and a hopeful sign for a developing convergence in the Marian doctrines of different churches.

One may well ask what is at stake in the immaculist debate, especially since both the Eastern and Catholic churches agree that Mary did not sin, and the disagreement essentially boils down to when and how her sinlessness began. Mindful also of Marina Warner's and other feminist scholars' cautionary depictions of how Mary's privileges and exceptionalism have historically been used to malign women, we should also ask how Gregory's support for the immaculate conception fits in with his general spirituality and desire to make the church more engaged with the people. For in emphasizing distinctions between Mary and the rest of her sex, he risks turning Mary into an unapproachable, forbidding demigod rather than a real woman who shares in the experiences of other women. In response to this concern, one may note that in some ways the immaculate conception teaching may have a reverse ef-

[56] The Armenian for "was purified" is *mak'rets'aw*. This passage occurs in both recensions: *MH* 12:960.70; Terian 2016, 301 (first recension) and *MH* 12:972.69; Terian 2016, 320 (second recension).

fect.[57] By revealing that a mortal being can be conceived free of sin even as the result of normal sexual intercourse, the teaching undoes an Augustinian-inspired disparagement of sexuality, and indeed of marriage, as the conduit of original sin—a belief that in many ways has had a negative effect on the course of Christian history. In this way, Mary's immaculate conception may actually help to affirm the inherent goodness of ordinary life and sexuality that is sanctified by God's will. It is perhaps no accident that the most forceful advocates of the immaculate conception in the West were Franciscans, whose spirituality, inherited from their founder, St. Francis of Assisi, emphasized simplicity and humility as well as the sanctity of ordinary life. Gregory's own spirituality, informed by the school of Narek's emphasis on the virtue of humility, bears many similarities with Franciscan ideals and perhaps, also not coincidentally, comes very close to affirming the immaculist doctrine as well.

In this rarefied air of grand theological disputations, though, we should not forget Mary the human being, chosen by God for the most sacred of responsibilities. Gregory never loses sight of the person of Mary and her place in popular piety. For Gregory, Mary is to be treated not simply as an object of theological speculation, but above all else as his intercessor with her Son and the Mother of God to whom we "lift up our arms, believing with unwavering hope that we will live."[58]

[57] My thoughts here about the anthropological implications of the doctrine are not original but based on Sarah Jane Boss's observations and especially her use of the fourteenth-century Franciscan mystic St. Bridget of Sweden's writings to illuminate these implications. See Sarah Jane Boss 2007b, esp. 214–17.

[58] *MH* 12:973.81; Terian 2016, 323.

Chapter Ten
From Narek to Rome and Beyond

The previous chapter began with a passage from Pope John Paul II's encyclical on Mary, *Redemptoris Mater*, that mentioned with admiration Gregory's devotional prayers to the Virgin. It was this reference to Gregory and his veneration of the Mother of God that set in motion his cause to be declared a Doctor of the Universal Church. In this chapter I will present some details on the process that led to Pope Francis's official declaration in 2015. But I also want to develop some thoughts on the broader implications of Gregory's new status as a universal Doctor not only concerning the more obvious ramifications for Christian ecumenism and unity but also for the insights that Gregory's writings and theology offer for the problems that the church and the world face today.

Becoming a Doctor

John Paul II was the first pope known to have mentioned Gregory in his writings and public statements. After his 1987 encyclical, he continued to refer to the Armenian monk in a number of speeches and homilies. For example, in his 2001 apostolic letter on the occasion of the 1,700th anniversary of Armenia's official proclamation as a Christian nation, he quoted several verses from the *Book of Lamentation* as well as the *Encomium on the Holy Virgin*.[1] There, the pontiff

[1] French text of the letter at http://www.vatican.va/holy_father/john_paul_ii/apost_letters/documents/hf_jp-ii_apl_20010217_battesimo-armenia_fr.html, retrieved December 4, 2017.

described Gregory as the "great Marian doctor (*vardapet*) of the Armenian Church." John Paul was himself noted for his profound devotion to Mary; his motto as both bishop and pope was *Totus Tuus* ("totally yours"), an expression of his personal entrustment to the protection of the Virgin Mother. It is therefore understandable that he would have a particular affinity for Armenia's gifted saint who shared his deep affection for Mary.

It was that affinity that prompted the hierarchy of the Armenian Catholic Church—the Eastern Catholic Church that follows the Armenian rite while also being in full communion with Rome—to propose that Gregory be named a Doctor of the Church. In 1988, the then-catholicos patriarch of the Armenian Catholics, John Peter XVIII Kasparian formally submitted to the pope a request that Gregory be granted the title of Doctor.[2] The pope forwarded this request to the relevant Vatican offices that would determine if Gregory was a suitable candidate. The Congregation for the Doctrine of the Faith is entrusted with the duty of establishing whether the candidate has a record of eminent teaching (*eminens doctrina*), while the Congregation for the Causes of Saints examines the evidence for a life of exceptional holiness (*insignis vitae sanctitas*). Gregory was already recognized as a saint of the Catholic Church since he has been venerated as such in the Armenian Catholic Church for centuries. But the Congregation for the Doctrine of the Faith at first responded that Gregory's work would need to be studied more carefully to enable an informed decision on the question of his *eminens doctrina*. Following this initial answer from the congregation, a number of academic conferences and symposia dedicated to Gregory's works were held, and scholars began to produce critical editions of his writings. With this scholarly work accomplished, in 2010, John Peter's successor as Armenian Catholic patriarch, Nersēs Peter XIX Tarmuni, asked John Paul's successor, Benedict XVI, to recommend that the congregation reopen its investigation. The patriarch also had the support of Archbishop Claudio Gugerotti, the apostolic nuncio to Armenia. Archbishop Gugerotti recommended that

[2] The details of the process of declaring Gregory a Doctor are based mainly on the comprehensive account in Regina Willi, 2015, "Gregor von Narek: Kirchenlehrer und Poet aus Armenien" in *Ostkirchliche Studien* 64, 313–34.

Gregory, who embodies the "sacrificial and penitential consciousness of his nation" be named a Doctor in 2015 as part of the commemoration of the centennial of the Armenian Genocide. In particular, the archbishop noted that Gregory is a symbol of his people and faith and a sign of unity for the faithful of the Armenian Apostolic and Catholic Churches, both of which venerate him as a beloved and celebrated saint.

With the extraordinary resignation of Pope Benedict in 2013 and the subsequent election of his successor, Jorge Mario Bergoglio, archbishop of Buenos Aires, as Pope Francis, the circumstances seemed especially favorable for Gregory's cause. The new pope had a history of close relations and friendship with the large Armenian community in Argentina and must have taken a special interest in expediting the process. On December 17, 2014, the Congregation for the Doctrine of the Faith decided unanimously that Gregory's writings were marked by eminent doctrine. Shortly after that, in the early days of 2015, the Congregation for the Causes of Saints certified Gregory's life as one of exceptional sanctity.

The third and final condition needed for elevation to the rank of Doctor of the Church is a declaration of the church (*Ecclesiae declaratio*), which is ordinarily made by the pope in his capacity as the supreme pastor of the universal church. Pope Francis made the solemn declaration that Gregory is a Doctor during the mass commemorating the Armenian Genocide on April 12, 2015, the Second Sunday of Easter and the liturgical feast of Divine Mercy. He did this in the presence of the Armenian Catholic patriarch, as well as the two Armenian Apostolic catholicoi, Garegin II, catholicos of all Armenians, and Aram I, catholicos of the Great House of Cilicia, the president of the Republic of Armenia, Serzh Sargsyan, and a large number of Armenian clergymen and lay faithful.

The Catholic Church has experienced some extraordinary changes in the years since Gregory's cause was first proposed. The church has witnessed the rare event of a papal resignation followed by the unexpected and unprecedented election of a pope from the New World, a Jesuit who took the name of St. Francis, a name never before taken by a pope. The course of events need not have turned out this way; the pope who named Gregory a Doctor could very well have been Benedict if he had remained in office, or a new pope other than Francis. But it is tempting to suppose that there is a special bond connecting Francis and the themes of his papacy with the first, and as of this writing, only Doctor proclaimed by him. Gregory's works are marked by a deep faith in and desire for God's mercy. The greatest of all God's gifts to us is his mercy, which is not given as payment for our works, but is offered freely to sinners:

> The rewards are yours, and yours too the mercies,
> And yet I exult not as much
> In your rewards, as in your mercy.
> For the latter increases your glory,
> While the former recognize the works of ascetics;
> The rewards are compensation for labor,
> But the mercies are acts of generosity toward sinners.[3]

The theme of mercy that runs throughout Gregory's poem is also central to Pope Francis's understanding of Christ's message. It may not be mere coincidence that Francis named Gregory a Doctor on the Sunday of the feast of Divine Mercy and that on the previous day he issued the formal proclamation of the Jubilee of Mercy. In an interview with Andrea Tornielli published in *The Name of God Is Mercy*, the pope said, "The message of Jesus is mercy. For me, and I say this with humility, it is the Lord's strongest message." Francis points out that we need mercy because "humanity is wounded, deeply wounded."[4] Gregory too speaks repeatedly of the wounds of humanity that need God's salvific healing:

> However much my wounds are incurable, hopeless,
> Twice as great is your artful wisdom;
> Illuminate me, O exalted, celebrated physician.[5]

To illustrate Christ's mercy, Francis recounts the story of the widow of Nain from Luke 7:11-17. He speaks of Christ's "visceral

[3] *BL* 13.2; *MH* 12:118.28–34.

[4] Pope Francis, 2016, *The Name of God Is Mercy*, Oonagh Stransky, trans., New York: Random House, 15.

[5] *BL* 9.3; *MH* 12:98.64–65.

love" that moves him to compassion for the widow. Her sorrow is compounded by her having no remaining close male relatives and thus she is left defenseless and vulnerable, given the status of women of her time and place. Jesus may also see his own mother's grief foreshadowed. As Francis says, "Jesus does not look at reality from outside. . . . He lets himself get involved."[6] So too as we have seen in chapter eight, Gregory depicts the widow's grief in Prayer 18 of the *Book of Lamentation*, remarkably identifying himself with her and crying out to God alongside her.

Another theme of Francis's papacy has been his insistence that we remember those on the peripheries and margins of the human community. He speaks of many kinds of peripheries: geographic, economic, and social. In going to the peripheries, he sees the church following the example of Christ, whose birth was announced in Galilee, "in a peripheral city whose reputation was not particularly good," as the pope remarked in a homily given in March 2017 in Milan.[7] Christ ministered to all but especially to the poor, the sick, those burdened by grave sins. We may add to these also those who live on the margins of life—the unborn, the elderly, the deathly ill—as well as those who subsist precariously along the boundaries of territorial nations, the migrants and refugees.

Here, too, it is evident that St. Gregory is himself a man of the peripheries. In terms of geography, he lived on the edge of Europe, on the frontier with Asia and the Middle East in a part of the world that has suffered and continues to suffer from oppression and violence. From an ecclesial perspective, he was a priest and monk of a church alienated from most of the major hierarchical sees and considered even by some today schismatic and heretical. Among his own people and by some in his church's hierarchy he was viewed with suspicion and accused of heresy. That he is today a Doctor of the Church testifies to how far the Catholic Church has advanced in its relations with separated churches. Gregory provides a clear historical model of how God's salvific

[6] Pope Francis 2016, 91–92.

[7] French text at http://w2.vatican.va/content/francesco/fr/homilies/2017/documents/papa-francesco_20170325_omelia-visitapastorale-milano.html, retrieved January 11, 2018.

grace operates outside the visible boundaries of the Catholic Church. This is not to imply that we should look for a Protestant doctor—much less a non-Christian—anytime soon. There are very few doctrinal differences between Gregory's writings and those of the other Catholic doctors. As I argued in the last chapter, on at least one matter of doctrine Gregory appears closer to modern Catholic teaching than the church's Doctor *par excellence*, St. Thomas Aquinas. But Gregory's status as a Doctor is nevertheless one more significant step along the path of reunion of the Western and Eastern churches and hope for the future of closer relation and eventual union with other Christians as well.

The confluence of these themes of mercy and the margins in Francis and Gregory suggests to me that Gregory's role as a Doctor is to provide one more sacred witness testifying on behalf of Francis's vision of the church that never neglects the peripheries. That this witness comes from the product of a medieval Christian culture far removed from our modern liberal and individualistic presuppositions underscores the fact that Francis's approach does not stem from a modernist rejection of tradition but flows from within the very heart of the ancient and venerable Christian tradition.

Gregory and the Contemporary World

Gregory's world, tenth-century Vaspurakan, is a long way from our modern condition. And yet there are some similarities that make his work especially relevant for us today. A significant segment of his contemporaries felt estranged by the established church that seemed to them too distant and formal. Instead, they opted for an interior spirituality that rejected the institutions of the church, even calling into question the church's traditional teachings on marriage. The church itself faced a crisis among its clergy, with many priests either ignorant of the liturgy's significance or involved in corrupt practices. In addition to being occupied in polemical conflict with other Christians, which at least in the case of the Byzantines had mercifully abated during much of Gregory's life, the church was challenged by its encounter with a new religion—even though many Christians did not recognize it as such—in the form of Islam, which would remain a dominant presence in the land, and whose adherents were at times tolerant and at others brutally violent. Powerful empires led by megalomaniacal rulers and menacing armies were a perennial peril to the peace of the country.

It was a different world, but we can recognize some faint gleams of our own condition. Especially in Western countries, not only in Europe but increasingly in North America as well, there is a growing indifference to organized religion.[8] The school of Narek, as we have seen, responded to a similar disengagement from the church. Their answer was to recognize that in many ways the church itself and its hierarchy were partially to blame, due either to venality or an overly cautious conservatism. As we have seen, Khosrov Andzewats'i embarked on a program of educating his clergy on the meaning of the religious rites and liturgical prayers. He studied practices in other traditions and recognized the need for reform in worship. That need to educate the clergy was an impetus for the founding of the monastery of Narek, which would become a center of learning that produced highly educated monks capable of preaching knowledgeably and effectively. Anania of Narek wrote of spiritual exercises that promoted a more personal, interior spirituality that would satisfy the spiritual needs of the faithful while also helping them to reconnect to the church, the sacraments, and the act of public worship. Their goals were most brilliantly realized in the body of spiritual poetry produced by their devoted disciple and son. The school of Narek was informed by the desire to chart a middle way between the excessive individualism and stifling interiority of private spirituality and the distant and ossified institutional church. They advanced a spirituality that would engage the people but at the same time was firmly moored in the traditions and practices of the church as the true body of Christ. They showed that genuine ecclesial reform should be guided by a fidelity to the beliefs and practices of the ancient church, even as those teachings and practices are renewed and developed according to the needs and circumstances of the time.

[8] See, for example, Elizabeth Drescher, 2016, *Choosing Our Religion: The Spiritual Lives of America's Nones*, Oxford: Oxford University Press.

Many Christians, alarmed by the growing secularism and even hostility toward religion in the mainstream culture, have called for a return to a kind of monasticism in which Christians live apart from the general community. The most prominent advocate of this idea is the American author Rod Dreher, who has called for Christians to form arks that would allow them to live through the storms besetting the post-Christian culture surrounding them.[9] He calls this the "Benedict option," a concept first described by the philosopher Alasdair MacIntyre in his book *After Virtue*.[10] The Benedict in question is St. Benedict of Nursia, recognized as the founder of Western monasticism and author of the rule that guides monastic life especially in the Western church. MacIntyre and Dreher are correct at least in the sense that there is a pressing need for a revival in and an expansion of our definitions of monasticism. Perhaps study of Gregory and his monastery with its intriguing synthesis of both eremitic and cenobitic life as well as its mission to educate and provide spiritual formation to those outside the monastery can serve as another model, one that shares many features with Benedictine monasticism but also has a number of distinctive qualities. Gregory's monasticism embodies both an inward-looking, contemplative, and penitential mode *and* an active and outward-looking zeal for reform of the church and the world. With MacIntyre we can say that perhaps the church and the world need not only a new Benedict but a new Gregory as well, bearing in mind MacIntyre's qualification that such persons will be very different from their original exemplars.

Another critical issue facing many churches today is the matter of the role of women, who are in both the Catholic and Orthodox churches barred from ordination. Indeed, in several ways there are fewer opportunities for women today than in earlier centuries when there was a more vibrant religious life available to female monastics. Likewise, the female diaconate has largely become

[9] Rod Dreher, 2017, *The Benedict Option: A Strategy for Christians in a Post-Christian Nation*, New York: Sentinel.

[10] Alasdair MacIntyre, 1984, *After Virtue*, Notre Dame, IN: University of Notre Dame Press, esp. 256–63.

obsolete in the Eastern churches.[11] There is now a growing movement in the Eastern churches to revive the diaconate for women, most notably in the Greek (Chalcedonian) patriarchate of Alexandria, which recently ordained several women as deacons.[12] The Armenian Apostolic Church has been exceptional in maintaining, albeit sporadically, the ancient tradition of ordaining women to the diaconate, and today has a few women deacons.[13] In the West, too, there is the promising development of a Vatican commission on the female diaconate, established by Pope Francis in 2016.[14] The virtual extinction of the practice of ordaining women to the diaconate, one that is ancient and biblical, is one of the major failings of the church today. Paradoxically, it has made the church in the modern, more egalitarian world even more male-dominated than it was during the Middle Ages, when there were many more women deacons, nuns, and esteemed hymnographers and theologians such as Gregory's fellow Doctor Hildegard of Bingen in the Latin tradition, Kassianē in the Byzantine, and in the Armenian, Sahakdukht, whom we have met and whose hymn to the Virgin is discussed in chapter nine. Gregory's willingness to speak of God as a woman and a mother was audacious in his day, but even today some may view this biblically and theologically sound characterization of God with suspicion. Perhaps a recovery of this way of thinking about God will help in fostering an open dialogue on the greater role of women in the ministry of the church.

While I have focused on Gregory's significance for unity of the church, we should also be mindful of the implications of his writings for relations with the world religions. One of the refreshing features of Gregory's works is the almost complete absence of polemics and hostility toward not only other Christian communions

[11] Phyllis Zagano, 2000, *Holy Saturday: An Argument for the Restoration of the Female Diaconate in the Catholic Church*, New York: Crossroad.

[12] Carrrie Frederick Frost, 2017, "Not a Novelty: The Eastern Orthodox Case for Deaconesses," in *Commonweal* 144: 9–11.

[13] Roberta R. Ervine, 2007, "The Women Deacons of the Armenian Church," in *St. Nersess Theological Review* 12: 17–56.

[14] http://en.radiovaticana.va/news/2016/11/25/vatican_commission_on_female_diaconate_holds_first_meeting/1274887, retrieved December 31, 2017.

but even other religions. His intemperate outburst at Nestorians, Jews, and Muslims in one passage in the commentary on the Song of Songs as well as his apparent enthusiasm over the execution of the T'ondrakean leader Smbat are isolated and uncharacteristic exceptions to his overriding irenic and conciliatory tone.[15] The general graciousness of his writing is all the more striking when compared with other Armenian authors who rarely shy away from invective and triumphalism. One need only compare him with Stephen of Siwnik', whose exegetical works are preoccupied with the principle of Christian supersessionism and frequently express a contempt for Judaism.[16] In contrast, Gregory asks us to focus on our own sins rather than berate others for their apparent failings:

> No one is as sinful as I, . . .
> I alone, and no one else,
> I am all this, and the sins of all are in me.
> Not the pagans, for they did not know,
> Not the Jews, for they became blind.[17]

His generally merciful approach to other nations and religions, all the more striking in the context of the often antagonistic language of medieval theological discourse, as well as the hints of universalism in his writings, make his works promising resources for contemporary interfaith and ecumenical dialogue. In particular, his relationship with Islamic culture is an auspicious area for further research and encounter between Armenian and Islamic scholars. I have already suggested that Gregory, at least in his poetic style, may have been influenced by Islamic spiritual poetry, perhaps even the Qur'an. As well, future research on Gregory's work will no doubt be enriched by comparative study with the monasticism

[15] *MH* 12:830.154; Ervine 2007, 157; and *MH* 12:1087.1.

[16] Even more hostile than Step'anos is the ninth-century exegete Hamam Arewelts'i, who, as Thomson notes, regularly assailed Jews for foolishness and impiety. See Robert W. Thomson, trans., 2005, *Hamam: Commentary on the Book of Proverbs*, Leuven: Peeters, esp. 10 and 25. Compared to both of these medieval commentators and theologians, Gregory is remarkably irenic and averse to invective.

[17] *BL* 72.3; *MH* 12:446.50–59.

and mysticism of other religious traditions, not only the Sufi tradition in Islam and its great poets as well as the mystical tradition in Judaism, but also the Eastern religions such as Buddhism that have eminent monastic traditions.

While decidedly not a political thinker, Gregory does in a few passages express his thoughts about politics. Though he extols the Byzantine emperors Basil and Constantine for their struggles on behalf of Orthodox Christianity, he expresses pessimism about the moral worth of political power, noting that "the kingdoms of this world, perhaps, are always more artful in killing than giving life."[18] Maybe he had some premonition of Basil's policy toward the end of his reign of relocating the Armenian nobility to estates farther west in the empire, a policy that would have devastating consequences for the Armenians as their lands became more vulnerable to invasions from the East. He does however recognize the biblical injunction to obey kings and political authorities, by which he justifies his acquiescing, albeit with reluctance, to compose the commentary on the Song of Songs at the command of Prince Gurgēn. He praises the prince for his interest in scripture and learning and for his avoidance of impure pursuits.[19]

All legitimate political authority, Gregory avers, ultimately derives from God, symbolized by the anointing of rulers with holy oil:

> The kingdoms of this world could not boast,
> Of conforming to your image, O Creator,
> Were they not anointed with the horn of the oil of your blessing
> Nor were they not adorned on their head with a crown,
> a diadem in your name, Christ.[20]

Among the responsibilities of the church and temporal rulers is the solemn duty to care for the poor. An equitable distribution must favor the needs of the indigent over the wealthy, based on the description of God's distribution of manna to the Israelites in Exodus 16:18:

[18] *BL* 51.1; *MH* 12:325.15–16.

[19] *MH* 12.761.5; Ervine 2007, 77–78.

[20] *BL* 93.5; *MH* 12:570.4.

That the poor may not want
Nor the rich be proud,
You have distributed your grace equally to all,
Like the air and sunlight,
The waters of flowing streams,
Like the manna given in common to all,
But to the poor more than the wealthy.[21]

Though not as pronounced in his writings, in a number of passages Gregory indicates that Christ's redemption is extended not only to all humans but to nature itself. Perhaps the most striking expression of this concern for all living things is found in the *Ode for the Holy Cross*, where the bird on Christ's cross is informed that the good news of the resurrection is addressed to it as well.[22] The implications of Gregory's thought on our responsibilities to the environment, an important concern of Francis's papacy, would also be a fruitful area for further investigation.[23]

A full study of Gregory's works will reveal many other areas in which his writings provide us with rich resources for the renewal of the pilgrim church in its journey on earth toward the final place of rest in the eternity of God. Gregory's writings, his monuments of prayer, have provided spiritual shelter and sustenance for generations of Armenians dispossessed of their lands. Today, as his writings become known more widely, his work can serve a similar role for all the migrants and pilgrims—both physical and spiritual—of this world.

Compline

Having come to the end of this book, it is fitting for us to join St. Gregory in his prayer of rest at the end of the day. This request

[21] *BL* 93.10; *MH* 12:579.4.

[22] *MH* 12:736.27-8; Terian 2016, 198.

[23] See the encyclical discussing environmental degradation and the instrumentalizing of nature: Pope Francis, 2015, *Laudato Si': On Care for Our Common Home*, Boston: Pauline Books and Media.

for rest is from Prayer 12 of the *Book of Lamentation*. Many believe it to have the power to ward off the demons of the night and grant peaceful sleep:

> Grant me the joyful rest
> Of death-like slumber
> In the depths of the night,
> Through the intercession
> And the petitions
> Of your Holy Mother,
> And of all the Elect.
>
> Cover and surround
> The window of my sight,
> The senses of my mind,
> In unshakable firmness;
> Secure them from agitation
> And the worldly distractions
> Of dreams, reveries,
> Foolish delusions.
> I am safe and guarded
> By the memory of your hope.
>
> And when I wake again
> From this heavy sleep,
> Most vigilant and alert,
> Spirit renewed by joy,
> Firmly grounded in You,
> Then will I send my voice of prayer,
> Redolent of faith, to heaven,
> All-blessed King of glory beyond words,
> In harmony with the heavenly choirs
> That sing of your glory.
> For You are glorified by all of creation,
> Forever and ever,
> Amen.[24]

[24] *BL* 12.4; *MH* 12:115-6.66-93.

Index